THE CREATIVE CIRCLE
Art, Literature, and Music in Bahá'í Perspective

WHEN YOUR WORST FEARS COME TRUE!
by Fritz A. Mann.

THE CREATIVE CIRCLE

Art, Literature, and Music in Bahá'í Perspective

Edited by Michael Fitzgerald

Kalimát Press
Los Angeles

First Edition

Copyright © 1989 by Kalimát Press
All Rights Reserved

Manufactured in the United States of America

"Can Bahá'í Art Become Distinctive?"
Copyright © 1989 by Ludwig Tuman
All rights reserved

"Poetry and Self-Transformation"
Copyright © 1988 by Association for Bahá'í Studies
All rights reserved

CONTENTS

Preface *by Michael Fitzgerald* viii

Foreword *by Charles Wolcott* xi

Poetry and Self-Transformation
by Roger White 1

The Creative Act and the Spirit
by Bonnie Wilder 17

But . . . My Mother Was a Singer
by Maya Kaathryn Bohnhoff 39

The Dilemma of the Artist: A Perspective
on the Development of Bahá'í Aesthetics
by Anne Gordon Atkinson 51

Can Bahá'í Art Become Distinctive?
by Ludwig Tuman 97

The Artist As Citizen
by Thomas Lysaght 121

Restating the Idealist Theory of Art
by Geoffrey Nash 159

Poetry and the Arts in Rebuilding Society
by Duane L. Herrmann 175

Ladder of the Soul
an interview with Lasse Thoresen 193

Looking Forward in the Visual Arts
by Fritz A. Mann 213

Biographical Notes 241

"Painting is a way of being."
—Jackson Pollock

"It is as difficult to write simply as it is to be good."
—W. Somerset Maugham

"I will hear in Heaven."
—Beethoven's last words

Preface

> *"The artist creates the uncreated conscience of the race."*
> —James Joyce

> *"What bestowal could be greater than this, that one's art should be as the act of worshiping the Lord?"*
> —'Abdu'l-Bahá

ART IS THE LAST vestige of the mysterious in an age that rejects religion. The twentieth century is widely known for its themes of alienation and a profound despair over the state of human affairs. Religion has abused its office. Responding, existentialists put forward a serious, but incomplete, philosophy which sought to address the situation of modern man, impotent in the face of titanic destruction. Humanists by and large have reserved themselves to intellectual labor, disdaining the world's spiritual traditions. There is thus a gaping void in human values.

The Bahá'í Faith has emerged as an artist's impetus and as an instrument for the renewal of society. Bahá'u'lláh (1817–1892), its Founder, anticipated the need for the inclusion of religion in a thinking person's modern repertoire of ideas. His expansive teachings on the oneness of mankind and the oneness of religions lead to a Whitmanesque embrace of diverse and conflicting cultures. Thus, the artist informed by a Bahá'í sensibility will be able to build on a wide variety of cultural raw materials that another artist might not accept. Pericles said that "where there is no vision the people perish." The planetary vision of a Bahá'í artist will lead him or her to relish the gifts that an exploding world culture offers. Without the need to be restricted by a parochial view, the artist with access to the Bahá'í Writings can glean a rich pool of ethical and aesthetic inspiration.

Poetry is often termed a "contact" with the natural world, as by Whitman; or "contact" with the locality, as by William Carlos Williams. When the "locality" is the whole planet, the frontiers of the imagination are expanded beyond provincialisms of every sort. Thus, prejudice can be overcome and the threat of war due to misunderstanding will be forestalled.

Still, artistic integrity for the Bahá'í must be foremost. Without preaching, without didacticism, the Bahá'í artist can form the themes of his faith into an individual vision that is authentic. In seeing art as both a service and as a means of healing, the development of young and mature talent must become a major priority in an evolving world culture. If James Joyce is right, and "the artist creates the uncreated conscience of the race," then here is a major responsibility.

The Bahá'í will be eager to practice art in a web of merging world visions, be determined to maintain the highest ethical standards, be assured that the effort to be consistent in public and private life will provide new sources. The prospects of authentic visionary work for a Bahá'í, in contrast to the documentation of an age at odds with itself, stirs the real longings of artists for honest, serious work. In harmony with the best that the contemporary world offers, expressing the unique value of diverse cultures, and committed to the highest standards of artistic and personal integrity, the Bahá'í artist can create a new world.

Michael Fitzgerald
Winchester, Virginia

CHARLES WOLCOTT
musician and member of the Universal House of Justice,
c. 1982.

Foreword

IT CAME IN A CLUTTER of mail one morning—an invitation to contribute an essay on music for inclusion in a book on the arts. The opening sentence was intriguing: "As a piano player and a Bahá'í, you must certainly, or one would think, have experienced the dynamics of artistic endeavor in the context of the pull toward community." My instincts cautioned me to forget it, but as in a movie flashback, my thoughts went scurrying pell-mell through time and space to what can best be described as another life, a professional life spanning some forty years—encompassing, yes, being a "piano player" early on, but widening in scope to include being a leader of dance bands, a music arranger, a composer, a conductor of studio orchestras, and eventually the General Music Director of not one but two major motion picture studios. (Not at the same time of course!)

Though my professional piano playing days are long gone, and little time is available for composing, opportunities to listen to music are abundant. From that viewpoint, acceptance of the invitation became a definite possibility. So I did just that. And you, dear reader, must judge whether the exercise was worth the doing.

What is music? According to that time-honored tome, the Oxford English Dictionary, music is defined as:

That one of the fine arts which is concerned with the combination of sounds, with a view to beauty of form and the expression of thought or feeling.

Listening to some of the noise that pours out incessantly from television screens or radio makes me wonder whether the creators of such incoherent mish-mash were ever conscious of the dictionary's precise definition.

Where did music get its name? In Greece there is an ancient mount, Parnassus, and legend has it that the mount was (and maybe still is!) the home of the nine sister goddesses, daughters of Zeus, who collectively bore the name of the Muses. Individually, each related to an expression of artistic endeavor. For example, Terpsichore was the goddess associated with dance. But since music is inexorably intertwined with all art forms, it seems logical to accept it as the offspring of the collective name of the "Muses."

Before concentrating on music as an art form, we may benefit from a few thoughts expressed by some serious thinkers about art as a whole. Albert Schweitzer, in addition to his medical skills, possessed a truly professional facility for playing the pipe organ. That immortal contrapuntist, Johann Sebastian Bach, observed that art can be categorized according to the material the artists use to express the world around them: The artist "is not only a painter, or only a poet, or only a musician, but all in one. . . . The distinction consists only in that one idea is dominant and artists choose the language that suits them best."[1] It is said that Goethe fancied himself a painter and Schiller reckoned himself a musician, though both are known as poets.

Then there is the remarkable comment purportedly made by an eminent though highly controversial nineteenth-century French poet: "A toy is a child's first introduction to art." While accepting the possibility that a child's interest in some form of art might, or even should, be stimulated in this way, it seems to me that the little one who becomes a great artist has been blessed by the Almighty with a special gift. And so, this brings us to a thought-provoking question: How is music related to religion? Given that records pertaining to the origins of the handful of ancient, divinely revealed religions with adherents in today's world go back less than a few thousand years, we must rely on findings of archeologists and other scholars who are diligently trying to uncover more information about our forebears.

It is more or less commonly accepted that in ancient times mankind's basic relationship to the gods was one of appeasement, that is, seeking protection from the elements—drought, flood, thunderstorms, earthquakes—by raising one's voice in praise of the gods. We may assume that in the beginning it was an individual effort: one voice plaintively chanting a supplication. Later, a communal petition came into being, many voices joined in the chanting, and primitive instruments were added. Probably the first of these were skins stretched over wooden frames, some to be struck by sticks and others with strings to be plucked.

Migrations of Chinese and Hindus added their contributions of traditions handed down orally through the generations. It is thought that the ancient Greek traditions probably came from Asia Minor importing the novel idea of one God—Zeus. And after the advent of Abraham, in time there came the psalmist, David, who contributed some one hundred fifty Psalms, texts dedicated to one God, which live today through being sung in synagogues and churches. Originally, the psalms were accompanied by the psaltery, a dulcimer-like stringed instrument which the player plucked.

Allow me a momentary digression for the benefit of today's youthful generation of Bahá'ís—many of whom are musicians who can, at a moment's notice, produce an instrument case and from it whip out a guitar, ready to accompany themselves in song or to encourage the eager group surrounding them to participate in a sing-along. This is in the tradition of the troubadors, twelfth-century lyric poets who traveled throughout southern Europe, accompanying themselves on stringed instruments. Often they were the purveyors of news picked up as they went back and forth through eastern Spain, southern France and northern Italy. Today's troubadors, Bahá'í youth on projects throughout the world, share songs they have picked up along the way, as well as their own tunes.

Returning to the subject of music related to religion, the most famous hymn of the Greek Church, Akathistos, thought to be from the fifth century A.D. is still sung today in the Feast of Annunciation service.

Then came the surge of great music suffused with religious emotion—the cantatas of Bach and oratorios of Handel (undoubtedly inspired by Luther's impassioned Protestantism), and the masses and requiems of Mozart, Berlioz, Brahms, Dvorak, and a host of other well-known eighteenth- and nineteenth-century composers. The western world is familiar with these compositions sung by huge church choirs, the texts of which are rooted in Christianity.

In his great work on Bach, Dr. Schweitzer pays this tribute to the man: "Music is an act of worship with Bach. His artistic activity and his personality are both based on his piety." In another passage: "All great art, even secular, is in itself religious in his eyes; for him the tones do not perish, but ascend to God like praise too deep for utterance."[2] Schweitzer quotes from the rules and principles of accompaniment that Bach prescribed to his pupils: "Like all music, the figured bass should have no other end and aim than the glory of God and the recreation of the soul; where this is not kept in mind there is no true music, but only an infernal clamor and ranting." Hmm—one could almost imagine Bach had a forewarning of the music of the last half of the twentieth century.

At this juncture, it would be pertinent to ask what Bahá'u'lláh, Founder of the Bahá'í Faith, had to say about the work of artists, craftsmen and scientists. The following brief excerpts will serve to show the high regard in which He held this pursuit.

> *The third Tajallí (Effulgence) is concerning arts, crafts and sciences. Knowledge is as wings to man's life, and a ladder for his ascent. Its acquisition is incumbent upon everyone.*

And:

> *The fifth Taráz (Ornament) concerneth the protection and preservation of the stations of God's servants. . . . In this Day the sun of craftsmanship shineth above the horizon of the occident and the river of arts is flowing out of the sea of that region . . .*

Finally:

> *It hath been revealed and is now repeated that the true worth of artists and craftsmen should be appreciated, for they advance the affairs of mankind.*

Though Bahá'u'lláh is addressing all humankind, and we are aware that all work done with care is akin to worship, we must distinguish between the exceptional and the pedestrian when assessing the work of those who place the results of their creative endeavors before us. The burden falls on fallible human beings—all of us. In my view, with regard to music, people can be classified as those who create, those who perform, and those who listen. Those who listen constitute by far the greater proportion of humankind. They may never compose or perform on an instrument, though they may attain the joy of raising their voices in song. And it is to them my plea to read and digest the above words of wisdom from Bahá'u'lláh is addressed.

We should all be concerned about the state of music today.

Parents of young children and soon-to-be parents need especially to be aware of what is happening to the current crop of teenagers according to the findings of a California State University study, published in the *Los Angeles Times*, June 1986. The intent of the study was to ascertain the impact of song lyrics on youth. Two excerpts from that study will suffice:

> [Only] 2% or 3% of all teenagers devote their full attention to lyrics; most use rock'n'roll as background noise. Teenagers cannot accurately describe their favorite songs, they are seriously lacking in literary skills to understand and interpret metaphors and symbolism.

This sad state of affairs didn't just appear in the 1980s. It is an insidious virus that has been slowly developing since the 1950s. However, before further commenting on the present, let's take a peak at the past.

The use of music to enhance drama wasn't a discovery of the twentieth century. Ancient Greek dramas rediscovered by the Renaissance were not just plays with spoken verses but dramas requiring actors and actresses who could sing! Seventeenth-century Claudio Monteverdi, composer of madrigals and part songs, delighted by this new development, set about to write music for the stage—his works were called operas. We are the beneficiaries of Monteverdi's zeal. Operas by Mozart, the Italians—Verdi, Puccini, Bellini, Rossini—and others too numerous to mention grace today's opera house stages. Even seventeenth-century works of Monteverdi, *Orfeo* and *The Coronation of Poppaea*, have been revived. Opera lives today because it communicates through its music. Arias are carried in one's head to be savored over and over again.

Now to revert to the plight of today's teenager and his inability to absorb the incoherent lyrics of so many of the current songs. Two instances that occurred during my stint at MGM studios in the 1950s will illustrate the importance of understanding the words of a pop song. The writer/director of a black-and-white movie about the pupils and teachers in a high school located in a New York slum district asked me to hear a record he had which he felt caught the spirit of the film he was about to make. He was right. The music *and* the lyrics supplied the color he was looking for to set the mood of his picture. The record he played for me had been released by the record company some two or three years before and, as they say in show business, it died. I wrote a 24-measure drum solo in the style of Gene Krupa which built up in intensity to the first words of the record—"Rock Around the Clock." The film, *Blackboard Jungle*, became a sensation. The record by Bill Haley and His Comets was reborn; to date it is second only to Bing Crosby's 'White Christmas" in the number of records sold. The point is, while the rock'n'roll rhythm was loud and incessant, *every word* of the lyric was heard distinctly. The young people dancing in the theatre aisles were singing along with the movie! It happened every time the picture began.

The second instance involved a rising young pop singer who was making his first movie at the studio. Listening in the control booth at his first recording session, it was impossible for me to distinguish the words he was singing. The sound engineer was asked to adjust the microphone set-up, but the singer's manager objected, saying, "That's the sound we get with all his records and they sell." His argument was that if a teenage buyer couldn't understand the lyrics, he (or she) would buy another copy.

And that, I'm sorry to say, was his method of selling the records of his singer. This incident underscores my belief that the deterioration in pop music started in the late 1950s. Teenagers today react to the loud, driving rhythms of what they see and hear on television and videos. If you were to read the lyrics of a Top-40 song without being distracted by the superstar charisma, the flashing colored lights, the gyrations of the performer, you would discover another reason why youth are unable to describe their favorite songs. In the vast majority of cases, the words are incoherent or utterly devoid of meaning.

Having examined the art of music, where its name comes from, and its historical relationship to religion. Now we need to determine, as Bahá'ís, how we can use music to support the thesis that man is created to carry forward an ever-advancing civilization. Those who comprise the largest group—the listeners—are reminded of Bahá'u'lláh's words in the Kitáb-í Aqdas: *"We have permitted you to listen to music and singing. Beware lest such listening cause you to transgress the bounds of decency and dignity."*[3] They can also follow the advice given by 'Abdu'l-Bahá. That is, from the earliest age, teach the child the verses of God, expose him to music that, in the words of Bach, are tones that "do not perish, but ascend to God like praise too deep for utterance."

Those who create music have an enormous responsibility. We know that in bygone days, composers were given sustenance by royal patrons. Mozart, for instance, composed for the royal court. Bach was a church organist and composed for the weekly services held throughout the year. Today, to earn his livelihood, a composer may find it necessary to spend much of his time and God-given talent on producing music of a secular nature. But in whatever he does he should maintain the highest standards. God willing, in the future, national governments will recognize their responsibility to provide subsidies to qualified artists who will then be able to contribute to the well-being of mankind. The performer may or may not also be a composer, but he should be guided, as is the composer, to so develop his artistic talent that his performance provides a *"ladder by which souls may ascend to the realms on high."*[4]

CHARLES WOLCOTT
editing music at his desk at the Walt Disney Studios, c. 1945.

What about the teenage Bahá'í composer and/or performer? Everything depends on God-given talent. Is it present? If so, that person should be given whole-hearted encouragement by parents and peers. Talent is an elusive thing. Proficiency is often confused with talent and can be the source of eventual heartbreak for the proficient but untalented musician. Nevertheless, there is a place for those who lack talent, but have sufficient ability to give enjoyment to an audience. They belong to a category into which falls the majority of Bahá'ís who are guitarists, drummers, or other instrumentalists. They constitute the reservoir of manpower on which Bahá'í youth projects often depend.

We can't all be stars, but we can all be Bahá'ís!

Charles Wolcott
Haifa, Israel

Editor's Note: Charles Wolcott, musician and member of the Universal House of Justice, passed away on the day he dictated this essay.

Notes

1. Johann Sebastian Bach, Vol. II, Chap. 20, p.8.
2. Ibid., Vol. I, Chap. IX, p. 167.
3. Compilation of Extracts from the Bahá'í Writings on Music.
4. Ibid.

Baha'i World Centre

ROGER WHITE (center)
Canadian-born author and poet, with Anne Gordon Atkinson (left) and Deborah Chicurel Conow (right) who frequently give dramatic readings of his poetry.

Poetry and Self-Transformation*

by Roger White

MY NON-BAHÁ'Í FRIENDS who are poets frequently complain that among friends and members of their families to whom they show their work they encounter indifference, contempt, embarassment, or sometimes hostility, which heightens their sense of alienation and uselessness. They are made to feel frivolous and somewhat less than respectable. They have no experience of audience and feel that they are writing in a void, speaking to themselves in a vacuum, presenting their private view of the world with no confidence that anyone else might see the world as they do.

Poetry is no longer very accessible to the average reader; it is rare to find families and groups of friends gathering together to read poetry; it is increasingly seen as a specialized and elitist interest divorced from real life, and few consider it a source of pleasure and insight. Poetry is still written and read, of course, but it has taken refuge in universities, creative writing workshops, and obscure coffeehouses. Seldom is it recognized as a vital means of communicating information of a kind that is found only in poems—bulletins

---

*Reprinted from *The Journal of Bahá'í Studies*, vol. 1, no. 2 (1988) pp. 61–69. Copyright © 1988 Association for Bahá'í Studies.

from the unconscious, "those sly reports on private experience, voices of the inner self . . . " as Louise Bernikow has remarked.[1]

Poets are in part to blame for the diminished regard in which poetry is held that results in society's impoverishment and deprives the poet of an audience. Without a common world perspective, poets are forced to delve in to their own psyches with the result that much modern poetry is despairing or seemingly deliberately difficult—one might say written in a private code. Many modern poets who write confessional verse invite us charmlessly to follow them not only into the bedroom but also the bathroom, and might dismiss our reluctance to do so as squeamishness, not noticing our yawns. Poetry that celebrates natural speech and activity can make unnatural demands on our sympathy and psychic fastidiousness. In an age of instant gratification a consumer society seeks consumer-oriented entertainments; we have perhaps deserved the disposable poems and novels we are given in such abundance, thirst as we might for literature that affirms life and identity, and reinforces our humanity in its struggle to resist the assault of all that is mechanistic and robotic. It remains the task of poetry to translate into words, with intensity and economy, the inexpressible with an immediacy that is not achieved in other art forms. The poet must not just describe the loaf but provide readers with the experience of eating it; the poet places the bread on the tongue. When the poet fails in this duty, readers will turn to films and novels for the kind of information about life that it is the poet's responsibility and privilege to provide.

Poets learn to live with the disquieting knowledge that more people aspire to write poetry than read it, and that more read it than buy it. This situation, it might be supposed, will gradually change in a Bahá'í society whose members are trained not to confuse who they are with what they do; who accept the necessity of inhabiting a social persona without having it overshadow the soul within that stands naked before its Creator; and whose interior lives are privately called into account each day, not morbidly, but in a spirit of creative self-interest that fosters growth towards fuller human development. If the best poets are indeed, as has been said of them, the antennae of civilization, we might do well to consult them. Their wisdom, Inder Nath Kher insists, "cannot be translated into discursive prose."[2] One of the highest services they perform is to reacquaint us with our true feelings which we put away in our need to manipulate our workaday world. But if we are correct in respecting poets as servants, we err in demanding that they be slaves to or propagandists of our view of reality. Very fine poetry has been created by poets writing both within and without a religious framework. It is chastening for the Bahá'í poet rising rapturously from devotions, and bent on "committing literature" (I accept blame for the phrase) by enshrining pious thoughts in poems, to recall T.S. Eliot's admonition that people who write devotional verse are usually writing as they want to feel, rather than as they do feel.

Many serious poets and other artists feel that they are at war with the age. Through this estrangement, both the poet and potential readers are the losers. Most of us have forgotten our discovery of poetry as children through nursery rhymes when we were fascinated to learn that words dance and resonate and have the capacity to provide the epiphanic moment, to transport, to express something we didn't know how to say, to reveal something we didn't know we knew. If the writer has done a valid job, the act of writing a poem has changed the writer, and we in reading it are put in touch with a power that transforms us—if only by reminding us that transformation is possible. This is what we look for in art. Cyril Connolly would have it that, "The true function of a writer is to produce a masterpiece . . . no other task is of any consequence . . . writers engaged in any literary task which is not an assault on perfection . . . might as well be peeling potatoes."³

Carol Sternhell, writing in the *New York Times*, relates how her friend, Michael, aged two, tried to climb inside a book. "Unwilling to believe that so wonderful a world [as described in the story he had heard read to him] was unreachable, he simply opened the tale to his favorite page, carefully arranged his choice on the floor and stepped in. He tried again and again, certain he would soon get it right, and each time he was left standing out in the cold he cried in bewilderment." Few of us are as innocent as Michael: we take revenge on the authors by refusing to read them, study them with calculation in order to expose their tricks, or withdraw from magic trnasport to take refuge in reading what we fondly believe are facts, revered because so manipulable. Most newspapers, how-to manuals, and interoffice memos have the virtue of being written in mind-numbing, heavisome prose. They have designs on our opinions and attitudes, and sometimes on our purses and our votes, but they are not usually concerned with our interior selves on any profound level. Newspapers and periodicals are adored by politicians. Emily Dickinson's father, who was a politician, displayed a misplaced kindness in indulgently allowing her to read the local newspaper, while urging her not to read books—especially the poetry she loved—lest they "jostle" her mind. Dickinson herself was, of course, a great poet although her father appears to have successfully avoided recognizing this. "Everybody must have wished at some time that poetry were written by nice ordinary people instead of poets—and, in a better world, it may be," as Randall Jarrell ruefully observes.

But the cockroaches of poetry lurk beneath the floorboards of even the loftiest mansions of the rational mind. It fell to my lot, as Associate Editor of *Hansard*, the record of the debates of the Canadian Parliament, to edit the following sentences, given here in the pristine form in which they fell from the honorable orators' lips:

Hon. Member for Grey North: Yes, Mr. Speaker, pessimism is the scarecrow that fear erects in the watermelon patch of the future to frighten away the timid souls so the feast may be richer for the few who are not afraid.

Hon. Member for Niagara Falls: I have thrown the Minister an orchid, and if you think I am throwing him a beanball at any time, merely point it out to me, and I will try to get the engine back on the track.

Hon. Member for Halifax: [In Divorce Bill Committee] It is extremely difficult to track down adultery and you seize upon it if you are lucky enough to find it.

Hon. Member for Timiskaming: Gossip sometimes creates a condition, a condition that would mean a man's reincarnation [*sic*] in prison. Parolees are not supposed to drink, go into public houses or associate with women of easy virtues—there are a number of conditions they are asked to observe that are not necessarily conducive to rehabilitation.

Hon. Member for Cartier: It is possible by law to say that only those who are born are qualified to serve in Her Majesty's Forces.

An Hon. Member for a Maritime Constituency: It is my privilege to represent fishermen, those brave men who go down to the sea in ships and do their business in great waters.

If a capacity to jostle the mind were a characteristic exclusive to poetry, these utterances might be considered poetry of the highest order.

Bahá'ís who write poetry—indeed any Bahá'í artists—are able to look forward to a different reception from that which my friends describe, and this will be increasingly true as the Bahá'í community expands and matures. Not only do Bahá'í poets have a common worldview shared with a community towards whose members they have a family feeling, but they are also aware of the high regard in which their craft has been held since the beginning of the Revelation. Without in any way confusing the Creative Word with poetry—one does not pun in saying they are a "kingdom" apart—Bahá'í poets might rejoice to remember that Nabíl records the Báb as saying that exalted or inspired poetry is the result of "the immediate influence of the Holy Spirit," and the Báb was heard to quote the tradition "Treasures lie hidden beneath the throne of God; the key to those treasures is the tongue of poets."[4] Writers of verse also know that many of the early Bábís were poets, including Ṭáhirih—at least a stanza from one of whose odes we have in the Guardian's own translation.[5] They also know that Bahá'u'lláh Himself wrote poetry; that, indeed, ten years before revealing his station to his followers, He alluded to it in Odes.[6]

'Abdu'l-Bahá, too, wrote poetry of a most exalted and devotional nature which, admire it though we may, we should resist imitating, just as we should resist writing poems in the style of the Revealed Word, which does not need our attempted compliment.

I am convinced there exists in the Sacred Writings and in the recorded talks of 'Abdu'l-Bahá a foundation upon which will be built a greater system of aesthetics for all the arts than the world has yet known, and that time and the patient researches of scholars and the creative efforts of artists will bring it to light. At this early stage in the development of the Bahá'í world community, one can only speculate that before Bahá'í artists can contribute significant advances they must dedicate themselves to the restoration and preservation of the ideals of beauty and perfection and order. In describing the high calling of the artist, David Bosworth hints at the intensity of the creative engagement: "To bear witness, to be an author, to make art, is a profound act; there is no work more serious or demanding or finally audacious."[7] Bahá'ís who write should not be surprised to discover that in addition to audacity the task confronting them may require heroism—Bahá'ís in almost everything they do are pioneering in one form or another. Kathleen Raine, the British poet and critic, laments:

> I have found myself wondering why the present age seems positively to shrink from beauty, to prefer the ugly, to feel safer, more at home with it; and I have come to realize that there is a reproach in the beautiful and the perfect; it passes its continual silent judgement and it requires perhaps a kind of courage to love what is perfect, since to do so is an implicit confession of our own imperfection. Can it be that the prevalence of the low and the sordid in contemporary writing is a kind of easy way, a form of sloth, an avoidance of that reproach which would call us, silently, to [aspire to] a self-perfection it would cost us too much to undertake? And yet it is in order to work upon us that transformation . . . that works which embody the beautiful alone exist. That is their function . . . [8]

The situation obtaining in the arts is too well known to require comment. The Universal House of Justice on 10 February 1980, in a general letter to Iranian Bahá'ís "resident in other countries throughout the world," did not labor the point. After drawing attention to 'Abdu'l-Bahá's reference to deepening chaos and confusion, the House of Justice stated: "Even music, art and literature, which are to represent and inspire the noblest sentiments and highest aspirations and should be a source of comfort and tranquillity for troubled souls . . . are now the mirrors of the soiled hearts of this confused, unprincipled, and disordered age."

Unquestionably, Bahá'í writers have their work cut out for them. Alex Aronson, a respected Shakespearian scholar, observing from outside the Bahá'í community, has been quick to discern that Bahá'í authors may play a role in addressing themselves to "dimensions of living reality . . . long ago consigned to oblivion" under the weight of "the triviality of our everyday experience" and in restoring the "grammar of belief."[9]

Language is the meduim of the poet. One has only to turn to the words of 'Abdu'l-Bahá to discover its purpose: " . . . the function of language is to portray the mysteries and secrets of human hearts. The heart is like a box, and language is the key."[9] And since, in *The Hidden Words*, Bahá'u'lláh tells us, *"Thy heart is My home"* (No. 59, Arabic), and that *"All that is in heaven and earth I have ordained for thee, except the human heart, which I have made the habitation of My beauty and glory . . . "* (No. 27, Persian), Bahá'í poets will not lack for subject matter and will be challenged to excellence of diction. Nor are they restricted to the solemn and devotional, for the heart is the seat also of joy and laughter and passion. Bahá'í poets might well write of "the intimate presence of the divine in the lives of men"[10] but will not confine their appreciation to poetry of that stamp, for they will probably recognize with Louis MacNeice, who felt "the drunkenness of things being various," that the world is "incorrigibly plural" and "suddener than we fancy it."[11] Humility will inform Bahá'í artists that they do not possess truth, though they may feel they have glimpsed its wellspring and will remain receptive to the poetry of quest. An emergent Bahá'í community, grown secure, will not, dare I guess, content itself with didactic and exhortative verse but will espouse poetry that celebrates an improved quality of life and will explore its ceremonial and recreational uses, its capacity to delight, inform, and inspire. Yeats pleaded for "the old passion felt as new" and declared heroic and religious themes, passed down from age to age, modified by individual talent, to be the unchanging substance of sublime poetry. Louise Bogan noted sadly that the generation of rising young poets in America whose work she reviewed wrote unambitious poems and were "positively terrified" of the sublime.

"It is certain that with the spread of the spirit of Bahá'u'lláh a new era will dawn in art and literature," Shoghi Effendi's secretary wrote on his behalf to a Bahá'í who had sent him a poem. "Whereas before the form was perfect but the spirit was lacking, now there will be a glorious spirit embodied in a form immeasurably improved by the quickened genius of the world."[12]

It remains for the poets and other artists of today and tomorrow to give expression to that spirit. The distinguished black poet, Robert Hayden, who was a Bahá'í, writing in *World Order* a publication he served as poetry editor, said of this process: "The making of a poem, like all other creative endeavors, is in the Bahá'í view a spiritual act, a form of worship," and reminded us of 'Abdu'l-Bahá's words that, "If a man engages with all his power in the acquisition of a science or in the perfection of an art, it is as if he has been worshipping God. . . . What bounty greater than this that science should be considered as an act of worship and art as service to the Kingdom of God?"[13] Would that not be, human society so ordered as to reflect divine ideals and virtues?

Hayden continued:

> It seems especially significant that 'Abdu'l-Bahá makes no distinction between "secular" and "religious" art. And we may infer from this that poetry, for example, need not be limited to religious themes (in the usual sense of the term) in order to serve "the Kingdom of God." 'Abdu'l-Bahá sees the creative act as essentially a religious act. The serious artist is involved in a spiritual enterprise. The poet's efforts to master form and technique are in themselves a kind of prayer. . . . If there exists a "poetry of despair" and rejection, there is also a poetry that affirms the humane and spiritual.[14]

It could also be pointed out that 'Abdu'l-Bahá makes no distinction between women and men writers and artists, nor

ROBERT HAYDEN (1913–1980)
a distinguished Bahá'í poet.

does he make any other invidious distinctions. Bahá'í writers should have no need to write out of anger and frustration occasioned by discrimination against them on the grounds of race or sex; they should have no need to engage in special pleading. The Bahá'í woman poet will not find it necessary to adopt the humiliating and dissembling device of appending to her work a self-deprecating note like that which appeared in the first volume of poetry published by an Englishwoman, Katherine Philips (1631–1664), a tactic employed in various guises by women writers well into the nineteenth century because of their vulnerability in a literary world dominated by men:

> I am so far from expecting applause for any thing I scribble that I can hardly expect pardon; and sometimes I think that employment so far above my reach and unfit for my sex that I am going to resolve against it for ever. . . . The truth is I have an incorrigible inclination to that folly of rhyming and intending the effects of that humour only for my own amusement in a retired life, I did not so much resist it as a wiser woman would have done.[15]

The male writer will not be disconcerted or threatened by the news that the earliest poet whose work survives is the Sumerian moon priestess, Enheduanna, born circa 2300 BC, of whom a detailed likeness has come down to us on a stone disc. To mention that she was the daughter of a king would merely serve to underline the pernicious tradition of defining women and their achievements as minor subordinate stars in relation to the galaxy of great male planets. And the male writer might respectfully regard, as an early ancestor-in-craft, Anne Bradstreet (1612?–1672), the first published poet of the New World.

We should not doubt that the world needs and will accept what we fashion with our best effort. Kathleen Raine states it well:

> . . . people crave for the heroic and the beautiful; and when they cease to do so . . . can our civilization long survive? The ugly and the vulgar enable us not to feel, not to think, not to live; they save us from the anguish of living. Let us admit that our society as a whole has chosen death—death in small, painless doses. Fortunes are made by selling it.[16]

She points to the almost universally forgotten use of poetry and the other arts to hold up to us a mirror of our own spiritual and human potential, to strengthen our will to aspire and to transform our vision of ourselves. The true work of art, Rilke said, addresses humanity saying: You must change your life.

But note that he says *you* must change it. That is a great truth which many of us spend our lives evading. Transformation, we vainly hope, will come from an outside agent—the princess will kiss the frog—and it will be painless. But Rilke has the support of Bahá'u'lláh in saying that we must transform ourselves. He makes it clear that growth and change, rescue from stasis, are achieved at a cost. In one of his odes written in Sulaymáníyyih, Bahá'u'lláh declares:

> *If thine aim be to cherish thy life,*
> *approach not our court;*
> *but if sacrifice be thy heart's desire,*
> *come and let others come with thee.*
> *For such is the way of Faith,*
> *if in thy heart thou seekest reunion with Bahá;*
> *shouldst thou refuse to tread this path,*
> *why trouble us? Begone!*[17]

And again, in the afterword to the *Hidden Words*:

> *I bear witness, O friends! that the favor is complete, the argument fulfilled, the proof manifest and the evidence estab-*

lished. Let it now be seen what your endeavors in the path of detachment will reveal.

Because I believe in the truth of the statement that change must be self-initiated, I have made it the theme of a poem in which I hope I have made a legitimate use of irony in depicting rescue as I think many of us would have it be: effortless, dramatic, and imposed by a congenially romantic agent who yet tells us, had we ears to hear, that transformation and transcendence must passionately engage our volition:

RESCUE

It cannot continue like this.
Surely the stranger will come at midnight
burst into the room on quick light feet
shake spring rain spangles from his ripe-wheat hair
the eyes blue opals iridescent with decision
to draw you from your reading chair
to say—the words hard-edged, distinct as
gems on velvet, his voice ascending in excitement—
You must change all of this!

Or next Thursday come
pensively at twilight
to sit coiled in silence on the low divan
then rise with lithe grace
dark locks luxuriant above the flawless brow
grave eyes mushy with thought
to say in slurred excruciating tenderness—
the tone a dreamer's—
Come away, this will not do!

Or come the Morn of Popinjay
stride through the sunlit garden

appear suddenly, filling the doorway,
a lean column, urgent and ebony—
his strong white teeth a keyboard of annunciation—
to clasp your wrist, to say—the voice
a snapping twig—*Look, you must escape!*
his grasp resolute, compelling,
the bronzy knuckles deceptively shell-delicate
come to say—the voice precise,
huskily constricted—*This is the time for risks!*
to say, *Listen, there is no formula!*
to say, *There is a better way!*
to say, *It cannot continue like this!*

BONNIE WILDER
author, teacher, and painter.

The Creative Act and the Spirit

by Bonnie Wilder

Introduction. On becoming a Bahá'í over thirty years ago, I, like most other believers, continued the process I had begun as a seeker—exploring the Bahá'í Writings as they applied to my own life. Until that time, the visual arts had always been my major focus. From then on they would share double-billing with the Bahá'í Faith. Because I was convinced that both were vital I was soon to have a new problem—time management. Nonetheless, soon after my declaration, I began a two-fold program. I continued my work as a painter, initiating a career in art education; and I began to discover and experience the never-ending facets of being a Bahá'í.

The following two-part essay is the result of my attempt to learn more about the connection between art and the Bahá'í Teachings. As I delved into personal memories and books, I discovered that spiritual insights can emerge from any unlikely setting, such as an art classroom. I also learned, as so many others have before, that teachers are often taught by their students, and sometimes when they least expect it.

From Mike to Michelangelo. At about mid-point in my twenty-year career of teaching art in the public high schools of

Houston, Mike Chisenhall made his appearance. A stocky, sandy-haired youth with freckles across his nose and a bit of defensive macho in his walk, Mike was rarely seen without a grin on his face. I soon learned his goal was to become a cartoonist. His hero was Michelangelo. He was glad that their names were almost the same.

Mike could have easily passed through my class unremembered. Over the years, I have had more than four thousand students. After the first few semesters, they seemed to fall into a few general categories. Some were talented, but not serious about developing art abilities. Others took art because the class they really wanted to take was unavailable. Some chose art because they thought it would be so easy they wouldn't have to work. (An opinion not shared by their teacher.) A great many students loved the class from the beginning. They came into the room ready to work feverishly until the bell rang, dampening their elated spirits, causing them to complain the time was too short. They were my inspiration as an art teacher, my *raison d'etre*. They are, for the most part, also the ones I remember best.

Mike Chisenhall was not one of these. Because he loved cartooning so much, he was less than happy when other aspects of the art curriculum were covered. He fidgeted and talked with his neighbors. And despite his perennial happy grin, he would in due course get on his teacher's nerves. Still, I liked him. However, it was his response to a particular assignment that fixed his image on my memory.

Art education journals are replete with reasons school art programs are vital to the system. Some of the most quoted are development of manual dexterity and eye-hand coordination, improved self-image, a more balanced outlook on life, and the acquisition of skills for career and leisure time use. Another aspect, opportunity for creative self-expression, is also highly praised and is probably the most important of all. As a seasoned art educator, I accepted all of these as givens with little conscious thought.

THE STAIRS AT MAZRÁ'IH
by Bonnie Wilder, completed on her 1985 pilgrimage.

It took Mike to bring the last one into particular focus, causing me to internalize the value that creative self-expression can hold for high school students. It was also Mike who, by trusting me enough to express himself honestly, brought home how closely the creative is related to what we as Bahá'ís refer to as spiritual awareness. (I refer to the fleeting, euphoric state one sometimes feels during a visit to the Holy Shrines, in the midst of intense prayer, or when a particular state of detachment has been reached through sacrifice, and one's consciousness of self is thereby greatly lessened. Such moments of insight are often accompanied by an intense desire to give or share with others because of a felt outpouring of love.)

The assignment at hand was indeed a special one. This chosen class of third and fourth year art students appeared deserving of such an opportunity. Collectively, they were about to design a group of major graphics which would be drawn in miniature form and then enlarged and transferred to the walls of the art room—the entire room, as well as sections of the hall on each side of the entrance door. Enduring paint would be used, and the designs were expected to remain in place for years. I had never entrusted a class with such a responsibility before, and they had certainly never had such an opportunity. After seven years in the same classroom, I looked forward eagerly to a new environment, imaginative and color-charged. It never occurred to me to be afraid of what they might do.

They took to it like ducks to water. To get started, each student chose part of the room, such as a display area, a major wall, a door, or the sink alcove, and worked out a rough sketch in colored pencil to express an individual idea. With a minimum of teacher input, all sketches were reviewed and discussed. Seven designs were selected by student vote. The originator of each design would serve as group leader for the others who would assist in carrying out the individual plans. There was a design representing each of the focal points in the class environment.

The Creative Act and the Spirit

During most of this process, Mike sat at the back of the room, fitfully working with pencil and paper. Still bending over the submitted sketches, I realized I had momentarily forgotten him. I looked up to ask how he was doing and noticed his face had taken on an unaccustomed seriousness. He was fidgeting again, but rather than talking with his neighbors, his attention was riveted to his work surface. Paper wads were everywhere, and he continued to push his pencil across yet another sheet. He gave me several quick glances, as though gauging my mood. His eyebrows formed question marks while he tried to muster what could pass for a smile. He was clearly very uncomfortable.

"You're not going to like this. It's not what you asked for. It's crazy. Let me try something else." As I approached he tried to hide what appeared on the last sheet of paper. I was surprised to see that the result of his considerable effort was not the cartoon I had expected. It was not even a drawing. It was a string of words.

More than mere phrases, Mike had composed a paragraph in which he summed up, in his unique way, the meaning art had for him. The total effect was so powerful and unexpected that, for a moment, I could not speak. Immediately, I knew I wanted to have the entire message on view in a prominent place, and I told Mike so. Stunned, he couldn't believe his idea had received such quick acceptance. He answered with enthusiasm, "Yes, ma'am!" His face glowed with an almost fierce delight.

Most of the joy Mike felt came from the fact that he had risked expressing his deepest feelings about art and found a receptive audience, an experience not unlike a spiritual exchange or sharing. He was unaccustomed, I am sure, to discussing abstract concepts. In fact, I doubt if he had ever attempted communication of this kind about art before. Endowed with a small vocabulary, he was not at all the sort of student likely to be judged an "intellectual" by most people. In fact, his I.Q. was probably average. He would have been far more at home cheering at a football game than sitting in

THE SHRINE OF THE BÁB
by Bonnie Wilder, completed on her 1985 pilgrimage.

a library. He had simply put down his own words, although somewhat awkwardly. What they lacked in perfection of style, they compensated for with sincerity, courage, and gut-level truth. This was a fellow not lacking in male pride whose desire to express himself had overruled caution on this occasion. Those who have had frequent contact with seventeen-year-old boys in a peer-group environment can understand what Mike accomplished.

The transformation of the room required eight weeks. At the conclusion, a reporter and photographer from a leading newspaper were on the scene to record the results in the form of a major feature article.

As we had planned, arrows proved to be an appropriate motif in many of the designs, because their symbolism easily suggested the multi-directional nature of creative output. A major attraction was the fifteen-foot rainbow which began high and narrow at the left edge of a wall to allow for audio-visual projection on the white space beneath, looped around the ever-present school clock, and widened on its downward approach to the bottom right corner of the same wall. Turquoise clouds and a yellow sun rested on the top edge of the rainbow near the center. Around the corner, nearby in the sink alcove, a huge faucet appeared, spouting a stream of water, ending in large drops above the splashboard of the counter. This six-foot design repeated the deep, rich pastel colors used throughout—pink, orange, turquoise, yellow, and lettuce green. Strong arrows pointed to the sink and the trash can, carrying the words, "Keep it clean," as a continuing reminder to future hurrying students. Oversized lettering on the doors and display areas tied the whole together for a sophisticated, upbeat, yet unabashedly cheerful atmosphere.

It was usually as the viewer turned back toward the door to leave that Mike's contribution was noticed. Then it took center stage. At the beginning of the project, before any of the graphics were applied to the walls, the entire room had been painted a fresh milky white. However, since Mike

THE MANSION AT BAHJÍ

by Bonnie Wilder. One of three watercolors she completed on her 1985 pilgrimage.

planned to use white lettering, a two-foot band of deep turquoise was added across his area to provide contrast for his message, which spanned the fifty-foot length of the room in several rows of five-inch letters.

Every word had been reproduced along the top edge of the art room wall inside and above the entrance. Declining the help of any of the others, Mike had borrowed a ladder from the custodian's supply room, working relentlessly and alone to make his idea a part of the final scheme. Although the work was sometimes difficult and tedious, he never complained. In fact, he frequently borrowed time from other classes to help push the work to completion. Classmates called him Michelangelo, comparing his efforts to the Sistine Chapel ceiling frescoes. He loved it.

Spiritual Glimmerings and Connections. I mentioned earlier the similarity between the creative act and a heightened spiritual awareness which Mike had brought to my attention. I share with many others the belief that these two entities are part of the same realm. Otto Donald Rogers, an artist and art professor, has expressed in an article in *Bahá'í Studies* magazine the opinion that unity, a fundamental quality of art in its highest form, is a part of the divine world. When it takes shape in the material world through an artist's composition, it attracts, and thereby reflects, a divine message.[1] Viewed in this way, the artist becomes a channel of communication between the source and the recipient. Yet, sometimes (and I have experienced this myself in my own painting), when the act of creation is complete, the artist—as though awakened from a dream—feels he is seeing the results for the first time.

History is rich with examples of artists who credit their Maker as the source of their inspiration. Mike's hero, Michelangelo, sent a stream of letters to his father and brothers with frequent references to such. He wrote in January 1507: "I think I shall be ready to cast my statue . . . pray God that it turns out well."[2] In March of the same year, he

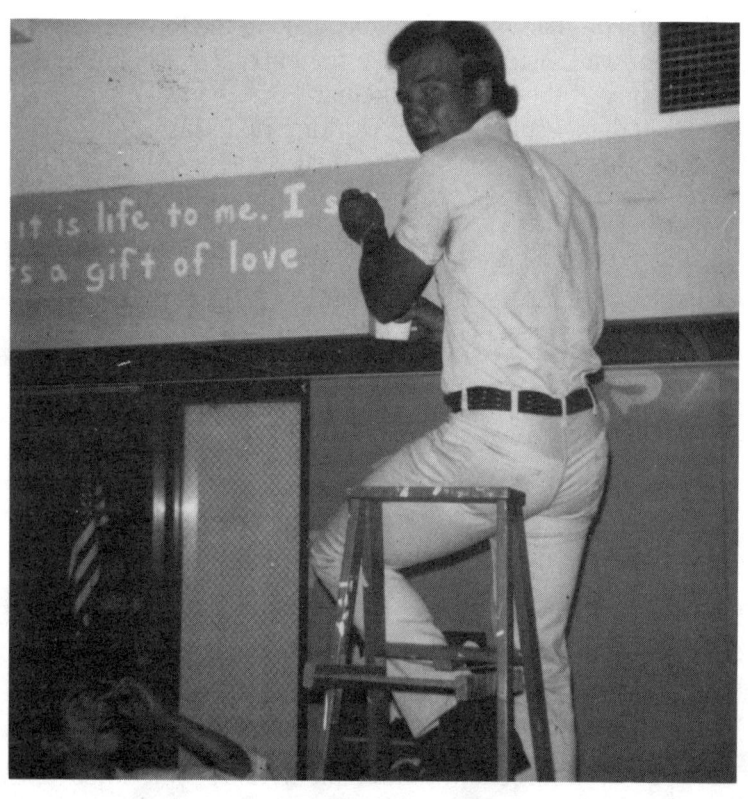

MIKE CHISENHALL
expressing his feelings about art through words, rather than through images.

followed with: "Pray God that my task shall come to a good end."³ Finally, in October he concluded: "My work will bring much honor upon me. I owe all of this to the grace of God."⁴

Michelangelo, who was less known as a poet than he was as a painter and sculptor, wrote a poem entitled "The Artist and His Work" which alludes to his belief both in the immortality of art and the power of the artist to bestow life. I quote it here in part:

> . . . Shapes that seem alive
> Wrought in hard mountain marble, will survive
> Their maker, whom the years to dust return!
> Thus to effect cause yields. Art hath her turn,
> And triumphs over Nature. I, who strive
> With Sculpture, know this well; her wonders live
> In spite of time and death, those tyrants stern.
> So I can give long life to both of us
> In either way, by color or by stone,
> Making the semblance of thy face and mine.⁵

A lesser artist of Michelangelo's time was Leon Battista Alberti, another Italian who had similar thoughts. In 1436, he stated:

> Painting is possessed of divine power, for not only, as it is said of friendship, does it make the absent present, but it also, after many centuries, makes the dead almost alive, so that they are recognized with great admiration for the artist, and with great delight.⁶

Vincent Van Gogh, the Dutch expressionist painter whose tragic life has been made legendary through song, film, and in countless books, demonstrated his high regard for religion by attempting to become a minister as a young man. His humanitarian efforts to assist the poor coal miners of Belgium, where he was sent, caused him to be judged a failure by church officials. They were of the opinion that he was excessively concerned with the miners' welfare, which caused him to lose dignity as a minister. Because he had failed at earlier endeavors, Vincent believed them. Later in life, he brought up the subject in letters written to his brother, Theo, who supported him financially when he changed to art. In 1888, during his most intense and productive period as an artist, he wrote from Arles to Theo in Paris:

> The subject (I am painting) is frightfully difficult, but that is just why I want to conquer it . . . and it does me good to do difficult things. . . . That does not prevent my having a terrible need of—shall I say the word—religion . . . [then] I go out at night to paint the stars . . . [7]

The result was one of his most well-known paintings, Starry Night.

In another letter during the same period, he wrote:

> My dear boy, sometimes I know so well what I want . . . but I cannot, ill as I am, do without something which is greater than I, which is my life—the power to create.[8]

Over the years I've made it a point to include a few days study of both Michelangelo and Van Gogh, among others, in my beginning level art classes, hoping to give them a taste of the heroic which is often an ingredient in an artist's life. I believe once a student is captivated by this quality, he is more likely to look beyond the superficial characteristics of art works new to him, which can sometimes appear awkward to the unpracticed eye. Thus he opens himself more readily to the artist's real message. On at least one occasion, a student was brought to tears after exposure to Van Gogh.

The Bahá'í writings contain many passages which exalt the arts to a lofty rank. One of these even indicates where the artist's "power" referred to in earlier quotes originates:

O people of Baha! The source of crafts, sciences, and arts is the power of reflection. Make ye every effort that out of this ideal Mine there may gleam forth such pearls of wisdom and utterance as will promote the well-being and harmony of all the kindreds of the earth.[9]

In seeking to define "reflection" the dictionary indicates loosely that it is a state leading to ideas or conclusions. Of all creatures on earth, only the human being has the ability to think to the extent that the process may be called reflection.

Several Bahá'í artists have documented their thoughts and experiences in the making of art, relating them to matters of the spirit. Some of these, including the American abstract-expressionist painter, Mark Tobey, and the English potter, Bernard Leach, have achieved international recognition, each leaving behind a major body of work.

Mark Tobey, who was largely self-taught, developed his talent and worldview simultaneously through travel and exchange of ideas on many continents. He also accomplished a near miracle by establishing himself as one of this country's foremost avant-garde painters without ever dwelling at length in New York, the long-accepted stage for the serious artist's debut.

Tobey learned of the Bahá'í Faith from Juliet Thompson when they were both young art students attending classes together. This was at a time when he had begun to search for other and possibly greater forces in the world than the artistic impulse. His acceptance of the Faith in 1918 marked the beginning of its influence on his work, which proved to be lasting. His unique "white writing" style emerged from his studies of oriental calligraphy, resulting in an art that blended East with West both materially on paper and spiritually in concept. Through usually small, subtle paintings Tobey speaks to the viewer in a mystical manner, mirroring his responses to Bahá'í historical events and teachings. For example, he was known to depict effects of light, perhaps of

THE RAINBOW WALL
expressed the elation students felt upon the completion of their eight-week mural project.

moonlight or city lights, and would by this imply a parallel with the spiritual world. Light is known to represent the spirit in the Bahá'í scriptures.[10] The titles of some works are potently revealing in meaning such as "Conflict of the Satanic and Celestial Egos," relating to man's dual nature; "The Void Devouring the Gadget Era," referring to the pervasive materialism in our society; and what could be considered a depiction of spirituality itself, "Lovers of Light," a beautiful painting reminiscent of frost on a windowpane. Tobey's success as a painter, in which the Faith played such a great part, led him to be the first American artist to be given the honor of a solo exhibition at the Louvre Museum in Paris during his own lifetime.

Expressing himself in a second creative medium, Tobey has written poems and essays relating to the spiritual. In 1972, connecting the core of Bahá'í teachings with art, he stated:

> ... the future of the world must be this realization of its oneness, which is the basic teaching as I understand it in the Bahá'í Faith, and from that oneness will naturally develop a new spirit in art, because that's what it is. It's a spirit and it's not new words and it's not new ideas only. It's a different spirit. And that spirit of oneness will be reflected through painting.[11]

Tobey's words connecting the spirit of unity proclaimed by the Faith with painting, can be compared with the following statement of Bahá'u'lláh:

The light which these souls radiate is responsible for the advancement of its peoples. They are like unto leaven which leaveneth the world of being, and constitute the animating force through which the arts and wonders of the world are made manifest.[12]

A resident of Switzerland at the time, Tobey attended the National Bahá'í Convention of that country held in Bern in 1962. As a pioneer to Switzerland during the Ten-Year World Crusade, I was also in attendance and had an opportunity to meet him. I remember thinking he looked something like the *Uncle Sam Wants You* posters of the Second World War, although not as formidable. The Swiss believers stood somewhat in awe of him. They described him as something of a recluse. I decided to speak to him anyway. Thinking he probably didn't wish attention drawn to himself, I was very brief. I told him I also had a deep involvement with art. He looked with interest at the small photographs of my work which I carried in my billfold, offering polite encouragement in a tone that was kind but not condescending. I was with Tobey no more than five minutes and still remember this encounter as one of the many unexpected rewards of pioneering.

The British potter, Bernard Leach, is even more well-known as a potter than Tobey is as painter. Both traveled extensively, and went together to the Orient on at least one occasion. Both incorporated elements of oriental design into their works, and both were profoundly affected by Bahá'í teachings. Leach spent eleven years in the East, traveling to Japan, Korea, and China in particular. He saw himself as a "courier between East and West," although he also visited many other parts of the world during his lifetime. One of his major accomplishments was the establishment of the St. Ives pottery works in Cornwall, England.

Leach saw his art, which began at the age of six, as only one of his "vocations." The other, initiated at about age seventeen, was his search for truth stimulated by the reading of William Blake's poetry. Through experiences he called "stepping stones of belief," he used two approaches to the gaining of knowledge: intellect and intuition. Of these he said:

> The genuine artist requires and uses both all the time, and finds that to place intellect above intuition is simply to mis-

guide his footsteps: count your footsteps and you may fall down the stairs. . . . Intellect is a very good servant but a very bad master.[13]

Leach justified his remarks by referring to a statement of 'Abdu'l-Bahá which connects the word of God with the power to awaken intuition within us. He did not give the written source.

Bahá'ís know of Juliet Thompson as the artist who, in 1912, painted a portrait of 'Abdu'l-Bahá in New York. Many don't realize, however, that she was a painter of some renown who had studied art extensively in New York and Paris, exhibited frequently, and had been received at the White House to paint the First Lady, Mrs. Calvin Coolidge. Juliet was very pretty and enjoyed an active social life, although she never married. Besides being skilled at art, she was an able writer who delighted 'Abdu'l-Bahá with her ability to express herself honestly.

Juliet had a close relationship with 'Abdu'l-Bahá, and he openly admitted that she was one of his favorites among those who attained his presence while he was in New York. We get a glimmering of the spiritual nature of this closeness as we read her diary. Juliet, in describing the sessions of painting 'Abdu'l-Bahá, alluded to the power which seemed to take over her senses at those times:

> Oh, those sittings: so wonderful, yet so humanly difficult! We move from room to room, from one kind of light to another. The Master has given me three half hours, each time in a different room, and each time people come in and watch me. But the miraculous thing is that nothing makes any difference. The minute I begin to work the same rapture takes possession of me. Someone Else looks through my eyes and sees clearly; Someone Else works through my hand with a sort of furious precision.[14]

Marzieh Gail, writing the preface to the diary, stated that 'Abdu'l-Bahá greatly encouraged Juliet's overall involvement in art, telling her it was the same as worship, but toward the end she no longer wanted to go on with it . . . and all she wanted to do was teach the Faith.[15]

Conclusion. On these pages we have touched on diverse time periods and artistic viewpoints, both Bahá'í and non-Bahá'í, in an attempt to discover the connection between the creative act and the spirit. Such an objective probably can never be achieved in an absolute sense, but we have gathered a harvest of hints. Michelangelo spoke of the "grace of God" and the "immortality of art," certainly spiritual terms. Alberti supported this by referring to painting as a "divine power." Van Gogh described his crying need for religion, which he seemed able to satisfy by the act of painting. Mark Tobey gave us a "spirit of oneness," while Bernard Leach offered "intuition awakened by God." Juliet Thompson described a "rapture taking possession," borrowing her eyes and hands.

Time itself will bring us more complete answers. Shoghi Effendi, the Guardian of the Bahá'í Faith, had this to say when questioned by an individual believer concerning future Bahá'í artists:

> We have to wait only a few years to see how the spirit breathed by Bahá'u'lláh will find expression in the work of the artists. What . . . you and other Bahá'ís are attempting are only faint rays that precede the effulgent light of a glorious morn. We cannot yet value the part the Cause is destined to play in the life of society. We will have to give it time. The material this spirit has to mold is too crude and unworthy, but it will at last give way and the cause of Bahá'u'lláh will reveal itself in its full splendour.[16]

The end of this essay brings us back to where we started, for I have not yet shared with you the message Mike Chisenhall wrote with such fervor long ago in my art class. (Forgive me for saving my favorite part for the last.) This was his way of expressing what art meant to him. His words are made more significant by the fact that he was a young, inexperienced student, as yet relatively untouched by the world. He was certainly no Van Gogh, no Tobey. However, I can't help but believe that, while he was writing, some celestial being must have been holding his other hand:

> My first love is art. It is life to me. I seek not the money that is in art, nor do I seek the glory that it might give. I find truth and understanding through the things I draw. What I draw is a part of me and a gift from me to you and the world to share. My gift is simple. It's a gift of love that can't be described. Art is the only way I can truly express my feeling to you. I try to show you the world today and my world that is in my mind. My gift is true. It is a gift of love. My gift is a part of me to you.

(Right before graduation when I asked about possible college plans, Mike answered he thought he would work for a while as a truck driver. He wanted to see the country in an eighteen-wheeler, recording it all on the pages of his sketchbook. He said this with a confident, almost breathless enthusiasm.

After graduation, I didn't see Mike again. About six months later a student who had known him in school told me he was working in a local corrugated cardboard factory, making boxes. Whatever he is doing now, I like to think that Mike followed through on his sketchbook plans and continued to broaden his understanding of the meaning of art.)

Notes

1. Otto Rogers, "The Effect of Revelation on Artistic Expression" in *Bahá'í Studies*, vol. 10 (1982) pp. 53–59.

2. In I. Stone (ed.), *I, Michelangelo, Sculptor* (New York: Signet Books, 1964) p. 40.
3. Ibid.
4. Ibid.
5. Ibid., p. 123.
6. L. B. Alberti, "On Painting" in R. Goldwater and M. Treves (eds.), *Artists On Art* (New York: Pantheon Books, 1945) p. 34.
7. In I. Stone (ed.), *Dear Theo* (New York: Signet Books, 1969) p. 391.
8. Ibid., p. 382.
9. Bahá'u'lláh, *Tablets of Bahá'u'lláh* (Haifa: The Universal House of Justice, 1978) p. 72.
10. A. Dahl, *Mark Tobey: Art and Belief* (Oxford: George Ronald, 1984) p. 34.
11. Ibid., p. 40.
12. Bahá'u'lláh, *Gleanings from the Writings of Bahá'u'lláh* (Wilmette, Ill.: Bahá'í Publishing Committee, 1951) p. 157.
13. B. Leach, *Beyond East and West: Memoirs, Portraits, and Essays* (New York: Watson-Guptill Publications, 1978) p. 305.
14. Juliet Thompson, *The Diary of Juliet Thompson* (Los Angeles: Kalimát Press, 1983) p. 308.
15. Ibid., p. xix.
16. In Helen Hornby (ed.), *Lights of Guidance* (New Delhi: Bahá'í Publishing Trust, 1983) p. 168.

MAYA AND JEFF BOHNHOFF
as the music duo SYNTAX.

But . . . My Mother Was A Singer

by Maya Kaathryn Bohnhoff

WHEN I WAS ENTERING junior high school, I was signed up automatically for the usual requisites: math, English, history, social studies, etc. I was then given a list of electives and told I could choose two. I immediately chose art and music, reasoning that creative writing would probably be covered in my required English class.

The counselor frowned. "That's two art courses," she said. "How about art *or* music, and home economics, typing, or business English?"

"No," I said, "I want art and music."

"Well, what do you want to be when you grow up?" (Ah! *The Question*.)

"A musician," I said.

"You're planning on majoring in music in college?"

"Yes. With a minor in writing—journalism, maybe."

Her nose threatened to wrinkle. "All you can do with a music major is teach. And teachers don't make a good living."

"I don't want to teach it," I said. "I want to *do* it. I want to be a singer. My mother was a singer."

The frown deepened. "Isn't there something else you'd like to be."

"A writer," I answered, "or an artist."

She got tough. "You really need to be more practical about this. Why don't I sign you up for art and business English?"

No music? I panicked, my insides squirming. "I have to have music!" My voice squeaked.

"Well, okay. Music and business English. You could be a secretary."

"I'm already taking English. And I don't want to be a secretary. I want to be a singer."

"I think two art electives is impractical," she said. "I'm signing you up for music and typing."

And so it went. My mother, the singer, couldn't even convince them to let me take the art class. It waited till my sophomore year in high school.

High school offered little change. Athletic programs thrived—art and music strangled in red tape and budget cuts. Arts people (music/writing/art/drama) were "different." I added *weird* to the growing list of adjectives (*impractical, unrealistic, trivial, frivolous*) that seemed to go with *artist* the way cream cheese goes with bagels.

Being a musician was something I was alternately proud of and guilty about. Shouldn't a Bahá'í be driven to go into social services or education? "Why," I asked myself constantly, "Why don't I have a hunger for something *useful?*"

> O Servant of Bahá! Music is regarded as a praiseworthy science at the Threshold of the Almighty.
> —'Abdu'l-Bahá[1]

For something that's supposed to be a "praiseworthy science" music has certainly earned a suspect reputation. Although it permeates every corner of our society—humming in markets and elevators, crooning in doctor's offices, crackling from tiny, tinny pocket radios, weaving its way through movies, TV shows, and commercials, holding halls full of rapt concert goers in thrall—yet we seem to accord music very little importance. When we do, we are more concerned with its evils and excesses than with its sublimity and beauty.

Indeed, those excesses seem to attract more attention than the music itself. And this creates several problems. For one thing, it distracts the audience from the virtues inherent in a particular song and prejudices it into debating the virtues (or lack of them) inherent in a particular genre. For another, it redefines the goal of musicianship. "I want to be a singer" may also mean "I want to be a celebrity," or "I want to make lots of money." This, in turn, creates a situation wherein natural talent and love of the artform need not play any part in being a "successful musician."

And what is a successful musician? Or successful anything, for that matter?

> *O My Servant! The best of men are they that earn a livelihood by their calling and spend on themselves and upon their kindred for the love of God, the Lord of all worlds.*
> —Bahá'u'lláh[2]

There are millions of successful bankers, lawyers, doctors, car mechanics, computer programmers, and electricians who do exactly what Bahá'u'lláh commends in that passage. They earn a living by their calling. They're neither excessively rich nor starvingly poor. There are perhaps equal millions of successful bankers, lawyers, doctors, et al, who are earning a living at something other than their calling because banking, barristry, medicine, or whatever, was more sensible, more respectable, more acceptable, more lucrative, and generally more secure than what they really wanted to do. And also out there are musicians and other artists, either excessively rich or desperately poor, who are actually following that call. There is virtually no "middle class" in the world of art.

Naturally, it's the starving musicians and the excessive

ones who draw the most attention. Mentioning that I was a musician usually drew comments from my elders to the effect that music was a nice hobby for a teenager, but hardly suitable for an adult career. If I really wanted to be of service to mankind, I'd enter the social services in some way.

> ... although sounds are but vibrations in the air which affect the ear's auditory nerve, and these vibrations are but chance phenomena carried along through the air, even so, see how they move the heart. A wonderous melody is wings for the spirit, and maketh the soul to tremble for joy.
> —'Abdu'l-Bahá[3]

"*Tremble for joy* ... " Yes, that's exactly how I respond to music. More than that, it's become a tool for self-knowledge—a shot of quick energy for flagging spirits; a soothing, healing balm to a wounded heart or an aching head; a means of dealing with anger, frustration, and depression; a focus for meditation. It can empty my mind or fill it with stories that, in turn, fill numerous well-worn notebooks. It's a touch from the Unseen Friend—a touch that lifts me toward a higher understanding of who I am and what potential lies within me. I feel the presence of God in music—feel the movement of some divine Spirit. I'm awed by it ... and frustrated by it.

When I try to explain this to anybody—even to other musicians, I find myself at an impasse. First of all, the genre is wrong. Classical music might qualify as spiritually uplifting, but rock and roll? And secondly, this is music I'm talking about, not a religious experience.

Or is it?

> *Every word that proceedeth out of the mouth of God is endowed with such potency as can instill new life into every human*

frame.... Through the mere revelation of the word "Fashioner," issuing forth from His lips and proclaiming His attribute to mankind, such power is released as can generate, through successive ages, all the manifold arts which the hands of man can produce. This, verily, is a certain truth. No sooner is this resplendent word uttered, than its animating energies, stirring within all created things, give birth to the means and instruments whereby such arts can be produced and perfected. All the wondrous achievements ye now witness are the direct consequences of the Revelation of this Name.
—Bahá'u'lláh[4]

"... *instill new life* ..." Now that sounds like a religious experience to me. And why not? If we are created in God's image, and our ability to create is a direct consequence of the revelation of one of God's names, then responding to that name ("Creator"), vibrating to it, reflecting it, is the very essence of our purpose here.

Having created the world and all that liveth and moveth therein, He, through the direct operation of His unconstrained and sovereign will, chose to confer upon man the unique distinction and capacity to know Him and to love Him—a capacity that must needs be regarded as the generating impulse and the primary purpose underlying the whole of creation.
—Bahá'u'lláh[5]

Whatever is in the heavens and whatever is on the earth is a direct evidence of the revelation within it of the attributes and names of God.... To a supreme degree is this true of man who, of all created things, hath been invested with the robe of such gifts.... For in him are potentially revealed all the attributes and names of God to a degree that no other created being hath excelled or surpassed.... Even as He hath revealed: "We will surely show them our signs in the world and

> *in themselves."* Again He saith: *"And also in your own selves: Will ye not then behold the signs of God?"* . . . *In this connection, He who is the eternal King* . . . *hath spoken: "He hath known God who hath known himself."*
>
> —Bahá'u'lláh[6]

We create because God creates. He has endowed us with His most basic attribute, the very cause of our own existence—creative power. This is part and parcel of our purpose for being here: fulfilling that purpose—knowing God—is predicated on the recognition in ourselves of His attributes. But it cannot end with mere recognition. We must use those attributes to fulfill yet another purpose—a collective one:

> *All men have been created to carry forward an ever-advancing civilization. The Almighty beareth me witness: To act like the beasts of the field is unworthy of man.*
>
> —Bahá'u'lláh[7]

That last sentence provides a key to discovering why we do not take the arts as seriously as the Bahá'í Faith would have us do. Taken to the level of the "field," to carry forward an ever-advancing civilization shrinks to simple survival instinct. Our basic animal instincts tell us that our purpose here is to survive. In the field, that may mean hunting successfully, defending territory, digging a burrow. In a highly evolved cultural structure, the hunt is replaced by a foray into the job market and the selection of an education necessary to enter it. Territorial imperative is transmuted into the building of job security. A well-dug burrow becomes a fat bank account or a piece of property.

At first glance, and using our cultural criteria, the arts may seem to have little to do with survival. But they have a tremendous amount to do with carrying forward an ever-advancing civilization, while material security (chimera that it is) has very little to do with it.

Unfortunately, this fact is lost on a good many people. At least it was lost on the teachers and counselors of my acquaintance. With the exception of a college music professor, who decided I was destined to be the next great contralto at the New York Metropolitan Opera, they all told me that music was "a nice hobby," but that I should look elsewhere for a profession.

Ultimately, I even disappointed my music professor. I got involved in drama, an evil distraction from the discipline of music in his view. When I joined a folk-rock band he informed me that I had to make a choice between "serious music" and the other kind. I chose. I left drama, opera, and school, and became a practicing musician.

The choice wasn't easy. Ultimately, it came back to knowing myself and fulfilling a purpose. Singing other people's lyrics in a language I didn't understand, acting out other people's lives, was rewarding—everyone likes applause—but when I sang my own music, the product of my own creative impulse, people reacted with more than just pleasure at being entertained. They were moved in the same way I was moved when I listened to my "muses" and mentors. Music was a spark that jumped from Burning Bush to human heart, and I had some ability to pass the spark along.

It was a strong drive. It took me through years of food stamps and rice cakes, the disappointment and frustration of losing band members and starting over—struggling again and again to find other musicians with the same vision. It helped me survive the inertia when playing "wall-paper" music to crowded dining rooms provided a living for a time, the "Top 40" club act, the living of a double life, with a nine-to-five week and nine-to-two weekend gigs.

Compromise. It can mean solving problems, easing polarities, or the frustrations of dreams. Caught between the energy drain of nine-to-five existence and the desire to pursue my own calling, I found I was truly successful at neither. The need to survive materially precluded having the energy and time to give to a musical career, while my devotion to my creativity kept me from pursuing career goals in more "practical" areas.

Bosses, aware that even at the best of times my heart wasn't entirely on my work, suggested I give up music and concentrate on my job. Or, sympathetic to my dilemma, they told me: "You know, you don't belong here." Coworkers who held a somewhat fictionalized view of the musician's lifestyle seemed to resent the fact that my evenings and weekends were spent in ways they couldn't relate to. They soon grew wary of asking me what I did over the weekend or on holidays. There was also the attitude: "Well, if you're any good, what are you doing working here?" "When are you going to make it big?" Minor setbacks in my "career" provided intensely embarrassing situations at work.

The musical battle has not been without its victories through. After many years of effort my husband and I now produce music we are deeply satisfied with. Our songs have been aired by major rock radio stations in California. We have self-produced a professionally recorded album. But always, on the verge of seeing our labor bear fruit, the awful questions rear their heads: Am I good enough at this? Do I deserve this? Should I even want this?

The knowledge that parents and other interested parties were waiting expectantly for us to grow up was a constant source of self doubt. So, for a while, was the fear that my motives for wanting to be a musician were somehow less than pure. I, too, love applause, and to me the act of sharing music is more rewarding than writing it. Perhaps, I worried, what I longed for was never having to do "an honest day's work" again. (Musicians, I'm told, are notoriously lazy.)

A trip to Fantasy Studios in Berkeley to record an EP (extended play album) put an end to those particular doubts. (After years of unpaid rehearsals I should never have had any.) I have never worked so hard, or so long, or been so emotionally involved in the product of my labor. Exhausted by fifteen-hour days and an eight-month pregnancy, I left Fantasy knowing two things: 1) The studio was aptly named, and 2) This was the best kind of exhaustion I had ever known. I came home with the conviction that I was a musician and a writer by natural inclination, not a celebrity. I loved the *process* of creation. I simply wanted that process to be my "daily grind," and to provide my daily bread.

Somewhere in that studio, I found a deeper understanding of Bahá'u'lláh's admonition to be independent of all save God. Listening to parents, peers, and practicality, it became all too easy to accord them a controlling interest in what I ultimately became. I can't, at this juncture in my life, say whether I will ever earn my living by my calling. But at least I understand now that it is *my* choice to pursue that dream, not someone else's. The time constraints are a definite problem, but I no longer feel guilty about trying to circumvent them. Finding a calling and pursuing it is what God intends for each and all of us. There should be no guilt involved, as long as our creativity never comes between us and the One who gave it to us.

I am optimistic enough to hope my son never feels obligated to choose between his calling and a "practical" career. I hope he will never experience first-hand the problems of purposelessness, apathy, lack of direction, energies turned inward, energies turned destructive—a picture of the general state of affairs among the youth in our present-day culture.

Because of Bahá'u'lláh, I believe that picture will be, to future generations, a mere snapshot of a darker, spiritually insecure age. Something to be stored in a time-capsule as a reminder of what can happen when we lose touch with ourselves, and thereby with our Creator.

For every one of you his paramount duty is to choose for himself that upon which no other may infringe and none usurp from him. Such a thing . . . is the love of God, could ye but perceive it.

—Bahá'u'lláh[8]

In the third Tajallí, Bahá'u'lláh tells us that: "*The possessors of sciences and arts have a great right among the people of the world.*" I believe that great right walks hand-in-hand with a great responsibility—a responsibility which has both individual and social implications.

For the individual—for ourselves, our children and youth—I believe our responsibility is to help every soul find the creator within, that spark deposited by God with a purpose. And when found, to provide an education that will develop the skills necessary to fan that spark into a full, constant blaze. If that fire happens to burn for music instead of science, art rather than social service, we can encourage, not confuse with lectures on practicality and realism. To lecture in that vein, in view of what Bahá'u'lláh and 'Abdu'l-Bahá have written about the arts, would only label us as hypocrites.

It is through the creative spark "stirring within" each of us that we fulfill our purpose—that we come to know God and return His love for us. Any musician who has ever heard a song come to life out of the weave of rhythm and melody, any writer who has ever created a set of characters, any painter who has ever laid brush to canvas, any sculptor who has ever been up to his elbows in clay or marble dust, any woman who has ever given birth to a child, any and all have experienced something central to understanding the love that motivated the First Creator.

> *O Son of Man! Veiled in My immemorial being and in the ancient eternity of My essence, I knew My love for thee, therefore, I created thee, have engraved on thee Mine image and revealed to thee My beauty.*
>
> —Bahá'u'lláh[9]

On a social level lies another responsibility: to reflect the names and attributes of God to our fellow beings; to use our music, our poetry, our prose, our art to enhance the human experience; to strive to cast our spark into the world in the hope that it will take fire in other hearts—or at the very least, give them warmth and joy.

> O bird that singeth sweetly of the Abhá Beauty! . . . In this new age the manifest Light hath, in His Holy Tablets, specifically proclaimed that music, sung or played, is spiritual food for the heart and soul. The musician's art is among those arts worthy of the highest praise, and it moveth the hearts of all those who grieve . . .
> —'Abdu'l-Bahá[10]

Notes

1. From *Bahá'í Writings on Music*, A Compilation of the Universal House of Justice, p. 5.
2. *The Hidden Words of Bahá'u'lláh*, from the Persian, #82.
3. Quoted in *Bahá'í World Faith*, p. 334.
4. *Gleanings from the Writings of Bahá'u'lláh*, LXXIV, pp. 141–42.
5. Ibid., XXVII, p. 65.
6. Ibid., XC, p. 177.
7. Ibid., CIX, p. 215.
8. Ibid., CXXIII, p. 261.
9. *The Hidden Words of Bahá'u'lláh*, from the Arabic, #3.
10. *Selections from the Writings of 'Abdu'l-Bahá*, #74, p. 112.

EARTH MEETING HEAVEN
Dance-Sculpture, 1976. Elaine Phillips (left) and Anne Gordon Atkinson.

The Dilemma of the Artist: A Perspective on the Development of Bahá'í Aesthetics

by Anne Gordon Atkinson

At a recent party I was telling some of my friends about a liturgical dance to the Lord's prayer that three of us (Christian, Jew, Bahá'í) had been invited to do as part of a peace service at a Lutheran Church.

"That's sacrilegious!" responded a Bahá'í listener.

"It is not!" I thought, believing that art is (or at least can be) holy and that there is an appropriate place for art and worship to merge. I gaped back at the friend for several seconds in speechless disbelief.

"Well, I guess it depends on how it's done and what you wear," said the Bahá'í apologetically.

If we look at artists as a diverse subgroup of human society with particular concerns, challenges, and characteristics, we can appreciate the importance of integrating the artistic element within ourselves, our Bahá'í communities, and our larger universe, in much the same way that we strive to integrate other diverse elements into the World Order of Bahá'u'lláh—diversity being its hallmark and quintessential foundation.

Some might argue that artists are not a species separate from the rest of humanity, that this is an artificial classification, and that all human beings have the potential for vast creativity. However, in this essay, I would like to examine some of the general qualities, dualities, and dilemmas associated with artists and those who interact with artists, particularly as they relate to the Bahá'í teaching work and development of the Bahá'í community. In doing so, I will draw upon Bahá'í writings, aesthetic theorists, artists, philosophers, and other spiritually minded thinkers of the nineteenth and twentieth centuries.

What is the role of the artist at this time of explosive change? How can Bahá'í communities encourage the artist to produce "that which will manifest the greatest beauty and perfection before the eyes of men?"[1] How can we know when art has attained its highest purpose? And what kind of art, ultimately, will be produced by the inspiration of this age?

In thinking about these and other related questions we discover various dilemmas faced by artists, art appreciators, critics, and society at large. Seen from one perspective, these dilemmas seem to represent a world of duality and paradox from which there is no escape. From another perspective, they represent challenges that might apply to any facet of life—myriad in its complexity, simple in its essence.

Bahá'u'lláh, writing to a poet, remarked, *"Every word of Thy poetry is indeed like unto a mirror in which the evidences of the devotion and love thou cherishest for God and His chosen ones are reflected. . . . Its perusal hath truly proved highly impressive, for it was indicative of both the light of reunion and the fire of separation."*[2]

Reunion and separation. Joy and sorrow. Light and shadow. These dualities are part of the human experience, and we are often sensitively aware of their dichotomous relationship. Perhaps as the *Tao Te Ching* says, "Under heaven all can see beauty as beauty only because there is ugliness. All can know good as good only because there is evil."[3] Being "under heaven" as we are, we are aware of dichotomies and difficult choices. But perhaps, as Shivas Irons remarks in *Golf in the Kingdom*: "Our relationship to paradox is a barometer of our enlightenment."[4]

Certainly our education, largely based on linear thinking, contention, polarities, and categorization, does not foster a unific view in which dualities might naturally be resolved. But our cultivation of a spiritual vantage point does. In sifting through some of the dilemmas of the artist we may discover that the paradoxical elements are not as irreconcilable as we may think.

"Materialistic" vs. "Spiritual" Art. It is difficult to define what is material and what is spiritual in art. In an article entitled "What Is Sacred in Architecture?" Keith Critchlow, architect and writer, says:

> To raise the issue of the Sacred immediately causes a response in the modern mind which conjures up its opposite—the profane. . . . We may say the profane is concerned only with appearances and not essence, and at worst sets out, as profanation, to obscure the hidden essence of things. The Sacred, on the other hand, sets out to reveal the absolute within the relative and transitory.[5]

He goes on to contrast the material world (subject to the laws of gravity) to the "realm of life" dominated by "levity"—a word meaning "to uplift" that has fallen out of use. The human psyche, he says, is attracted to this elevating principle. He adds:

> Architecture as sacred expression, is concerned with the power of levity in the physical, emotional, intellectual, inspirational and ontological realms, always dedicated to raising experience to a more inclusive and comprehensive unity and integrity. Therefore, it is not without relevance that the vertical dimension is so often the dominant one in so much of sacred architecture.[6]

When the sacred predominates, "the relationships between peoples are increased in harmony and understanding. This in turn raises up and gives birth to expression in the arts in the form of inspiration and beauty." [7]

But what happens when art reflects a materialistic outlook, is weighed down by gravity? "Hatred, partisanship, cliques, jealousy, intrigues are the natural consequences of an aimless, materialist art," says the painter Kandinsky in an essay called "Concerning the Spiritual in Art."[8]

> At those times when the soul tends to be choked by materialist lack of belief, art becomes purposeless, and it is said that art exists for art's sake alone. The relation between art and the world, is, as it were, doped into unconsciousness. The artist and the public drift apart, until at last the public turns its back, or regards the artist as a juggler whose skill and dexterity alone are worthy of applause. It is important for the artist to gauge his position correctly, to realize that he has a duty to his art and to himself, that he is not a king but a servant of a noble end. He must search his soul deeply, develop it and guard it, so that his art may have something on which to rest and does not remain flesh without bones.[9]

Bahíyyih Na<u>kh</u>javání, Bahá'í author, speaks of the result of this materialistic effect upon both artist and mystic:

> What happens to us when art is separated from its spiritual goals and when the mystic is sealed away from the need to communicate is that the "high sort of seeing" which is our birthright becomes inaccessible to us. The artist becomes absorbed in the forms he encounters and uses them like talismans for their own sakes. The mystic appears to be occupied by thoughts and visions that have little or nothing to do with our everyday lives. We find ourselves deprived and unable to celebrate the praise of this matchless Day.[10]

Yet how can we determine what is sacred and what is profane in, for example, modern Western works of art? Mircea Eliade, the late mythologist, said that the "sacred" has not disappeared in the West but has become unrecognizable. It is no longer expressed in conventional religious language, as it was, for example, in the Middle Ages. Nevertheless, he maintained that the sacred is still present. Though modern man:

> wants to be, and declares himself to be areligious, he continues to participate in the sacred through his dreams and his daydreams, through certain attitudes (his love of nature, for example), through his distractions, through his nostalgias and impulses. . . . The artist penetrates . . . into the depths of the world and of his own psyche. From cubism to tachism, we are witnessing a desperate effort on the part of the artist to free himself of the "surface" of things and to penetrate into matter to lay bare its ultimate structures.[11]

Joseph Campbell, another mythologist, spoke about the role of the artist as mythmaker, shaman, healer—one whose "ears are open to the song of the universe."[12] To Campbell, "the function of the artist is the mythologization of the environment and the world."[13]

Mondrian, the painter, expressed the idea that art and artists strive to reflect what is universal:

> We have a nostalgia for the Universal, and that nostalgia must bring a completely new art into being. . . . Art—although an end in itself—like religion—is the means through which we can know the universal and contemplate it in plastic form.[14]

He spoke of the past as being "oppressive as darkness" and in 1920 wrote that "we are at a turning point of culture, at the end of everything ancient. . . . The new culture will be that of the individual—open to the universal and tending to unite more with it."[15]

Tolstoy, the great novelist, historian, and philosopher spoke of the activity of art as being more important than speech, serving to transmit feelings that unite people:

> Art is not, as the metaphysicians say, the manifestation of some mysterious Idea of beauty or God; it is not, as the aesthetic physiologists say, a game in which man lets off his excess of stored-up energy; it is not the expression of man's emotions by external signs; it is not the production of pleasing objects; and, above all, it is not pleasure; but it is a means of union among men joining them together in the same feelings, and indispensable for the life and progress towards well-being of individuals and of humanity.[16]

The poet Guillaume Apollinaire futher emphasized this unifying point when he said:

> Without poets, without artists, men would soon weary of nature's monotony. The sublime idea men have of the universe would collapse with dizzying speed. The order we find in nature, and which is only an effect of art, would at once vanish. Everything would break up in chaos. There would be no seasons, no civilization, no thought, no humanity; even life would give way, and the impotent void would reign everywhere. Poets and artists plot the characteristics of their epoch, and the future docilely falls in with their desires.[17]

This last view is an extremist one, and perhaps it more clearly mirrors the Bahá'í perspective on the need for religion rather than art, but it also suggests a link between the two.

Those of us who have paid heed to the summons of Bahá'u'lláh subscribe to the theory that the highest purpose of art is "to show forth the praise of God."[18] Further, it is the Messengers of God that *"constitute the animating force through which the arts and wonders of the world are made manifest,"*[19] and it is the word of God that releases the power to generate *"all the manifold arts which the hands of man can produce.... No sooner is this resplendent Word uttered, than its animating energies, stirring within all created things, give birth to the means and instruments whereby such arts can be produced and perfected."*[20]

When we contemplate how religion has historically influenced art, we are awed. Looking at, for example, the great Hindu and Buddhist iconography; Jewish music, literature, and theatre; Christian painting, architecture, and sculpture; Islamic calligraphy and inlay tile work, we wonder what will be produced within the scope of the Bahá'í Revelation.

Shoghi Effendi, in a letter written on his behalf, explained that:

> we cannot possibly foresee, standing as we do on the threshold of Bahá'í culture, what forms and characteristics the arts of the future, inspired by this Mighty New Revelation, will have. All that we can be sure of is that they will be wonderful; as every Faith has given rise to a culture which flowered in different forms, so too our beloved Faith may be expected to do the same thing. It is premature to try and grasp what they will be at present.[21]

And he predicted a link between the development of the arts and the spread of the Bahá'í Revelation itself:

> That day will the Cause spread like wildfire when its spirit and teachings are presented on the stage or in art and literature as a whole. Art can better awaken such noble sentiments than cold rationalizing, especially among the mass of people.[22]

How then can we underestimate the role of art in our lives and in our Bahá'í communities? How can we content ourselves with a shallow, materialistic art that does not strive to fulfill its highest purpose?

At present, we have a strongly developing architecture, rich in its multicultural influence, and we have a glimmer of the emergence of dance forms, drama, music, literature, and the visual arts, which are slowly becoming visible through the efforts of individual "pioneers" in these fields.

In another letter written on his behalf, the Guardian expressed the hope that:

> as the Cause grows and talented persons come under its banner, they will begin to produce in art the divine spirit that animates their soul. Every religion has brought with it some form of art. . . . The Temple with all its beauty is only the first ray of an early dawn; even more wondrous things are to be achieved in the future.[22]

Bahá'ís, of course, are not the only ones who have a transcendent view of the purpose of art. Many artists and art enthusiasts have linked art with the power of the spirit. Speaking of art's transformative potential, the mystic Thomas Merton wrote that "art enables us to find ourselves and lose ourselves at the same time."[24] The potter Cecilia Davis Cunningham stated that "in that rather large task of world salvation the artist plays a modest but real role: to create epiphanies of beauty in the mundane surroundings of everyday life."[25] The writer Anais Nin declared: "Art must be for women like a personified ancient ritual where every spiritual thought is made visible, enacted, represented. Art must be like a miracle. Art is a miracle."[26] Theologian Paul Tillich expressed the thought that "art strives to communicate ideas about ultimate meaning, the most profound apprehension of reality."[27] For Tillich, the twentieth century is "a period in which the religious dimension has appeared with astonishing power in non-religious works."[28]

Perhaps the most dramatic statement on visionary art I have found is a description of Russian composer Alexander Scriabin's "Mysterium"—an multimedia symphony-dance-poem that he believed would culminate in the enlightenment of his audience. Scriabin died in 1915, before he fulfilled his vision.

> Scriabin had planned for the "Mysterium" to be a systhesis of the arts that would include colored lights and various scents, as well as musicians and dancers. It would present "the development of the cosmos, the emergence of all mankind, and the individual growth of individual personalities: from Oneness to Duality, into multiplicity and finally to return to the initial oneness. [It] would take seven days, and at the end of the twelfth hour of the seventh day, a new race of men would be born. Each day's performance would elevate the audience and performers to a new plane or level of sensation and vibration."
>
> The work was to be performed in India. A universal temple was to be built in the form of a semicircle that would hold two thousand people with no differentiation between the audience and the performers. Sunrises and sunsets were to be incorporated into the work and Scriabin even planned to employ bells suspended from the clouds over the Himalayas. [It] was to end in enlightenment and universal brotherhood. . . . "Mass joy would be like the ocean endlessly shifting and unchanging. Soul and matter would be released from their corporeal bondage one to the other. Male and female polarization would vanish."[29]

Certainly art does not have to go to the extent of Scriabin's vision to be "spiritual." Nor is there any guarantee that "spiritual" art will have the desired effect upon the viewer, reader, or audience. Artistic experience is often personal, subjective, and conditioned by our cultural background and our ability to create and respond to "spiritual" stimuli. But we can see that art that "seeks to represent the invisible by means of the visible" (in Eliade's words) and that does not present a denigrated view of humankind could trigger a "spiritual" response in both artist and recipient of the art, regardless of whether either or both are aware of the Bahá'í Revelation.

Perhaps the dilemma here is in attempting to define what constitutes a "spiritual" or "materialistic" response to art. Like the response to anything we encounter in life, our ability to respond spiritually is subjective and dependent upon where we are on the pendulum of paradox.

Nurturing and Protecting the Spiritual in Art. Mark Rothko, a modern painter who may be the only artist of our times to have a chapel designed with the sole purpose of displaying a collection of his enormous works, hesitated in his later years to discuss publicly the spirituality behind his work.[20] Roger Lipsey, writing of him, says:

> The spiritual in art requires strategies for its protection. It is easily debased or simply mislaid by too many or incorrect words. It can become a burden for artists who acknowledge a metaphysical dimension but do not wish to be construed as "spiritual," as if they were wearing clerical garb and must behave. And then, no matter how spiritual the artist, his or her struggle has been to achieve a sensuous sign that is astonishing in its own right. The work of art may point beyond itself, but it points to itself as well. "Sensuality," Rothko said, "[is] the basis for being concrete about the world."[31]

We live, after all, in a material world, and it is often in being touched by aspects of this world that we gain a perspective on what is transcendental and immortal.

The Bahá'í writings clearly link the practice of art to worship itself. 'Abdu'l-Bahá explains this link:

> All art is a gift of the Holy Spirit. When this light shines through the mind of a musician, it manifests itself in beautiful harmonies. Again, shining through the mind of a poet, it is seen in fine poetry and poetic prose. When the Light of the Sun of Truth inspires the mind of a painter, he

produces marvelous pictures. These gifts are fulfilling their highest purpose, when showing forth the praise of God.[32]

He emphasizes the sphere of action and its impact upon the development of art and science: "Our actions will help on the world, will spread civilization, will help the progress of science and cause the arts to develop."[33] And He gives general guidance regarding the acquisition of both the sciences and arts:

> In accordance with the Divine Teachings, the acquisition of sciences and the perfection of arts are considered as acts of worship. If a man engages with all his power in the acquisition of a science or in the perfection of an art, it is as if he has been worshipping God in the churches and temples. . . . What bounty greater than this that science should be considered as an act of worship and art as service to the Kingdom of God.[34]

In addition, there is specific guidance written to individuals, such as the passage below:

> I rejoice to hear that thou takest pains with thine art, for in this wonderful new age, art is worship. The more thou strivest to perfect it, the closer wilt thou come to God. What bestowal could be greater than this, that one's art should be even as the act of worshipping the Lord? That is to say, when thy fingers grasp the paint brush, it is as if thou wert at prayer in the Temple.[35]

It is clear, then, that we must find ways to protect and nurture this element of "worship" in our midsts.

But Is Aesthetics a Matter of Concern to Religion? In a paper called "Sin and Bad Taste: Relations between Religious and Aesthetic Criteria," Professor Frank Burch Brown points out that from one point of view aesthetic tastes are a matter of indifference to religion. Impeccable taste is not one of the requirements of religion; the beatitudes do not mention those with "good taste" among the blessed. On the contrary, the poor and the outcast, who might be the least likely to have "good taste" are the ones for whom the Kingdom is said to be most accessible.

Yet he argues that those whose aesthetic taste is dull or perverse are in a poor position to respond to the sacred narratives, rituals, and metaphors central to religious life. Hence, having "bad taste" becomes a moral problem, a mark of profound deprivation. He concludes by suggesting that the answer to "bad taste" may not be "good taste" but a state of grace.[36]

Certainly in the Bahá'í Faith the capacity to discern and to reflect beauty is essential, and our "taste" in artistic matters is expanded when our worldview embraces cultures other than our own. Participating in another's artistic expression may, in fact, be one of the most effective ways of ridding ourselves of prejudice. Consider the effect, for example, of incorporating into Bahá'í gatherings more flexibility, improvisation, sharing, and the aliveness of rich music found in black churches? Or, cultivating and celebrating extended family ties—and enjoying dance as a means of social interaction—as is characteristic of Persian culture. When a culture's expressive forms are accepted, people themselves feel valued, and greater integration and unity become possible.

Although art has played a great part in religion, particularly in the use of liturgical music and dance, educational drama, architecture, symbols, icons, and so forth, matters of aesthetic concern have not always been considered by theology. In an essay entitled "Dramatic Art and Religion: An Uneasy Relation," Lloyd Eby speaks of the tension that often exists between art and religion. He contends that religions have historically been concerned with subject matter or content—the correct performance of rituals, the authority of the institutions—while art depends more on style than subject matter.[37] Addressing the problem of freedom versus authority, he describes art as primarily an expression of an individual's sensibility, representing and reproducing a received culture and tradition ("traditional" art) or protesting some feature of the received culture or tradition ("iconoclastic" art). The latter, he says, is almost certain to be opposed by religious institutions and traditions. According to Eby, religions are based on and embody authority; art, though created against a background of tradition, is inherently antiauthoritarian.

John Stuart Mill, in his celebrated work "On Liberty," describes the kind of climate that individuals who are particularly creative need:

> Persons of genius, it is true, are, and are always likely to be, a small minority; but in order to have them, it is necessary to preserve the soil in which they grow. Genius can only breathe freely in an atmosphere of freedom. Persons of genius are . . . more individual than any other people—less capable, consequently, of fitting themselves, without hurtful compression, into any of the small number of moulds which society provides in order to save its members the trouble of forming their own character. If from their own timidity they consent to be forced into one of these moulds, and to let all that part of themselves which cannot expand under the pressure remain unexpanded, society will be little the better for their genius. If they are of a strong character, and break their fetters, they become a mark for the society which has not suceeded in reducing them to commonplace, to point at with solemn warning as "wild," "erratic," and the like; much as if one should complain of the Niagara river for not flowing smoothly between its banks like a Dutch canal.[38]

The recent letter on the subject of individual rights and freedoms in the World Order of Bahá'u'lláh from the Universal House of Justice to the Bahá'ís in the United States addresses the need for balance between respect for the authority of our embryonic institutions and fostering the individual's right to free expression. The letter has vast implications for artists and for communities and Assemblies dealing with artists. It states:

> As to freedom of expression, a fundamental principle of the Cause, the Administrative Order provides unique methods and channels for its exercise and maintenance; these have been amply described in the writings of the Faith, but they are not yet clearly understood by the friends. For Bahá'u'lláh has extended the scope and deepened the meaning of self-expression. In His elevation of art and of work performed in the service of humanity to acts of worship can be discerned enormous prospects for a new birth of expression in the civilization anticipated by His World Order.[39]

The letter calls for institutions truly to honor and draw upon the talents and expressions of the friends and for individuals to exercise discipline, moderation, and absolute respect for the authority of our institutions. For persons whose individuality and "genius" are well developed the latter can be a formidable task. And for people and institutions unused to dealing with such individuality and its expressions, appreciating and utilizing them to serve the goals of the Cause can be an equal challenge.

Unfortunately, Bahá'í artists are too often slighted, cut out of programs, unacknowledged, disrespected, misunderstood, or damaged by the way they are treated by immature community members and institutions. For some Bahá'í artists, serving the Faith through their art becomes too painful, and retreat from the community is chosen as an easier path. Yet in time—all too often after their passage into the next world—their efforts may be lauded and finally seen as contributing to the development of the Faith.

Current research in terms of other religions corelates religion and aesthetics by taking theological understanding beyond its verbal dimension to embrace the parameters of "religious" art. Writers such as Jacob Neusner, for example, are showing how the study of art is essential for the study of ancient (and contemporary) Judaism.[40] John Dillenberger in *A Theology of Artistic Sensibilities* connects the visual arts with the Christian church and deals with some artists of other faiths. Writing of Bahá'í painter Mark Tobey, Dillenberger says:

> Tobey's Congregationalism was superceded by a conversion to the inclusive Bahá'í Faith, in which all religions are considered to be separate paths to one reality. Tobey believed that this outlook determined the content and aesthetic form of his art; and, indeed, among artists in the twentieth century, Tobey seems unique in feeling the direct influence of religion upon his art. . . . *Conflict of the Satanic and Celestial Egos*, for example . . . discloses the forces which threaten humanity and which can be overcome only if humanity identifies itself with the forces of peace and victory. *Rising Orb* is a self-conscious Bahá'í painting in which horizons from beyond are breaking into the horizon of this time, a hopeful portent for the future.

It is suggested here that the message conveyed in these paintings is didactic rather than spiritual and that other influences that led Tobey toward a more abstract style resulted in a more spiritual art, in exact proportion to the disappearance of an exact religious iconography. Tobey himself recognized this. Although acclaimed by the Bahá'í movement, he was not interested in Bahá'í art, maintaining that in our world, where literacy is high, art especially must be free of particular moorings in order for it to express its transcendent thrusts. Tobey himself was a cosmopolitan spirit, at home in skid row and in affluent society, in the East and in the West, always open to widening influences in the quest for the fullness of humanity.[41]

Dillenberger (like Eliade) feels that "in the modern world, the spiritual perceptions of artists and the full scope of a religious tradition seldom coincide." He also claims, interestingly enough, that "the world of art is more aware of the role of religion in the arts than the world of religion is of art." And, he says, since being creative is a relative matter and "in its special form as art, it is not universally shared, only a tamed creativity is prized by the rank and file, including that of the American church."[42]

Is it too soon to look at how Bahá'í theology and aesthetics interact? I think not. But as with the church, I think we can expect resistance within the Bahá'í community to anything but a "tamed creativity." Hence much of the nurturance and protection we as artists or supporters of the arts might want or expect from our spiritual "family" must come from within and from the fragile (and sometimes barely existent) network of likeminded souls.

Despite the explosive potential of the new revelation and the necessity of utilizing the arts in our teaching work and in the development and integration of our communities, it seems that our communities—like the rest of society—may be wary of much flourishing of creative ideas. Creativity, the lifeblood of cultural change, is generally resisted by any society—"old world" or "new world." As norms are established and maintained, creative thinking of any kind becomes suspect.

What Is the Effect of Creativity on the Artist? Despite attempts to understand creativity and its effects on the artist, it remains illusive. The painter Kandinsky says:

> A work of art is born of the artist in a mysterious and secret way. . . . The artist's life is not one of pleasure. He must not live irresponsibly; he has a difficult work to perform, one which often proves a crown of thorns. He must

realize that his arts, feelings and thoughts are the imponderable but sound material from which his work is to rise; he is free in art, but not in life.[43]

The philosopher Kierkegaard once asked, "What is a poet?" And he answered that "a poet is an unhappy man who in his heart harbors a deep anguish, but whose lips are so fashioned that the moans and cries that pass over them are transformed into ravishing music."[44] The artist, in addition to experiencing the wounds of his/her culture and an oppression that manifests itself most noticeably in terms of economic difficulties, has the added burden of having a vision that is not in sync with others. This leads to inner turmoil and a kind of fragmentation of being bordering on utter existential confusion.

The poet W. B. Yeats described this state when he said, "We who are poets and artists, not being permitted to shoot beyond the tangible, must go from desire to weariness and so to desire again, and live but for the moment when vision comes to our weariness like terrible lightning."[45] For Yeats, "[It is no little thing] to achieve anything in any art, to stand alone perhaps for many years, to go a path no other man has gone, to accept one's own thoughts when the thought of others has the authority of the world behind it." And he asked, "Why should we honor those that die upon the field of battle, a man may show as reckless a courage in entering into the abyss of himself."[46]

Bahá'í painter and Counselor Otto Donald Rogers, in an essay called "The Effect of Revelation on Artistic Expression," described this need for courage in another way:

> In art, the young artist is often unable to give himself to the creative act which alone can transform the work and the artist. We fear that if we give ourselves to evolutionary process, we will lose our identity, our individuality. The opposite is true. When we sacrifice our immediate likes and dislikes to an order greater than ourselves, we

are surprised to find in ourselves a depth of individuality we had dared not hope for.[47]

Bahá'ís, of course, are not exempt from the loneliness that accompanies this kind of courage. Bernard Leach, writing of his close friend, the Bahá'í painter Reginald Turvey, says:

> The genuine artist is usually speaking a language which the average man does not understand. Those of us who have a natural gift which leads to a vocation like painting accept a responsibility guaranteed by our conscience alone, but we desperately need the corroboration of the informed few at least in order to be assured from without that the long years had a meaning and a value.[48]

The artist, then, must be committed to the cultivation of his or her soul without the reassurance that there will be others who will understand—a feat that requires great discipline and sacrifice. Rare are the Mark Tobeys, the Marion Jacks, the Robert Haydens, the Roger Whites of the Bahá'í world who are able to pursue singular devotion to an art form and still maintain a strong Bahá'í identity.

Solitude is often quite essential during the creative process. Even loneliness, though difficult to bear, can at times be a boon to the artist. Natalie Goldberg in *Writing Down the Bones: Freeing the Writer Within* urges writers to

> take the bitter taste of isolation, and from that place feel a kinship and compassion for all people who have been alone. . . . Use loneliness. Its ache creates urgency to reconnect with the world. Take that aching and use it to propel you deeper into your need for expression—to speak, to say who you are and how you care about light and rooms and lullabyes.[49]

At times the artist will wish that he or she was *not* given the desire to create. "Talent is not necessarily a blessing," writes the great psychologist C. J. Jung "It is so only if the rest of the personality keeps pace with it."[50] And although 'Abdu'l-Bahá says that "joy gives one more freedom to create,"[51] it is also true that an inner angst is often necessary to drive the artist to create.

Nietzsche speaks of this condition of turmoil when he says, "One must have chaos inside to give birth to a dancing star."[52] Yet our goal as Bahá'ís is to reflect calmness, moderation, and certitude as we develop our talents and follow our callings. Perhaps as we experience being "called up" by a spiritual longing to create rather out of our own morass, the cultivation of these attributes will present less of a challenge.

Artistic Content. Matisse yearned for "an art of balance, of purity and serenity devoid of troubling or depressing subject-matter, an art which might be for every mental worker, be he businessman or writer, like an appeasing influence, like a mental soother, something like a good armchair in which to rest from physical fatigue."[53]

Art, however, unless it is striving to express pure lyricism, often reflects some kind of dynamic tension. It is the interplay of light and shadows, turmoil and resolution that makes art not only interesting but more effective. Trials are certainly a part of our spiritual and physical life, and art can reflect these conditions and at the same time offer transformation from them. Art calls our attention not just to the beautiful, but to the unjust and painful as well. Hence, it can serve as a catalyst for greater awareness and social change.

I can vividly remember the artistic work that had the greatest effect upon me, a work whose powerful artistic content was fused with a social message and spiritual significance. It was Phillip Glass' opera "Satyagraha," which dealt with Gandhi's years in South Africa. The story, of course, had its tragic elements. Yet the depiction of struggle and death, so beautifully rendered through the symbolic stage movement and music, uplifted me to the point of religious ecstasy. We can imagine how powerful the episodes of our own Faith will be expressed in the future, when wider acceptance and greater resources will be available to us.

As Bahá'í artists living in the "half light," we sometimes wonder if we will more effectively inspire others if we choose to engage in art that does not mention the Faith or art that does. Shoghi Effendi advised us on this point when he said, "The believers are free to paint, write, and compose as their talents guide them."[54] An instrumentalist, for example, may inspire the audience through the sound of his or her instrument alone, whereas a dramatist may feel that by choosing a "spiritual" or Bahá'í-related script the audience may be more moved than if the content were more general.

In terms of the development of Bahá'í drama, we can reflect on 'Abdu'l-Bahá's prophetic statements: "The drama is of the utmost importance. It has been a great educational power in the past; it will be so again;"[55] "The stage will be the pulpit of the future."[56] Dance and drama are natural vehicles for education and upliftment. When these art forms reflect theme and content that convey a spiritual message, an audience can be greatly moved. Mark Tobey reported that while he was on his second pilgrimage, in 1932, the Guardian said that he had translated *The Dawn-Breakers* so that dancers would have Bahá'í motifs for the dance, as he believed that this art would be first to be developed along Bahá'í lines.[57]

The dilemma in producing art with Bahá'í motifs is the constant feeling of inadequacy the artist may feel in portraying so great a subject. The architect Antonio Gaudi said, "Art aspires to the fullest possible expression of the effect it proposes. Religious subjects require the employment of all means in a higher key."[58]

We are told by Shoghi Effendi that "although now is only the very beginning of Bahá'í art, yet the friends who feel they are gifted in such matters should endeavor to develop and cultivate their gifts and through their works to reflect, however inadequately, the Divine spirit which Bahá'u'lláh has breathed into the world."[59] The phrase "however inadequately" helps to quell the awful doubts the artist may have about rising to such a task.

As an artist develops, the methods of reflecting divinity may become more refined and more effective in terms of their impact upon others. Certainly, we are promised that "there will be a new art, a new architecture, fused with all the beauty of the past, but new."[60] When we aspire to play a part in the development of a new art, we are allowing ourselves to contribute to an ever-advancing civilization in a unique way.

Our task is to come to terms with "the tension between the expectations harbored by custom and the introduction of new ways of doing things,"[61] according to philosopher Gadamer, whose collection of essays, *The Revelance of the Beautiful*, addresses the need for continuity between the world of art and our everyday world. In Gadamer's thinking, if art is divorced from everyday life, aesthetics comes to be viewed as separated from the truth. This separation is somewhat like the mutilation to which the Guardian refers when he speaks of separating the spirit of the Cause from its Administrative Order.

Our choice of artistic content relates greatly to our ability to inspire others through our art. And of course we must consider our audience when making choices related to artistic content.

The Problem of Interpretation. "The artist is the mouthpiece of the secrets of the psyche of his time," says Jung. "He believes himself to be speaking out of himself; but the spirit of the age speaks through him."[62] Maintaining a perspective of humility will help us to realize that we are channels that are seized by a spirit larger than ourselves when we create. Jung's perspective is that "the artist is essentially the instrument, and he stands below his work, for which reason we should never expect from him an interpretation of his own work. He achieved his highest with his composition. He must leave the interpretation to others and to the future."[63]

Thus the artist is faced with another dilemma when asked to explain the meaning of the work. My own response to this when asked about the symbolism of a dance or drama work is, "If I could reduce it to words, I would not have done the piece." Yet an audience will frequently want to assign a concrete meaning to the symbolism, unable to recognize that the artist is still being formed by the process of creation, and his or her inability or unwillingness to articulate its meaning may be related to the degree to which the creative energy is still being manifested. Too, artists will often hope that the recipient of the art will derive unique meaning from the piece.

Jung explains that:

> creative expression, which is the absolute contrary of ordinary expression, will be forever hidden from human knowledge. We may continue to describe it and sense it, but in appearance only, and we will never understand it. The creative energy lives and waxes in the man as a tree in the earth from which it takes its nourishment. It might be well, therefore, to regard the creative process as a living thing, implanted, as it were, in the souls of men.[64]

The artist may experience being seized, taught, formed, or transformed by the creative process. Jung comments, "It is not Goethe [the author] who makes Faust [his character], but Faust who makes Goethe."[65] In her classic meditation on craft, *Centering*, Mary C. Richards describes herself as potter at the center of the wheel, being mastered by her clay. Transformation of the self can often be the byproduct of art, particularly if we are sensitive to the spirit flowing through us.

Aware as we are of this age as a time of spiritual reformation, it can be through our art that we struggle to understand this universal reformation, shed our egocentric views, and heal ourselves from the pain of the "old world." Interpreting our work may be nearly impossible, especially as we are in the process of being transformed by it.

The Role of Criticism. Shoghi Effendi assures us that "it is certain that with the spread of the spirit of Bahá'u'lláh a new era will dawn in art and literature. Whereas before the form was perfect but the spirit was lacking, now there will be a glorious spirit embodied in a form immeasurably improved by the quickening genius of the world."[66] As we arise to participate in bringing about this new era, we will inevitably be met with criticism. Some critics will judge the form of our work, others the content. Undoubtedly there will be some who deny the spirit behind it.

The positive side of criticism was expressed by Oscar Wilde when he said, "Diversity of opinion about a work of art shows that the work is new, complex, and vital."[67] Certainly criticism for the sake of evaluation and progress in any field is essential. Yet criticism can also be a deadly enemy of creativity.

Brenda Ueland, in a work entitled *If You Want to Write: A Book about Art, Independence, and Spirit,* discusses the tragic effect that criticism can have upon the writer. "The critics rap us savagely on the head with their thimbles, for our nerve. No one but a virtuoso should be allowed to do it," she says.

> This is one of the results: that people who try to write become anxious, timid, contracted, become perfectionists, so terribly afraid that they may put something down that is not as good as Shakespeare. . . . I hate it [criticism] because of the potentially shining, gentle, gifted people of all ages that it snuffs out every year. It is a murderer of talent. And because the most modest and sensitive people are the most talented . . . these are the very first ones to get killed off. It is the brutal egotists that survive.[68]

Author Virginia Woolf asks in her diary, "Is the time coming when I can endure to read my own writing in print without blushing—shivering and wishing to take cover?"[69] In her case, illness would often follow the publication of a major work, even after successful public recognition. But she would use this time of illness, isolation, and fear of public judgment to "incubate" the next creation.

Bahá'í artists are sometimes acutely sensitive to criticism, especially from fellow Bahá'ís. Certainly the cultivation of detachment on the part of the artist is essential in order to deal with the dilemma of criticism. Here the community's role in the cultivation of encouragement and appreciation is also crucial. Bahá'u'lláh instructs us on this point: "*The people of Bahá should not deny any soul the reward due to him, should treat craftsmen with deference, and unlike the people aforetime, should not defile their tongues with abuse.*"[70]

Geoffrey Nash, at the conclusion of an essay entitled "Can There Be a Bahá'í Poetry?" voices the following appeal:

> To the communities of Bahá'ís we say: be kind to all those with artistic gifts—to those who invariably are introverted and ineloquent in all but their art. To the lonely Bahá'í poet, writing in inhospitable circumstances among aliens or not always enlightened friends, we say: persevere in what you have been given, in what you have to do; do not hide your light under a bushel.[71]

Separateness and Fusion; Order and Chaos. Though artists may remain behind or above their handiwork, they may also be at one with it. Jamake Highwater describes the Native American approach to dance as a form of prayer: "When the Eagle Dancer puts on his costume, when he begins to dance to the music, he doesn't simply perform it; he actually becomes the Eagle itself. The dancer is virtually inseparable from the dance."[72]

Actors at times describe profound experiences that resem-

The Dilemma of the Artist 75

ble those of mystics. Brian Bates in a book entitled *The Way of the Actor: A Path to Knowledge and Power*, describes the role that actors play in traditional societies:

> They are people chosen for their abilities to communicate directly with the "spirit world"; the powers and forces of life which we know to exist but cannot see, visions of truth that lie beyond our normal senses. Actor shamans manifest the "spirit" in dramatic performance, in which they are believed to "fly" to the spirit world, or be possessed by and become the spirits themselves. This view of actors as people with extraordinary abilities is still widespread in Oriental cultures, and in South America and Africa. But in times past, hundreds of years ago, actors in Western societies also performed the role of visionary, healer, and sage. Actors were essentially performing mystics.[73]

Bates contrasts modern ambivalent views regarding the abilities and qualities of the actor, who is often seen as neurotic, insecure, in need of constant attention and applause. Consigned to the frivolous category of "entertainers," actors are not seen as people who can teach us something about life.

Perhaps modern artists experience a greater tension between separateness and fusion because life itself has become so full of tension. Yet the challenge to create order out of chaos has always been a part of the artist's task. The search for order, for wholeness, for unity, is a significant motivating force to create. And perhaps, as author Anthony Storr says in his study of solitude, "the greater the disharmony within, the sharper the spur to seek harmony, or, if one has the gifts, to *create* harmony."[74]

Poet William Wordsworth expresses this idea in the following lines:

> Dust as we are, the immortal spirit grows
> Like harmony in music; there is a dark

> Inscrutable workmanship that reconciles
> Discordant elements, make them cling together
> In one society.[75]

And Yeats, addressing the concept of the reconciliation of divergent realities, tells us that "the nobleness of the arts is in the mingling of contraries, the extremity of sorrow, the extremity of joy, perfection of personality, the perfection of its surrender, overflowing turbulent energy, and marmorean stillness."[76]

As important as ordering discordant elements is to art, we should not confuse love of order for love of art. John Ruskin, who wrote many treatises on aesthetics, remarked:

> It is true that order, in its highest sense, is one of the necessities of art, just as time is a necessity of music; but love of order has no more to do with our right enjoyment of architecture or painting, than love of punctuality with the appreciation of an opera. Experience, I fear, teaches us that accurate and methodical habits in daily life are seldom characteristic of those who either quickly perceive, or richly possess, the creative powers of art; there is, however, nothing inconsistent between the two instincts, and nothing to hinder us from retaining our business habits, and yet fully allowing and enjoying the noblest gifts of Invention.[77]

Ruskin's comment dispels the myth of the erratic artist unable to function in society and still create, and certainly the kind of balance he suggests is a worthy goal for the Bahá'í artist.

The Problem of Time. Time is often against us in our pursuit of artistic development and creation. The need to compromise faces us at every turn. Yet how can we not compromise when our energy is directed into so many different undertakings, most of them worthy of our complete attention? How can we balance our work, family, artistic pursuits, committee meetings, and so forth, and maintain the vision that we are contributing to the birth of a new civilization that requires our full nurturing? Choices lean heavily on the artist.

We are repeatedly urged to reach perfection in our work. Bahá'u'lláh proclaims that *"in every art and skill, God loveth the highest perfection."*[78] With reference to the architecture of Bahá'í Temples, He says, *"It is incumbent upon you to build . . . Houses as perfect as can be built on earth."*[79]

Regarding music, 'Abdu'l-Bahá wrote:

> The art of music must be brought to the highest stage of development, for this is one of the most wonderful arts and in this glorious age of the Lord of Unity it is highly essential to gain its mastery. However, one must endeavor to attain the degree of artistic perfection and not be like those who leave matters unfinished.[80]

Those who think that full creative expression should come quickly might do well to reflect on the words of the Japanese painter Hokusai:

> From the age of six, I felt an impulse to draw the shapes of things. When I was around fifty, I exhibited a group of drawings, but I am not satisfied with anything done before the age of seventy. Only at seventy-three did I have, even approximately, an understanding of the true form and nature of birds, fish, and plants. Consequently, at eighty I will have made great progress; at ninety I will have penetrated to the essence of all things; at one hundred, I will have ascended to a higher and indescribable state; and if I reach a hundred and ten, everything, every dot and every line, will be alive. I invite those who live as long as I do to verify whether I fulfill these promises. Written at the age of seventy-five by me, once Hokusai, now known as Huakivo-Royi, the old man driven mad by drawing.[81]

(Hokusai died at the age of eighty-nine.)

But What About Service, Sacrifice, and Balance? In dedicating ourselves to reviving the world and serving the Cause, we are often called upon to sacrifice our own tastes and comforts. Shoghi Effendi writes:

> Let us scatter to the uttermost corners of the earth; sacrifice our personal interests, comforts, tastes and pleasures; mingle with the divers peoples and kindreds of the world; familiarize ourselves with their manners, traditions, thoughts and customs; arouse, stimulate, and maintain universal interest in the Movement.[82]

Many examples of heroic sacrifices lie at the root of the development of our Faith. We think of Lua Getsinger, who had a talent for drama, but used this gift to attract souls and to teach. Many others have utilized their artistic abilities to serve the Cause or have set them aside to step into a larger arena of sacrificial action. Advice to Bahá'í artists has often been to balance service with artistic goals. To an individual who wrote to Shoghi Effendi regarding whether or not he should pursue voice training, the following was sent:

> He [the Guardian] fully realizes that some decisions are very hard to take in life, and he urges you in this case to do two things: in the first place, are you quite sure two years voice-training will really carry you where you hope it will? . . . It would be a great pity to, in any way, sacrifice your service to the Cause for a career in which the end might not be a substantial one. And in the second he advises you to . . . continue your studies (once you are quite sure about the outcome), providing the Plan does not reach such a critical point that it is *imperative* for you to go as a pioneer in order to really help save the situation. If this need arises in such urgency, he certainly feels you should temporarily give up your singing lessons, for, of course, no

sacrifice is too great for the Cause. What we put into serving it we know serves as a useful and worthy purpose, whereas the outcome of our struggles in life is never assured completely and is certainly insignificant compared to the Faith's importance.[83]

Likewise, to an aspiring writer, a letter on behalf of the Guardian held this message:

> He feels that to devote all one's studies with the object of becoming a Bahá'í author is rather risky. We need Bahá'í authors badly, but you have to be assured that you have the talent to earn your living in that field, and also serve the Faith in it. He feels like the best thing for you to do is to devote your studies to acquiring a sound education, if you like along literary lines, and then see what develops.[84]

Whether an artist chooses to pursue an art form as a vocation or avocation, in one field or several, for a Bahá'í audience or a general one, the ramifications are many. Each decision is fraught with its own complexities. To survive financially, he or she may compromise with a system that requires sacrificing personal vision to produce a more commercial art. If art is pursued as a service (usually in addition to work in the home or outside world) attention to perfection must often be sacrificed. Faced with these kinds of dilemmas, we may experience a sense of tragic loss because there is a gap between our dreams and our reality.

The Dichotomy of Art and Life. Some artists perceive a dichotomy between life and art. Life, encompassing relationships, normality, the ongoing processes of living, can be seen as a kind of threat to the realm of art. Art, the crystalization of experience, the result of focused effort and vision, is likewise in opposition to the flow of life. The dancer Isadora Duncan, described the difference when she said, "Life is the root and art is the flower."[85] At another time she said, "My life has known but two motives—Love and Art. And often Love destroyed Art—and often the imperious call of Art put a tragic end to Love—for these two have known no accord but constant battle."[86]

The poet Rilke expressed this struggle in a letter to a friend:

> Whoever does not consecrate himself wholly to art with all his wishes and values can never reach the highest goal. He is not an artist at all. And now it can be no presumption if I confess that I feel myself to be an artist, weak and wavering in strength and boldness, yet aware of bright goals, and hence to me every creative activity is serious, glorious and true. Not as martyrdom do I regard art—but as a battle the chosen one has to wage with himself and the environment in order to go forward with a pure heart to the greatest goal. . . . But that needs a whole man! Not a few weary leisure hours.[87]

And novelist Gustave Flaubert wrote:

> "For an artist there is only one [principle]: to sacrifice everything to Art. Life for him must be no more than a means to an end, and the last person he must consider is himself."[88]

For a woman (socialized to nurture others) who is also an artist, this kind of sacrifice is particularly difficult. Yet the Bahá'í writings say: "She must become proficient in the arts and sciences and prove by her accomplishments that her abilities and powers have merely been latent."[89] What will happen when she does this?

The (male) poet Rimbaud predicted:

> When the unending servitude of women is broken, when she lives by and for herself, when man—hitherto abominable—has given her her freedom, she too will be a

poet! Women will discover part of the unknown! Will her world of ideas be different from ours? She will discover things strange and unfathomable, repulsive and delicious. We shall take them into ourselves, we shall understand them.[90]

Part of the problem for women is a lack of role models. Alice Walker, author of the best-seller *The Color Purple* and other novels, essays, poems, and children's stories, writes of this dearth of models, particularly for black women. "The absence of models, in literature as in life, to say nothing of painting, is an occupational hazard for the artist, simply because models in art, in behavior, in growth of spirit and intellect—even if rejected—enrich and enlarge one's view of existence." Walker says that she writes "all the things I should have been able to read, consulting, as belatedly discovered models, those writers—most of whom, not surprisingly, are women—who understood that their experience as ordinary human beings was also valuable, and in danger of being misrepresented, distorted, or lost."[91]

Judith Stone, a traditional corporate wife, mother, and homemaker, expresses the need for acknowledging the enormous creativity of women in the spheres of home, garden, and handicrafts:

> I had never been comfortable with the explaining away of women's creativity . . . [and] discovered that grace did abound where I had least expected and that these millions of women whose talents never saw the light of poetry, music, or architecture had nonetheless expressed their creative force, their spirituality, to light the way for their children.[92]

Yet handicapped by both the fear of failure and the fear of success, and caught up with external demands on their time, women will frequently ignore their deepest needs for creative expression.

Men who are denied access to the feeling and intuitive parts of themselves are also held back from creative directions; many would-be artists are pointed towards more "practical" careers. It is no wonder that people (of either sex) who are actualizing their creative potential have difficulty maintaining a balance between art and life. Some have lauded art over life; others have done the opposite. To Flaubert, art offered an escape from suffering. "Life is such a hideous business," he wrote in a letter in 1857, "that the only method of bearing it is to avoid it. And one does avoid it by living in Art, in the ceaseless quest for Truth presented by Beauty."[93]

The great statesman Gandhi, on the other hand, felt that "life is greater than all art. . . . The man whose life comes nearest to perfection is the greatest artist; for what is art without the sure foundation and framework of a noble life?"[94] He particularly felt that "art for art's sake" enslaved and degraded humanity.

The perceived duality of life and art extends itself to sexuality, which has been seen both as a force that is similar to art, and as an impediment to it. Supporting the first view, Rilke wrote: "Artistic experience lies so close to that of sex, to its pain and its ecstasy, that the two manifestations are indeed but different forms of one and the same yearning delight."[95]

The composer Chopin expressed a contrasting view in a priceless letter to his mistress:

> Fidelina, my one and only beloved:
> I will bore you once again with my thoughts on the subject of inspiration and creativity. . . .
> To me, inspiration and creativity come only when I have abstained from a woman for a longish period. When, with passion, I have emptied my fluid into a woman until I am pumped dry then inspiration shuns me and ideas won't crawl into my head. Consider how strange and wonderful it is that the same forces that go to fertilize a woman and

create a human being should go to create a work of art! Yet a man wastes this life-giving fluid for a moment of ecstasy. . . .

Of course, I am speaking only of those who have ability and talent. A fool living without a woman, will merely be driven insane by frustration. . . . On the other hand, unrequited love and unfulfilled passion, sharpened by the image of one's beloved and carrying unbearable frustration with it, can contribute to creativity. . . .

Sweetest Fidelina, how much of that precious fluid, how many forces have I wasted on you! I have not given you a child, and God knows how many excellent inspirations, how many musical ideas have gone to perdition! Works which could have come to life . . . so that you are filled with music and pregnant with my compositions!

Time flies, life runs on, no one can recapture wasted moments. It is with reason that the saints call woman the gate to hell!

No, I take that back. To me you are the gate of paradise. For you I will renounce fame, creativity, everything. To hell with inspiration and ideas. Let my composition disappear in the dark forever.

I kiss your beloved little body all over.

Your most faithful Frederic
Your entirely faithful Frederic
Your most gifted pupil, one who has
skillfully mastered the art of making love

P.S. I wasted time doing nothing yesterday and the letter did not leave so I am adding to it. I have just finished a Prelude.[96]

The kind of schism experienced by Chopin may be felt by Bahá'í artists struggling with the choice of marriage or celibacy. Mark Tobey found that "there are two hells—

marriage and celibacy. Take your choice."[97] Some artists, of course, manage to have successful marriages. But many, dedicated mainly to their art and/or unable to provide a living for a family, find that marriage is not compatible with following an artistic path. Remaining single as a Bahá'í brings its own particular difficulties, especially in the realm of sexuality. For the artist surrounded by liberal attitudes in the art world, this challenge can be hazardous.

Married artists (male and female) may find that they sacrifice artistic goals for the sake of the family or that their devotion to art creates tension within the marriage. On the other hand, marriage can provide the stability and support that artists need in order to create, particularly if the artist's partner is willing to shoulder financial burdens if necessary.

Whether or not "art" and "life" are seen as dichotomies from a Bahá'í perspective, the artist striving to be a Bahá'í or the Bahá'í striving to be an artist is probably affected by some aspect of this dualism.

What About Art and Religion? "Time and again I have been brought back sharply to the fact that art cannot save our souls," said Ruth St. Denis after long study of religion and art forms in Asia and many years of dancing as part of the regular church service in leading churches of this country.[98]

As Bahá'ís, we know that religion is the greatest means for the transformation of our lives and the establishment of the unity of our planet. Yet we can recognize that art that aspires to greatness will have an influence upon our souls. Bahíyyih Nakhjavání writes:

> Great art, therefore, is the expression of the soul's glimpse of certitude in the double-lensed burning glass of an aesthetic structure commensurate with the patterns it perceives. To be great it must also seize us with an entirety that leaves no word untouched by wonder, no line untouched by light. Whether in dance, in song, in color or

rhythm, art conveys us to a place at once familiar and strange. It invites crimson astonishment to leap through our veins. It may tell of pain and anguish; it may exalt with the lilt of every breeze. But whether it comes as lamentation or love, laughter or loss, it is impelled by an urgency that tells of the soul's flight and not the mind's ease.[99]

And she goes on to say that a Bahá'í aesthetic is a form of "seeing" that allows both artist and appreciator to respond as "true believers."

Some perceive a unity in the religious quest and the activity of art; others see these two as often at odds with each other. The great actor and movement artist Francois Delsarte had much to say in support of the former view:

> No true artist has denied his God. For him, art is a magnificent objective, upon whose field appears an entire transluminous world, and to whose visions he incessantly tends to unite himself. For him, art is still a mystic fountain from which escapes a celestial perfume and across which he feels, he sees, he touches in some sort that God who fills him with irrepressible raptures.
>
> Art is divine in its principles, divine in its essence, divine in its action, divine in its end. . . . Art and Prayer so confound themselves in one ineffable unity that I cannot separate the two things.[100]

But he adds, "To depend entirely upon inspiration is as bad as waiting for a shipwreck to learn how to swim."[101]

For others there are great differences between the "saint" —a person who strives to reflect the will of God—and the artist. It has always seemed to me that the saint renounces distinctions and sees with the eye of oneness. The artist, on the other hand, is constantly having to create distinctions, rejecting this to favor that, sharpening the perception of taste and choice.

The composer Wagner remarked that if he had not been an artist the one thing he would have wanted to be was a saint, which he felt it was impossible for him to be as an artist. Inside Wagner the artist, as he himself said, was a saint trying to get out. Yet he was engaged in a great spiritual task. He called his work "the agonizing labor of calling a nonexistent world into being."[102]

Sculptor and illustrator Karen Laub-Novak said:

> Those who find the spiritual quest difficult and think that the artistic quest will be easier are mistaken. It is hard to be an artist. It is even harder to be a developed moral person (a saint). To be both is not twice as hard, but twice squared.[103]

This is perhaps the ultimate dilemma for the Bahá'í artist, who wants his or her life *and* art to reflect the divine. We are called upon to develop saintly characters in the Bahá'í Faith. Perhaps we need to redefine our concept of "saintliness"; perhaps our new definition will incorporate more of what it means to be an artist.

Bernard Leach, Bahá'í potter and poet, articulated the relationship between an artwork and its creator in terms of the meaning both might represent when he asks: "If a pot does not speak, what can a potter say?"[104] Indeed, our works should reflect something of our own "voice" as well as an element of the spirit that lies behind it.

The Bahá'í civilization of the future will assuredly flower in terms of its culture and its art, a reality we can scarcely imagine today. Perhaps at that time, art and religion will have achieved a new kind of unity, and perhaps various artforms will have a greater unity with each other.

Visualizing the future, Isadora Duncan predicted that music, art, architecture, and drama would come together, and:

The Dilemma of the Artist 87

Our theatres will become temples. All drama should have its foundation in religion, for without that it becomes ignoble. . . . The dance of the future will have to become again a high religious art as it was with the Greeks. For art which is not religious is not art, is mere merchandise. The dance will return as I have envisioned it. Mankind will not always expect those with vision to put a seed in the ground and bring it to flowering in a single night.[105]

Cosmologist and physicist Brian Swimme has a different vision of the role of the arts in the future:

That day will come when the political and commercial leaders of all nations sing together. Board members of multi-national corporations will dance before every major decision. Nor will this seem strange, but rather the sanest activity, the most valuable for wisdom. Music will not be understood as entertainment, but as the fullness of life. Dance will not be seen as a side activity, but as the very discipline that leads to truth. . . . To be human is to enter this dance and celebrate this mystery of existence. There is no more powerful political act. To make music is to join with that power that created galaxies. Who can know this and refuse to dance?[106]

Artists, with all of these challenges, have a special mission in the creation of a new civilization. The composer Schumann summarized our task when he said, "To send light into the darkness of men's hearts—such is the obligation of the artist."[107] 'Abdu'l-Bahá more clearly enunciated our mandate in the following words:

Ye must therefore put forth a mighty effort, striving by day and night and resting not for a moment, to acquire an abundant share of all the sciences and arts, that the Divine

Image, which shineth out from the Sun of Truth, may illumine the mirror of the hearts of men.[108]

We have no choice but to embrace all of our dilemmas, offering our rich diversity of thought and talent to the emerging World Order, committed to the work of transforming the self through the agencies of both art and religion. The tests may be formidable; the rewards unquestionably will be sublime.

"I remember you," said the elderly Persian man with an enraptured expression on his face. He pointed a knarled finger at me in the midst of a crowd at the House of Worship. "Seven years ago I saw you dance," he said, shaking his head and placing his hand over his heart. "I never forget it."

At such moments the artist understands immortality. Dilemmas fade to a distant point on the far horizon.

Acknowledgements

I would like to thank the editors of Kalimát Press for their patience and encouragement. In addition, I would like to acknowledge the following (mentors, teachers, co-workers, friends, and family) who have influenced me and provided invaluable support and assistance: Gol Aidun, Mark Tobey, Roger White, Bahíyyih Nakhjavání, Deborah Chicurel Conow, Mark Ochu, Jocelyn Boor, Sasha Rogers-Hariri, Michele and Hossain Danesh, the Bahá'í Arts Council of Canada, Roland Rutland, Judith Hatcher, John Wolfe, Richard Grover, Rita Leydon, Maureen Haghighi, Gordon Kerr, Karen and Allan Washatko, Tom and Patty Kubala, Joni Lincoln, Richard Hill, Shiela Banani, Arthur Dahl, Sr., Joyce Dahl, Gregory Dahl, Kurt Hein, Larry McCullough, Ladjamaya Green, Donna Kime, Chris and Sarah Page, Erika Batdorf, Thaya Batdorf, Elaine Phillips, Danny Phillips, Judith Provost, Gerry O'Mahony, Eric Evans, Paula Henderson, Richard Quinn, Doug Quinn, Mark

Sadan, T. S. Gordon, Jean and Walter Clancy, Jean and Frank Gordon, Joan Campbell, Sara Murphy, Colette Smith, Michelle Broussard, Thomas Leabhart, Marguerite Mathews, Martha Channer, Janet Bucknell, Mona Carloni, Rosamund Brenner, Susan Engle, Robert Reneau, Kathy Magill, Janet Marks, Robert Stockman, Daniel Ware, Carol Rutstein, Charles Nolley, Jeannie Kuipers, Juliet Carson, Amy Krichko, Ellen Weiskopf, Donald Camp, Michael Penn, and the musicians and families of Do'ah.

Notes

1. 'Abdu'l-Bahá, *Selections from the Writings of 'Abdu'l-Bahá* (Haifa: Bahá'í World Center, 1978) p. 145.
2. Bahá'u'lláh, *Tablets of Bahá'u'lláh* (Haifa: Bahá'í World Center, 1978) pp. 175-76.
3. Lao Tsu, *Tao Te Ching*, trans. Gia-Fu Feng and Jane English (New York: Vintage Books, 1972) p. 2.
4. Michael Murphy, *Golf in the Kingdom* (New York: Dell Publishing Co., 1972) p. 164.
5. Keith Critchlow, "What Is Sacred in Architecture?" *Lindisfarne Letter: Geometry and Architect* (W. Stockbridge, MA: Lindisfarne Press, 1980) p. 4.
6. Ibid., p. 5.
7. Ibid., p. 6.
8. Wassily Kandinsky, "Concerning the Spiritual in Art," in *Art, Creativity, and the Sacred*, ed. Diane Apostolos-Cappadona (New York: The Crossroad Publishing Company, 1984) p. 6.
9. Wassily Kandinsky, "An Expressionist Credo," *The Modern Tradition*, ed. Richard Ellmann, Charles Feidelson, Jr. (New York: Oxford University Press, 1965) p. 710.
10. Bahíyyih Nakhjavání, "Artist, Seeker and Seer," *Bahá'í Studies*, Vol. 10 (Ottawa, Ontario: The Association for Bahá'í Studies, 1982) p. 17.
11. Mircea Eliade, "Divinities: Art and the Divine" and "The Sacred and the Modern Artist," *Symbolism, the Sacred, and the Arts*, ed. Diane Apostolos-Cappadona (New York: The Crossroad Publishing Company, 1926) pp. 55, 82–83.

12. Joseph Campbell with Bill Moyers, *The Power of Myth*, ed. Betty Sue Flowers (New York: Doubleday, 1988) p. 85.
13. Ibid.
14. Roger Lipsey, "Mondrian's Ideas," *The American Theosophist*: The Spiritual in the Arts, (Wheaton, Ill.: The Theosophical Society in America, 1982) pp. 100–01.
15. Ibid., p. 105.
16. Leo Tolstoy, "Art as Ethical Communication," *The Modern Tradition*, p. 301.
17. Guillaume Apollinaire, "The Doctrine of Purity," *The Modern Tradition*, p. 117.
18. 'Abdu'l-Bahá, quoted in Lady Blomfield, *The Chosen Highway* (Wilmette, Ill.: Bahá'í Publishing Trust, 1970) p. 167.
19. Bahá'u'lláh, *Gleanings from the Writings of Bahá'u'lláh* (Wilmette, Ill.: Bahá'í Publishing Trust, 1982) p. 157.
20. Ibid., pp. 141-42.
21. Shoghi Effendi, letter to an individual dated 12/23/42, quoted in "Extracts from the Writings and from Letters of the Guardian and The Universal House of Justice on the Arts and Architecture" (unpublished compilation from the Research Department of the Universal House of Justice) p. 2.
22. Shoghi Effendi, letter on his behalf to an individual, quoted in *Bahá'í News*, #73 (May 1933) p. 7.
23. Shoghi Effendi, letter on his behalf to Mrs. Nina Matthison dated 11/12/31, from her files.
24. Thomas Merton, quoted in Stephen De Staebler and Diane Apostolos-Cappadona, "Reflections on Art and the Spirit: A Conversation," *Art, Creativity, and the Sacred*, ed. Diane Apostolos-Cappadona (New York: The Crossroad Publishing Company, 1986) p. 24.
25. Cecilia Davis Cunningham, "Craft: Making and Being," in *Art, Creativity, and the Sacred*, p. 11.
26. Anais Nin, from the author's notes.
27. Paul Tillich, quoted in Lois Ibsen Al Faruqi, "An Islamic Perspective on Symbolism in the Arts: New Thoughts on Figural Representation," *Art, Creativity, and the Sacred*, p. 167.
28. Paul Tillich, "Address on the Occasion of the Opening of the New Galleries and Sculpture Garden of the Museum of Modern Art," *Criterion*, 3:3 (Summer 1964) p. 40.

The Dilemma of the Artist 91

29. Gary Brown, "Music as Magic: Composer Alexander Scriabin," in *The American Theosophist: The Spiritual in the Arts*, p. 157.

30. The Rothko Chapel, located in Houston, contains fourteen of Rothko's works, the number referring to the stations of the cross. The paintings have been described as "the quintessential statement of a unitive spirituality in art." Rothko's feeling about the creative impulse was that it originated from "God's claim on and call to man."

31. Roger Lipsey, "Mark Rothko: They Are Not Pictures," *Parabola: The Creative Response*, 8:1, (February 1988) p. 52.

32. Quote in *The Chosen Highway* (Wilmette, Ill.: Bahá'í Publishing Trust, 1967), p. 167.

33. 'Abdu'l-Bahá, *Paris Talks* (London: Bahá'í Publishing Trust, 1969) pp. 80–81.

34. Quoted in *Bahá'í World Faith*, pp. 377–78.

35. 'Abdu'l-Bahá, from a recently translated Tablet, "Extracts from the Writings and from Letters of the Guardian and The Universal House of Justice on the Arts and Architecture," p. 2.

36. Frank Burch Brown, comments from a paper delivered orally at the American Academy of Religions Annual Meeting, Atlanta, 1986, and from the AAR Book of Abstracts, 1986, p. 82.

37. Lloyd Eby, "Dramatic Art & Religion: An Uneasy Relation," *Dialogue & Alliance: A Journal of the International Religious Foundation, Inc.* 2:1 (Spring 1988) pp. 86–87.

38. John Stuart Mill, "On Liberty," *The Literature of England*, vol. 2 (Glenview, Ill.: Scott, Foresman and Company, 1979) p. 859.

39. The Universal House of Justice, letter to the Followers of Bahá'u'lláh in the United States of America, *Individual Rights and Freedoms in the World Order of Bahá'u'lláh* (Wilmette, Ill.: Bahá'í Publishing Trust, 1989) p. 22.

40. Jacob Neusner, "Studying Judaism through the Art of the Synagogue," *Art as Religious Studies*, ed. Doug Adams and Diane Apostolos-Cappadona (New York: The Crossroad Publishing Company, 1987) pp. 29–57.

41. John Dillenberger, *A Theology of Artistic Sensibilities: The Visual Arts and the Church* (New York: The Crossroad Publishing Company, 1986) pp. 148–49.

42. Ibid., p. 232.

43. Wassily Kandinsky, "An Expressionist Credo," *The Modern Tradition*, pp. 709–10.
44. Soren Kierkegaard, quoted in Langdon B. Gilkey, "Can Art Fill the Vacuum?" *Art, Creativity, and the Sacred*, p. 191.
45. W. B. Yeats, "The Anti-Self," *The Modern Tradition*, p. 763.
46. W. B. Yeats, "The Courage of the Artist," *The Modern Tradition*, p. 170.
47. Otto Donald Rogers, "The Effect of Revelation on Artistic Expression," *Bahá'í Studies*, vol. 10, p. 58.
48. Bernard Leach, "Reginald Turvey," *Reginald Turvey: Art and Life*, ed. Lowell Johnson (Oxford: George Ronald, Publisher, 1986) p. 14.
49. Natalie Goldberg, *Writing Down the Bones* (Boston: Shambhala, 1986) p. 141.
50. Carl Gustav Jung, *Psychological Reflections: A New Anthology of His Writings, 1905-1961*, ed. Jolande Jacobi and R. F. Hull, (Princeton University Press, 1970) p. 184.
51. 'Abdu'l-Bahá, quoted in a letter to an individual from Shoghi Effendi dated 10/5/52, *Unfolding Destiny* (London: Bahá'í Publishing Trust, 1981) p. 461.
52. Friedrich Wilhelm Nietzsche, *The Gay Science*, trans. Walter Kaufman (New York: Random House, 1974).
53. Henri Matisse, "Notes of a Painter," *Artists on Art* (New York: Pantheon Books, 1945) p. 413.
54. Shoghi Effendi, letter written on his behalf to the National Spiritual Assembly of the Bahá'ís of the United States, dated 7/20/46, quoted in *The Dynamic Force of Example* (Wilmette, Ill.: Bahá'í Publishing Trust, 1974) p. 172.
55. 'Abdu'l-Bahá, quoted in *Star of the West*, XIX, p. 341.
56. 'Abdu'l-Bahá, quoted by Loulie Mathews in *The Magazine of the Children of the Kingdom*, June 1923.
57. Excerpt from a pilgrim note by Mark Tobey contained in his "In Memoriam" submitted for *The Bahá'í World*, XVII, 1976-79.
58. Antonio Gaudi, from the author's notes.
59. Shoghi Effendi, letter dated 4/7/35 to an individual, quoted in *The Dynamic Force of Example*, p. 172.
60. 'Abdu'l-Bahá, *Star of the West*, V, p. 149.

61. Hans-Georg Gadamer, *The Relevance of the Beautiful and Other Essays*, ed. Robert Bernasconi (New York: Cambridge University Press, 1986) p. 10.
62. Jung, p. 182.
63. Ibid., p. 183.
64. Ibid., p. 175.
65. Ibid., p. 178.
66. Shoghi Effendi, unpublished letter on behalf of to an individual, dated 3/4/32.
67. Oscar Wilde, from the author's notes.
68. Brenda Ueland, *If You Want to Write: A Book about Art, Independence, and Spirit* (Saint Paul: Graywolf Press, 1987) p. 709.
69. Virginia Woolf, *A Writer's Diary* (New York: Harcourt Brace Jovanovich, Inc., 1954) p. 11.
70. Bahá'u'lláh, *Tablets of Bahá'u'lláh*, pp. 38–39.
71. Geoffrey Nash, "Can There Be a Bahá'í Poetry?" *Response to the Revelation, Bahá'í Studies*, vol. 7, p. 7.
72. Jamake Highwater, quoted in *The Dance Notebook* (Philadelphia: Running Press Book Publishers, 1984) p. 8.
73. Brian Bates, *The Way of the Actor: A Path to Knowledge and Power* (Boston: Shambhala, 1988) p. 3.
74. Anthony Storr, *Solitude: A Return to the Self* (New York: The Free Press, 1988) p. 132.
75. Ibid., p. 185.
76. A. Norman Jeffaires, ed., *W. B. Yeats: Selected Criticism* (London: Macmillan and Co., 1970) p. 164.
77. John Ruskin, "The Nature of the Gothic," *The Literature of England*, p. 950.
78. Bahá'u'lláh, quoted in *Extracts from the Writings Concerning Arts and Crafts* (unpublished compilation from the Research Department of the Universal House of Justice) p. 2.
79. Bahá'u'lláh, from a recently translated Tablet quoted in *Extracts from the Writings and from Letters of the Guardian and The Universal House of Justice on the Arts and Architecture*, p. 1.
80. 'Abdu'l-Bahá, from a recently translated Tablet quoted in *References from the Bahá'í Writings on Various Professions* (unpublished compilation by the Research Department of the Universal House of Justice) p. 2.

81. Hokusai, "Every Dot Will Be Alive," trans. Anne Twitty, *Parabola: The Creative Response*, p. 99.
82. Shoghi Effendi, *Bahá'í Administration* (Wilmette, Ill.: Bahá'í Publishing Trust, 1974) p. 69.
83. Shoghi Effendi, *Unfolding Destiny*, pp. 454–55.
84. Shoghi Effendi, letter on behalf of dated 5/14/57 to an individual, quoted in *Extracts from the Bahá'í Writings on the Subject of Writers and Writing* (unpublished compilation from the Research Department of the Universal House of Justice, July 1980) p. 8.
85. Isadora Duncan, *My Life* (New York: Boni & Liveright, 1927).
86. Isadora Duncan, *The Art of the Dance*, ed. Sheldon Cheney (New York: Theatre Arts Books, 1977) p. 143.
87. Rainer Maria Rilke, "The Mission of the Artist," *The Modern Tradition*, p. 172.
88. Gustave Flaubert, "An Aesthetic Mysticism," *The Modern Tradition*, p. 193.
89. 'Abdu'l-Bahá, *The Promulgation of Universal Peace* (Wilmette, Ill.: Bahá'í Publishing Trust, 1982) pp. 283–84.
90. Arthur Rimbaud, "The Poet as Revolutionary Seer," *The Modern Tradition*, pp. 204–05.
91. Alice Walker, *In Search of our Mother's Gardens* (San Diego: Harcourt Brace Jovanovich, Publishers, 1983) pp. 4, 13.
92. Judith Stone, "Creating the Possible," *Sacred Dimensions of Women's Experience*, ed. Elizabeth Dodson Gray (Wellesley, Mass.: Roundtable Press, 1988) p. 40.
93. Gustave Flaubert, "Art Without Conclusions," *The Modern Tradition*, p. 72.
94. Mahatma Gandhi, *All Men Are Brothers: Autobiographical Reflections*, ed. Krishna Kripalani (New York: Continuum, 1980) p. 163.
95. Rainer Maria Rilke, quoted in *The Lover's Quotation Book: A Literary Companion*, ed. Helen Handley (New York: Penguin Books, 1986) p. 23.
96. Frederick Chopin, letter to Delphine Potocka (c. 1835), quoted in Antonia Fraser, *Love Letters*.
97. Mark Tobey, quoted in Marzieh Gail, "The Days with Mark Tobey," *World Order*, II:3 (Spring 1977) p. 17.

98. Ruth St. Denis, *An Unfinished Life* (New York: AMS Press, 1939).

99. Bahíyyih Nak͟hjavání, "Artist, Seeker and Seer," *Bahá'í Studies*, vol. 10, p. 5.

100. François Delsarte, quoted in Ted Shawn *Every Little Movement* (New York: M. Witmark & Sons, 1963) p. 23.

101. Ibid., p. 24.

102. Richard Wagner, from opera notes in author's collection.

103. Karen Laub-Novak, "The Art of Deception," *Art, Creativity, and the Sacred*, p. 23.

104. Bernard Leach, *Drawings Verse & Belief* (London: One World Publications Ltd, 1988) p. 104.

105. Isadora Duncan, *The Art of the Dance*, pp. 135, 62, 136.

106. Brian Swimme, "Do-re-mi and the Galaxy," *Creation*, II:3, (July/August 1986) pp. 24–25.

107. Robert Schumann, quoted in Kandinsky, "Concerning the Spiritual in Art," *Art, Creativity, and the Sacred*, p. 5.

108. 'Abdu'l-Bahá, *Selections from the Writings of 'Abdu'l-Bahá*, p. 140.

Can Bahá'í Art Become Distinctive?*

by Ludwig Tuman

SHOGHI EFFENDI, the Guardian of the Bahá'í Faith, stated that the Faith will pass through three stages: the Heroic Age, the Formative Age, and the Golden Age. The first commenced in 1844, and was composed of the ministries of the Central Figures of the Faith. The second was initiated in 1921 by 'Abdu'l-Bahá's Will and Testament and is characterized by "the crystallization and shaping of the creative energies" released by the Bahá'í Revelation.[1] Now in its Formative Age, the Faith continues to progress rapidly. However, much remains to be accomplished before it can be said to have attained to that phase within the future Golden Age, when the Most Great Peace will be inaugurated and a world civilization founded. Ours, then, is "an Age of Transition to be identified with the rise and establishment of the Administrative Order," an age that is moving steadily forward towards its fruition.[2]

From this perspective, we see that there can be no distinctively Bahá'í art during our formative Age of Transition, for

*Copyright © by Ludwig Tuman 1989.

such art cannot emerge except as a natural outgrowth of the civilization to be established in the future Golden Age of the Faith. The Guardian clarified, in a letter written on his behalf, that "there is no cultural expression which could be called Bahá'í at this time (distinctive music, literature, art, architecture, etc., being the flower of the civilization and not coming at the beginning of a new Revelation) . . . "[3]

However, one finds that the Cause has evolved to the point that there is now a growing need felt throughout the Bahá'í world for art that is related to the aims and character of the Faith. Such art is often intended for specific purposes, is commissioned by Bahá'í institutions, brought into being under their auspices, and in some cases made available to the public through the mass media. Evidence of this world-wide development has been increasing, especially in the 1980s. In an enumeration of activities to be undertaken for the promotion of world peace, the Universal House of Justice, in 1985, requested all National Spiritual Assemblies to consider

> encouraging Bahá'í artists and musicians to contribute, and consider inviting their non-Bahá'í colleagues to contribute, to the effectiveness of such activities by giving expression through the various arts to important themes relating to world peace.[4]

One of the many responses to this request was a Peace Exhibit co-sponsored by the National Spiritual Assembly of the Bahá'ís and the National Arts Council of Belize. The exhibit included calligraphy, painting, drawing, graphics, sculpture, needlework, and stained glass—all the works being on the theme of peace.[5]

For the Six Year Plan, launched in 1986, the Universal House of Justice made suggestions to National Spiritual Assemblies regarding possible ways of achieving the major objectives of the Plan. Included among such suggested measures was the "use of drama and singing in the teaching and deepening work and in Bahá'í gatherings, where advisable."[6] Further, the Bahá'í Association for Arts has been formed and has held, in 1988, its first arts festival in Groesbeek, Netherlands.[7]

Bahá'í news organs have reported the formation of Bahá'í theatrical groups, or the presentation of theatrical works related to the Faith, in several parts of the world, among them India, Japan, Malaysia, Austria, St. Vincent, Canada, the United States, and Peru.[8] Such presentations sometimes employ puppetry or dance. Among the more recently formed is a Bahá'í youth theatre troupe called "El Teatro de Pan y Paz," based in Puno, Peru, and affiliated with Radio Bahá'í of that country. It has become a permanent institute and offers training in theatre "as a tool for achieving the purposes of the Faith among rural people."[9] Moreover, an international conference for Bahá'í musicians was held in Costa Rica in 1985, under the joint auspices of CIRBAL and the National Spiritual Assembly.[10] The conference deliberated upon and produced music for a variety of purposes, including music for the proclamation of the Faith by radio, by television, and by recording; music for the strengthening of community activities, for deepening, and for the education of children.

It is clear that art produced by Bahá'ís at the present time cannot be considered Bahá'í art, even when it is made for ends such as those mentioned above. However, it might be referred to as *Bahá'í-engendered art*. This term will be used with two applications in mind: in general, the term refers to any art inspired by the Faith and produced by Bahá'ís; and in particular, it refers to art designed for specified uses within the Faith. With the growing demand for this second, more specific kind of Bahá'í-engendered art, Bahá'í artists are finding themselves in a new and challenging situation. What we are witnessing recently is the emergence of a wave of art works in a wide range of mediums and forms, each work designed to meet a certain need or play a particular role within the framework of the aims of the Faith.

This is a different matter from the solitary artist who creates in a style determined exclusively by his own tastes and inclinations, and who relates his creative efforts solely to such themes as personally interest him. In this essay, we are concerned not only with art produced by Bahá'ís, but in particular with that produced by Bahá'ís expressly for the Bahá'í Faith.[11]

A Three-fold Responsibility. The focus here on the creation of art commissioned for specific Bahá'í uses should not be taken to imply that such art is in any way preferable to that created spontaneously without being intended for a particular use. The importance of individual initiative and the right to freedom of expression are affirmed in the Bahá'í teachings.[12] Such initiative and latitude of expression will no doubt play a fundamental role in the processes leading toward the emergence, in the distant future, of a distinctively Bahá'í art. In referring to the styles employed by artists, and the ends and occasions for which art is created by Bahá'ís, the Universal House of Justice in a letter written on its behalf has indicated the unhurried, unforced, and organic nature of cultural development within the Faith:

> Bahá'í artists are entirely free in all these matters to pursue and develop their arts as their inspiration moves them, and it is from their desire to glorify God through their creative activities that new arts and sciences will gradually develop to enrich a new culture.[13]

If we focus, then, on the problems raised by the advent of art created specifically for Bahá'í use, it is only because such problems are new to the Bahá'í community and have not yet been addressed.

When we make art solely for our personal satisfaction, we might not be overly concerned about how it is perceived by others. But when we undertake to make art to be used by the institutions of the Faith for specific purposes such as proclamation and the education of children, then our work becomes something larger than a personal testimony of faith. The dimension of service to mankind, inherent in all art-making, comes to the foreground, and we become responsible for the quality of the service. Moreover, art designed for such purposes is taken by the public to be in some way representative of the Faith of Bahá'u'lláh. This places upon the Bahá'í artist the special responsibility of aspiring to ever greater heights in his ascent toward an utterly unattainable goal: to apply such elevated standards in his art as would befit the sublime and majestic character of the Bahá'í Revelation.

Thus it would seem that the Bahá'í artist, when he works in the service of the Faith, is responsible to the Blessed Beauty (Bahá'u'lláh) for upholding the dignity of His Name; is responsible to the institutions, when it is under their auspices that he undertakes an artistic project; and is responsible to the public for the spiritual service he aspires to render. This three-fold responsibility, which would seem to constitute a new and challenging feature of our present historical juncture, raises certain questions which in some of their aspects are explored in the following remarks. In brief, though the day is distant when distinctively Bahá'í art can be said to have emerged, the time seems to have arrived to ponder and begin to articulate the values and the characteristics that art created expressly for the Faith should manifest. Though we cannot witness the breathtaking sights of the arts of the future Golden Age, nor yet hear their enchanting verses and tones, perhaps we can have the privilege of taking part, during this Age of Transition, in the process whereby new approaches to art-making, derived from the Sacred Writings, will gradually crystallize and take shape.

What Kind of Distinction? One of the questions raised by the prospect of creating art for use within the Faith, is this: what should its distinguishing characteristics be? 'Abdu'l-Bahá gave us a framework within which all Bahá'í endeavors, including those made in the arts, may strive toward distinction:

> I desire distinction for you. The Bahá'ís must be distinguished from others of humanity . . . It is not an ordinary distinction I desire . . . For you I desire spiritual distinction; that is, you must become eminent and distinguished in morals. In the love of God you must become distinguished from all else. You must become distinguished for loving humanity; for unity and accord; for love and justice. In brief, you must become distinguished in all the virtues of the human world; for faithfulness and sincerity; for justice and fidelity; for firmness and steadfastness; for philanthropic deeds and service to the human world; for love toward every human being; for unity and accord with all people; for removing prejudices and promoting international peace. Finally, you must become distinguished for heavenly illumination and acquiring the bestowals of God.[14]

All this is summarized in 'Abdu'l-Bahá's words *"spiritual distinction."* It is a distinction that manifests itself not only in what one says but in what one does. Commenting that it is common for ideals to be discussed but not carried into action, 'Abdu'l-Bahá, on another occasion, went on to say:

> Unhappily this is the road most men tread. But Bahá'ís must not be thus; they must rise above this condition. Actions must be more to them than words . . . They must on all occasions confirm by their actions what they proclaim in words. Their deeds must prove their fidelity, and their actions must show forth divine light.[15]

In this context, might we not regard the making of art as an action? When we consider the great effect art can have on people's lives, we realize that making art can indeed be a decisive action with far-reaching consequences. In our age of rapid acoustic and graphic reproduction and worldwide communication, a single work of art may enter the homes, touch the hearts, and influence the thinking of thousands, even millions, of persons. Can we, should we, separate art-making from everything else we do, and treat it as a self-enclosed terrain where universal religious values have no reason to enter? Should we regard it as a private world where the only criteria of value are one's personal tastes and preferences, likes and dislikes; or as a strictly commercial world where sales matter more than conscience? 'Abdu'l-Bahá's injunction "They must on all occasions confirm by their actions what they proclaim in words," would seem to apply to the action of art-making as well as to any other.

If we seek spiritual distinction in our inner lives, it appears to follow that we should attempt to carry that spiritual distinction into action in our art-making. We may surmise, therefore, that one of the first characteristics of art created for the Bahá'í Faith is that it should "show forth divine light," should manifest "the virtues of the human world," and be imbued with spiritual qualities.

Some Working Guidelines. Whether one is a poet, a musician, a rug weaver, or an architect; whatever the medium, one usually needs to answer four preliminary questions if work on a particular project is to be effective: 1) What is my purpose in general, and in this specific case? 2) For whom is my work intended? 3) What do I wish to say or convey? 4) How shall I say it? These questions may be reduced to four issues by which the work to be done is conceived and produced: purpose, public, content, and style.

In the communications of 'Abdu'l-Bahá we have an ideal example. The Master was always clear about His purpose in His dealings with people; He always took into account the beliefs, the attitudes, the spiritual strengths and weaknesses of the person with whom He conversed, or of the public for whom He wrote. And what He expressed, even the way He expressed it, was invariably derived from His purpose and carefully adapted to the qualities of His listeners or of His readers. This approach, summarized in the following words of the Guardian, might be equally fruitful if applied to the creation of art designed to attract receptive souls or to deepen the believers. Those who present the Faith to the public, he wrote, should bear in mind that

> . . . the fundamental prerequisite for any successful teaching enterprise . . . is to adapt the presentation of the fundamental principles of their Faith to the cultural and religious backgrounds, the ideologies, and the temperament of the divers races and nations whom they are called upon to enlighten and attract.[16]

When we undertake to produce art, then, for the promotion of the interests of the Faith and as a service to mankind, we need to have in mind the purpose of the work to be done, the public for whom our service is intended, and the content and style of what we wish to communicate. Even if we are unsure about the latter two, it is often sufficient to start with a clear notion of our purpose and of the intended public. From this working minimum, we can then usually feel our way toward a content and style that are appropriate.

Let us take, as an illustration, one of the subjects discussed at the 1985 International Conference for Bahá'í Musicians: music to stimulate the masses. The intended audience is "the masses." The purpose is "to stimulate." Both criteria are broad and permit a great variety of musical realizations, each of which would vary according to the characteristics of the specific case at hand.

Let us say that the masses in question are those of rural Ecuador, and that the purpose is to stimulate them to a greater appreciation of their traditional culture. This might result in songs written in the traditional styles of that people, performed with indigenous instruments, and supplied with texts which extol such traditional values as unity, truthfulness, and hospitality. Alternatively, if the masses in question are the city dwellers of New York and the purpose is to acquaint them with the Bahá'í teachings by radio, then obviously a very different content and other styles of music are called for.

Excellence in Technique, Excellence in Values. In the Bahá'í teachings, art, and also science, crafts, and professions, are regarded as "an act of worship," as "service to the Kingdom of God," and as a "service to humanity." On this theme 'Abdu'l-Bahá wrote:

> What bounty greater than this that science should be considered as an act of worship and art as service to the Kingdom of God.[17]
>
> In this great dispensation, art (or a profession) is identical with an act of worship and this is a clear text of the Blessed Perfection.[18]

In one of His talks, He also stated the following:

> In the Bahá'í Cause arts, sciences and all crafts are (counted as) worship. . . . Briefly, all effort and exertion put forth by man from the fullness of his heart is worship, if it is prompted by the highest motives and the will to do service to humanity.[19]

It was emphasized by Bahá'u'lláh, moreover, that the arts and sciences must be of benefit to mankind:

> Of all the arts and sciences, set the children to studying those which will result in advantage to man, will ensure his progress and elevate his rank.[20]

As the need and demand for Bahá'í-engendered art steadily grows throughout the Bahá'í world, those who are entrusted with producing such art, or with estimating its fitness for a given project, are frequently faced with the problem of evaluation. Statements from the Writings such as those given above establish a framework within which evaluation can be made: the arts are a form of worship and are to render a beneficial service to humanity. Within this broad framework, Bahá'í artists can and do aspire to render services of great value. Both artists and project coordinators often speak of the need for excellence in all art associated with the name of the Faith. The question, however, is how such quality is achieved and in what terms it can be gauged.

What is excellence in art? Surely all supporters of the Bahá'í Faith are agreed that what is produced for the Faith should be of high caliber, but there is little agreement in the world at large, and as yet no consensus in the Bahá'í community, as to what constitutes artistic excellence.

Where there is some agreement is in the area of technical quality. Each art form makes certain technical demands on its maker or its executor, and only when these demands are well met does the finished work become effective. One can say that a stage actor's rendition was technically excellent because he made no mistakes, spoke clearly, projected his voice well, and gave life to the role he was playing. One can say a certain song is technically excellent because its music fits well with its words, its form is well conceived, and it is written with consistent materials and economy of means. Thus, to achieve this kind of excellence, one need only meet the technical demands of the artistic medium and of the particular style in which one works.

But is there no more to art than this? Many would say there is not; or if there is, it is only a matter of personal taste. Yet how shall we explain the following experience which many of us surely have had? We go to see an award-winning film. We are impressed by its cogent plot, its imaginative script writing, its persuasive actors, its resourceful cinematography, its evocative background music, its well-paced drama, and its spectacular special effects. It is technically excellent. Yet as Bahá'ís we cannot help but feel disappointed when we find that the film portrays material gain and sensual pleasure as the highest good in life, raises selfishness to a virtue, presents sexual promiscuity as normal and acceptable, and makes a hero of someone for whom cold-heartedness, deceit, and violence are a way of life. "The director is just presenting life as it really is," our friends tell us. But the feeling persists within us that something is wrong. It persists with good reason. We know that art, like all other activities, should be of service to humankind. And to be of service it must speak not only of life as it is, but of life as it can be at its best. In other words, it needs to be motivated by a desire to draw mankind nearer to God, and should be imbued with spiritual values. When thus motivated, the making of art can take its place among those actions that "show forth divine light" and manifest "the virtues of the human world."[21]

If we respond to works of art not only in terms of their technical qualities but also in terms of the spiritual values they manifest or fail to manifest, might it not be possible then to speak of spiritual excellence in the arts? Might not this concept enable us to formulate more completely what it is we are aspiring toward in our creative work as artists? A work of art may be technically excellent but spiritually lacking. Or it may manifest some noble spiritual values, yet be weak technically. From this point of view, it would appear that the best art is that which combines technical excellence with spiritual distinction.[22]

Let us consider music as an example. How can we speak of music manifesting spiritual values? When we remove the words from a song, or when we listen to purely instrumental music, we are dealing only with tones and rhythms. Is it possible for sheer sound, organized into tones and rhythms, to manifest spiritual values? This is a subtle problem, but

'Abdu'l-Bahá has indicated its solution. In a Tablet to a believer, He once recommended the following:

> Try, if thou canst, to use spiritual melodies, songs, and tunes, and to bring the earthly music into harmony with the celestial melody.[23]

We see, then, that there is such a thing as spiritual melody. The implication seems to be that melodies may vary in the degree to which they possess the quality of spirituality, some manifesting this quality to a high degree, some to a lesser extent, and some hardly at all. Note that this concept does not refer to the words of a song, but to the actual *sound* of the music. This statement of 'Abdu'l-Bahá is exceedingly important for the arts, for it indirectly confirms what ancient philosophers often maintained and what modern philosophers are beginning to rediscover: that music, as well as the other arts, is capable of showing forth both those attributes that belong to man's lower nature and those attributes that spring from his divine nature.

Having found that music can, indeed, manifest spiritual qualities, we might look to the Writings to see what some of the attributes are that music ought specifically to show forth or to shun. In the Kitáb-i Aqdas, the Blessed Beauty declares:

> *We have permitted you to listen to music and singing. Beware lest such listening cause you to transgress the bounds of decency and dignity. Rejoice in the joy of My Most Great Name through which the hearts are enchanted and the minds of the well-favored are attracted.*

And again:

> *We have made music a ladder by which souls may ascend to the realm on high. Change it not into wings for self and passion.*[24]

Can Bahá'í Art Become Distinctive? 109

And in a letter written on behalf of the Guardian, we find the following:

> The element of music is, no doubt, an important feature of all Bahá'í gatherings. The Master Himself has emphasized its importance. But the friends should in this, as well as in all other things, not pass beyond the limits of moderation, and should take great care to maintain the strict spiritual character of all their gatherings. Music should lead to spirituality, and provided it creates such an atmosphere there can be no objection against it.[25]

Here we have a clear statement on the fundamental purpose of music: it should "lead to spirituality," so that it may serve as "a ladder by which souls may ascend to the realm on high." Bahá'u'lláh specifically warns not to turn music into "wings for self and passion," for music should be "the food of the soul and spirit"[26] rather than a stimulus to the desires and inclinations of man's lower nature. These passages also mention three values or spiritual qualities within whose bounds all music made for the Faith should abide: decency, dignity, and moderation. Surely we could find in the Writings many other spiritual qualities with which our art could be enriched, but with these three values perhaps it is possible to make a beginning.

Moreover, the spiritual values mentioned in the above quotations, such as decency and moderation, pertain not only to music but to all arts; indeed, such attributes are essential to the Bahá'í way of life itself in all of its manifestations.[27] Further still, on a moral plane, the arts share the same general purpose and the same spiritual orientation. In the words of the Universal House of Justice:

> Music, art, and literature . . . are to represent and inspire the noblest sentiments and highest aspirations and should be a source of comfort and tranquillity for troubled souls . . .[28]

Might we not find in this passage some of the principal criteria for measuring excellence, and some of the traits that should characterize Bahá'í-engendered art?

In sum, when we make art for use within the Faith, we need to ask ourselves: Is it well-crafted? Is it well-executed? This would assure technical excellence. But we need also to ask ourselves: Does it abide within the bounds of decency, dignity, and moderation? Does it "represent and inspire the noblest sentiments and highest aspirations?" Is it "a source of comfort and tranquillity for troubled souls?" This would be a step toward spiritual distinction.

Art Classification: A Sociological and a Spiritual Approach. There are many ways of classifying art. One of them is the sociological approach. For example, art can be classified according to the use it is given, the public for whom it is created, the style in which it is conceived, or the specific theme it deals with (when it has one). So we have art for proclamation (its use); art for children (its public); traditional ethnic art (its style); and art concerning the history of the Faith (its theme). Such classifications, focusing on art in relation to the poeple who use it and for whom it is intended, are derived from a sociological point of view.

We have found, however, that when viewed in spiritual terms, all the arts, even the nonverbal ones, may be said to carry a kind of message, for they can impart to the public an experience in which certain values are inherent. Such values are manifest not only in the words that may accompany an art form, but in the very substance of the medium, in the way that the elements of composition are ordered. The lines, shapes, and colors of visual art; the play of opposing forces and their manner of resolution in dramatic works; the gestures and patterned movements of dance; the relations of form and space, light and shadow in spatial arts such as architecture; the melodies, rhythms, and harmonies of music: all such phenomena are impregnated with, and inform us about, the artist's vision of life and his hierarchy of values.[29] From this point of view, all kinds of art, verbal and nonverbal, and including those which are called abstract, appear to have something in common: they communicate the beliefs, values, and attitudes of the people who create and produce them—even when the artist has no conscious intention of communicating a particular message, and even when the public has no motive for viewing, reading, or listening to his art work other than to be entertained.

The sociological view tends to classify types of art according to their social uses and their intended audiences. However, what we might call a spiritual view, as described above, makes it possible to classify art according to the kinds of values it manifests. It seems that both approaches are necessary. The sociological approach permits us to define the purpose, the public, and the other parameters of an artisitc project. The spiritual approach permits us to scrutinize the elements of which a given style of art is composed, to attempt to identify the values it manifests; and to ask whether it shows sufficient dignity, decency, and moderation, and whether it represents the noblest sentiments and highest aspirations, so as to merit being used in a Bahá'í project.

Music and Text. For an example of how the process outlined above might work, we could turn to the art of song-writing. Bahá'í themes are commonly set to music in a current musical style, in the confidence that the spiritual subject matter of the text will lend its dignity to virtually any musical style employed, and that the combination will thereby have an ennobling effect on the listener. This method has been widely used by some religious movements. From a sociological point of view, such a method seems quite reasonable, for it has the advantage of communicating with people in a musical style they understand and can identify with. But from a spiritual point of view, caution is called for.

We have seen that the degree of nobility of a musical style

depends on the degree to which it manifests spiritual qualities, entirely apart from what its text may say. Let us suppose that a text concerned with the life of the Blessed Beauty were to be combined with a musical style in which decency and dignity were lacking. Not even such a lofty theme would suffice to elevate the musical style, for the values manifested by the latter depend on its own musical substance and not on the text that accompanies it. The result of such a combination would simply be a clash between an exalted theme and irreverent music. Rather than ennobling the musical style, the composer or arranger would be running the risk of detracting from the image of the Faith. An indiscriminate use of this method, then, might end by allowing the sacred character of the message of the Faith to be compromised by an unbefitting medium. In this connection the Guardian's counsel seems especially relevant: he who presents the Faith to the public should "bear in mind the claims which his Faith is constantly making upon him to preserve its dignity, and station."[30]

But it should not be concluded that the method itself is unsuitable. Rather, the principle involved is that one needs to bear in mind the spiritual values inherent in a given Bahá'í theme, and then search for an existing style of art, or develop a new one, that manifests values which are compatible. In the case of songs on Bahá'í themes, when the spiritual values implicit in the textual subject are compatible with those manifested by the musical style, the result is pleasing and effective.

In this matter, there is naturally an important difference between song texts taken from the Sacred Writings and those written by Bahá'ís. Whatever the style in which they are set to music, the Sacred Writings would appear to call for a marked degree of sobriety and dignity.[31] With song texts written by Bahá'ís, however, the subject matter, the purpose, and the intended audience would allow for considerable latitude in the style employed and the kind of sentiment expressed. For a text intended to teach pre-school children the

Bahá'í subject of kindness to animals, a musical style would need to be sought which combines the simplicity, purity, and innocence of children with the love, delight, kindness, and mercy implied in the song's subject. By contrast, associated with the subject of Spiritual Assemblies are such values as order, stateliness, guidance, and authority. It seems evident that some musical styles, such as those placing a strong emphasis on diversion and sensual pleasure, would not be compatible with this theme and therefore would not lend themselves to being employed in a song whose text is concerned with Bahá'í Assemblies. But there might be other existing styles which do prove compatible. It is a matter of analysis, careful selection, and adaptation.

Unity in Diversity. We are living in a Formative Age destined to "witness the crystallization and shaping of the creative energies" released by the Revelation of Bahá'u'lláh. With regard to the arts, this shaping process has at least three important characteristics. First, the Sacred Writings make broad statements about the purpose of the arts but do not go into detail as to how to realize that purpose. Second, we cannot even dimly envision what the arts will be like in the future. And third, we cannot rely on art as it is practiced in contemporary society, to guide us through the Formative Age. Commenting on the chaos which has overtaken contemporary society, the Universal House of Justice wrote:

> Every discerning eye clearly sees that the early stages of this chaos have daily manifestations affecting the structure of human society; its destructive forces are uprooting time-honored institutions.... The same destructive forces are also deranging the political, economic, scientific, literary, and moral equilibrium of the world and are destroying the fairest fruits of the present civilization.... Even music, art, and literature, which are to represent and inspire the noblest sentiments and highest aspirations and should be

a source of comfort and tranquillity for troubled souls, have strayed from the straight path and are now the mirrors of the soiled hearts of this confused, unprincipled, and disordered age.[32]

Meanwhile, a demand is beginning to emerge worldwide for a Bahá'í-engendered art addressed to specific needs. We find ourselves, therefore, in an unusual and challenging situation. Though conscious of working toward something noble, we cannot envision the form our art will eventually take in the future. Though called upon to make art for people living in the present, the Bahá'í artist finds that present-day art has, by and large, "strayed from the straight path" and has become a "mirror of the soiled hearts" of his generation—a fact that renders much of it, whether popular or "serious," unsuitable for use in Bahá'í projects, and requires of him to exercise caution and sound judgment as to when and how it might be employed.

There are two things, however, on which we can safely rely. The guidelines laid down by Bahá'u'lláh, if we are faithful to them, will enable us and future generations to feel our way gradually toward a new world of art, within which unprecedented concepts and styles may well be generated. And while this evolutionary process is underway, we can rely, as did the Guardian, on artistic styles developed at various times in the past and in various parts of the world—styles whose basis is spiritual, whose values are consonant with Bahá'í values, and whose beauty and integrity have withstood the test of time.

What is being suggested here is not that we merely copy established styles of art, but rather that we creatively modify them according to our needs and adapt them to our purposes. Such a process of creative adaptation, over the decades, would gradually produce a worldwide pattern of unity in diversity in the arts. The result would be not one, but dozens or perhaps hundreds of styles of art being used for the Faith. This diversity, like the world's variety of flowering plant species that have adapted themselves to varying environments, would result naturally by adapting styles of art both to the specific needs and purposes of the Faith, and to the various cultural groups for whom the artwork is intended. One of the most important unifying elements in this diversity of styles would be found in their adherence to the high spiritual standards set for the arts by the Blessed Beauty.

Conclusion. In summary, the Bahá'í teachings appear to point toward several traits that should characterize, or that seem likely to characterize, the making of art for specific uses within the Faith. First, the practice of such art, and indeed of all arts, sciences, and professions, is regarded in the Bahá'í teachings as an act of worship, a service to the Kingdom of God, and a service to humankind, for whom it should prove to be a means to "ensure his progress and elevate his rank."[33] Second, it would seem that the Bahá'í who produces such art carries a three-fold responsibility: toward Bahá'u'lláh for upholding the dignity of His Name, toward Bahá'í institutions when it is under their auspices that he undertakes an artistic project, and toward the public for the spiritual service he renders. Third, the making of such art should aspire toward spiritual distinction; that is, it should "show forth divine light" and manifest "the virtues of the world of humanity."[34] It should seek excellence both in its technical quality and in its expression of spiritual ideals, by representing and inspiring "the noblest sentiments and highest aspirations" and by being "a source of comfort and tranquillity for troubled souls."[35] Fourth, such Bahá'í-engendered art is in each case intended for a specific purpose and a particular public to whose characteristics both the content and the style are adapted. Fifth, in view of the inadequacy of much of present-day art in the world at large, and considering the great cultural diversity in the Bahá'í world community, it appears likely that Bahá'í-engendered art, while it produces new approaches and concepts, will also manifest a broad-minded and receptive attitude toward the traditional art of the world's past and present civilizations, and a willingness to learn from and assimilate such of their stylistic elements as are compatible with Bahá'í teachings and standards. Sixth and finally, the adaptation of Bahá'í-engendered art to the multiple needs, aims and purposes of the Faith, and to the public's variety of cultural backgrounds, seems likely to generate in time a world-embracing pattern of unity in diversity in the arts—a pattern whose spiritual hub of unity would be found in the high standards set for the arts by Bahá'u'lláh.

Notes

1. Shoghi Effendi, *God Passes By* (Wilmette: Bahá'í Publishing Trust, 1944) pp. xiii-xiv, 411.

2. Ibid., pp. 325, 411.

3. *Bahá'í Writings on Music* (Oakham, England: Bahá'í Publishing Trust, 1973) pp. 12–13.

4. From a letter of the Universal House of Justice to all National Spiritual Assemblies, dated 23 January 1985, *Bahá'í News* (March 1985) p. 1.

5. See the newsletter, *Bahá'í International News Service* (hereafter *BINS*) (Haifa: Bahá'í World Centre) No. 156 (July 1986) p. 4.

6. "The Six Year Plan, 143–149, 1986–1992, The Major Objectives" sent by the Universal House of Justice to National Spiritual Assemblies, *Bahá'í News* (July 1986) p. 1.

7. See *BINS*, No. 180 (31 July 1988) p. 4.

8. For India, see *BINS* No. 146 (June 1985) p. 6; No. 124 (30 January 1983) pp. 7–8; and *Bahá'í News*, (February 1983), p. 13. For Austria, see *Bahá'í News* (October 1976) p. 16. For St. Vincent, see *BINS* No. 164 (March 1987) p. 7. For Canada, see *The Bahá'í World*, Volume XVI (Haifa: Bahá'í World Centre, 1978) p. 696. For

Japan, see *BINS*, No. 149 (Sept. 1985) p. 8. For Malaysia, see *BINS*, No. 172 (December 1987) p. 9.

9. See *BINS*, No. 151 (January 1986) p. 11. And *Bahá'í News* (December 1985) p. 5.

10. The term CRIBAL is composed of the initials of Centro para Intercambio Radiofónico Bahá'í en América Latina. At the behest of the Universal House of Justice, this institution has since merged with the International Bahá'í Audio Visual Centre, and is now known by the latter name. The music conference was covered in *BINS* No. 142 (February 1985) pp. 5–6; and in *Bahá'í News* (June 1985) p. 10.

11. Furthermore, we are concerned in this essay not only with the fine or aesthetic arts (such as poetry, music, painting, and film), but also with those in which the aesthetic element is combined with material or worldly utility, such as in urban design, architecture, industrial design, and advertising art. Most of the concepts in this essay would seem relevant, moreover, to the practice of art-making in general, whether or not the resulting work be intended for use within the Bahá'í Faith.

12. Shoghi Effendi, *Bahá'í Administration* (Wilmette: Bahá'í Publishing Trust, 1968 edn.) p. 63. Also Shoghi Effendi, *The World Order of Bahá'u'lláh* (Wilmette: Bahá'í Publishing Trust, 1974 edn.) p. 203.

13. From an unpublished letter, dated 22 February 1980, written to an individual believer.

14. Bahá'u'lláh and 'Abdu'l-Bahá, *The Pattern of Bahá'í Life* (London: Bahá'í Publishing Trust, 1963 edn.) pp. 47–8.

15. 'Abdu'l-Bahá, *Paris Talks* (London: Bahá'í Publishing Trust, 1969 edn.) p. 80.

16. Shoghi Effendi, *Citadel of Faith* (Wilmette: Bahá'í Publishing Trust, 1965) p. 25.

17. 'Abdu'l-Bahá, *Selections from the Writings of 'Abdu'l-Bahá* (Haifa: Bahá'í World Centre, 1978) p. 145.

18. Bahá'u'lláh and 'Abdu'l-Bahá, *Bahá'í World Faith* (Wilmette: Bahá'í Publishing Trust, 1956 edn.) p. 377.

19. 'Abdu'l-Bahá, *Paris Talks*, p. 176.

20. Bahá'u'lláh, *Tablets of Bahá'u'lláh* (Haifa: Bahá'í World Centre, 1978) p. 168.

21. Cited in references 14 and 15.
22. Technical excellence itself could be regarded as only one aspect of spiritual distinction.
23. *Bahá'í Writings on Music*, p. 4.
24. Ibid., p. 1.
25. Ibid., p. 11.
26. 'Abdu'l-Bahá, ibid., p. 7.
27. Shoghi Effendi, *The Advent of Divine Justice* (Wilmette: Bahá'í Publishing Trust, 1939) pp. 24–28.
28. From a circular letter, dated 10 February 1980, to the Iranian believers throughout the world.
29. For further discussion of this concept, see Ludwig Tuman, "Toward Critical Foundations for a World Culture of the Arts" in *World Order*, Vol. 9, No. 4 (Summer 1975) pp. 17–21. For the application of this concept to the art of music, see Wilson Coker, *Music and Meaning: A Theoretical Introduction to Musical Aesthetics* (New York: The Free Press, 1972).
30. Shoghi Effendi, *Advent*, p. 43.
31. To speak of sobriety and dignity is by no means to suggest that settings of the Sacred Word be necessarily dull or grave. The Writings themselves abound in passages of joy, bright hope, and thanksgiving. The music of Bach provides one example of a style in which sacred literature is set to music with a combination of dignity and spiritual joy.
32. From the circular letter cited in note 28.
33. See notes 17 to 20.
34. See notes 14 and 15.
35. See note 28.

SOCRATES
From *The History of Philosophy* by Thomas Stanley, 1687.

The Artist As Citizen

by Thomas Lysaght

But the wise and calm character, being nearly always the same and self-composed, is not easy to imitate, and when imitated is not readily understood, especially by a festival assembly of all sorts and conditions of men gathered in a theatre; for the condition of mind imitated is, I should think, alien to them. . . .

So the imitative poet is clearly not naturally suited to imitate this part of the soul, and his skill is not set upon adapting itself to it, if he is to be popular with the multitude, but rather to imitate the resentful and complex character because that can be imitated well. . . . Then we can rightly catch hold of him at once, and place him beside the painter as his counterpart, for he is like the painter in making things which are inferior, in point of reality, he is also like him in being intimate with an inferior part of the soul, not the best part. Thus we are justified at once in refusing to let him into a city which is to be ordered well; *because he arouses and fosters and strengthens this part of the soul, and destroys the rational part, just as in a city, when by putting bad men in power one hands over the city to them and ruins the finer people. The*

> *imitative poet, we will say, does just the same with each private person; he establishes an evil constitution in his soul . . .*
> —Plato quoting Socrates
> in The Republic, Book X

THUS, IN LAYING DOWN the guidelines for a utopia, Socrates—according to Plato—banished the creative artist from the ideal city. Writers often cite this bold fact out of context as if merely content with the Socratic comment as a curiosity, laughingly dismissing it as if smugly proud of our notorious reputation with our pens. But if we were to treat this harsh sentence of Socrates seriously, perhaps we might realize how correct he was in his judgment. Especially in light of most of modern artistic endeavor.

This essay will have two thrusts. First, we will justify Socrates' reservations—as recorded by Plato—about the Greek poet and other ancient Greek artists, and we will show how these reservations are equally justified when applied to the majority of modern creative artists. We then will proceed to prove Plato, and his mentor Socrates, wrong when their opinion is applied to the new age artist: the Bahá'í artist living in the nascent World Order of Bahá'u'lláh.

Prefatory Comments. For many Bahá'ís it is of little interest what any particular philosopher—however brilliant—has said. This can hold true even for those Bahá'ís who, prior to embracing Bahá'u'lláh's Cause, pored over the writings of countless philosophers in search of a viable worldview or way of life. For after encountering Bahá'u'lláh's teachings and recognizing Him as the Divine Educator and God-inspired Revealer of knowledge and solutions for the problems of this epoch in history, a Bahá'í's interest in man-made explanations of the universe may well wane. Clutching Bahá'u'lláh to his breast, he is then inclined to say to all philosophers, with something akin to Hamlet's condescension: "There are more things in heaven and earth, Horatio, than are dreamt of in your philosophy." And perhaps the Bahá'í is justified in adopting this attitude toward philosophers, even if in his smugness there is lacking a certain generosity of spirit and nobleness of heart. For the Divine Messenger, the Manifestation of God—Bahá'u'lláh, Muhammad, Christ, Moses, Buddha—are the "subjects" or sources of human knowledge; whereas the astute philosophers are the "objects" or receptors and reflectors of this knowledge. These philosophers are like the full moon reflecting the source of light that emanates from these Suns of God. However unobscured by cloudy human qualities, however burnished by learning as a polished reflecting surface, however brilliant the full moon guidance of these human philosophers, they are not the Day-Stars of knowledge and wisdom. They are sensitive receptors and transmitting instruments of the divine knowledge which emanates from the Manifestation of God.[1]

Therefore, if Socrates—a human philosopher—says through Plato that the poet should be banished from the utopian Republic; while Bahá'u'lláh, a divine Manifestation of God says that *"Great indeed is the claim of scientists and craftsmen on the people of the world"* and *"it is permissible to study sciences and arts,"*[2] we could dismiss Socrates' opinion without even reflecting upon it, for it is superseded by Bahá'u'lláh's words. We could avoid the issue of questioning the artist's worth and spare him from feeling even more insecure in a world largely indifferent to art. We could listen to Bahá'u'lláh and leave the subject at that.

However, Bahá'u'lláh qualified what kind of art should be pursued in His New World Order. In speaking of the arts and sciences, He stressed that only those "should be acquired as can profit the peoples of the earth, and not those which begin with words and end with words."[3] So let us utilize Socrates' reasoning in helping us to understand this cautionary tone of Bahá'u'lláh. For although he was not a divine Prophet or Manifestation, Socrates was a great philosopher. And a great philosopher is able to carry a thought or idea to a much farther point than the average short-distance-running mind. Like a track runner using a starting block, let us spring off Socrates' conclusions for an extra mental edge on the issue. For after all, Bahá'u'lláh points out that both Socrates and his chronicler Plato have earned our respect:

> .... Socrates who was indeed wise, accomplished and righteous. He practiced self-denial, repressed his appetites for selfish desires and turned away from material pleasures . . . He dissuaded men from worshiping idols and taught them the way of God, the Lord of Mercy, until the ignorant rose up against him. . . . What a penetrating vision into philosophy this eminent man had! He is the most distinguished of all philosophers and was highly versed in wisdom. We testify that he is one of the heroes in this field and an outstanding champion dedicated unto it.[4]

> After Socrates came the divine Plato who was a pupil of the former and occupied the chair of philosophy as his successor. He acknowledged his belief in God and in His signs which pervade all that hath been and shall be.[5]

The Socratic Dilemma. Let us first explain in more depth and less ambiguity precisely what Socrates was saying when he banished the poet from his utopian city.

Socrates distinguishes three levels of reality in existence. He speaks of the ideal, the real, and the image—or imitation—of the real. For example, there is the ideal bed, there is the bed one sleeps on, and there is the image of a bed in a picture. Socrates held that the creative artist functions at the last and lowest level; that he portrays (imitates) the actual or real, and not the ideal, bed. Therefore, art (sculpture, literature, theatre, etc.) is merely an imitation of an appearance of reality whose source of inspiration or essence is the ideal. It is twice removed from its source. Socrates felt that imitation is an activity inferior to doing or making (e.g., craftsmanship) and that moreover, a creative artist will never even be able to imitate particularly well, because his knowledge of his subject is bound in every case to be inferior to a practical knowledge of it. So Socrates concluded that art, however diverting, cannot be a serious occupation.

The key to Socrates' reasoning is that he held that an artist cannot have a "practical" knowledge of that which he imitates. Socrates' philosophy thus demonstrates that, as a product of his times, his reasoning is limited. For classical Greek thought maintained a static view of the universe. Physical bodies were regarded as being naturally at rest, and motion and change were viewed as abnormal. This view of the physical universe influenced the metaphysical outlook of the ancient Greeks also. Man was seen as organically flawed and imperfect. He was frozen in a predestined condition from which he could not free himself, and therefore was ever incapable of realizing the Ideal. We can see this "tragic flaw" most clearly at work in Sophocles' great play, Oedipus Rex. Although Oedipus knows the Delphic Oracle's prediction that he is destined to kill his father and to marry his mother, and he therefore reorganizes his affairs and does everything humanly possible to prevent such a frightful fate, he nonetheless is drawn relentlessly toward this horrible, inevitable destiny.

In this static view of the universe, there were three levels, ever separate and distinct, with the artist occupying and working at the lowest rung of reality's ladder:

Level of Reality	Agent
IDEAL	GODHEAD
REAL	MEN OF ACTION (craftsman, generals, educators, etc.)
IMITATION	ARTISTS/POETS

So when Socrates says that the artist cannot have a "practical" knowledge of that which he "imitates," he is speaking as a classical Greek, expressing his view of reality that art must ever be distinct and removed from that which is "real." Just as the real—or flawed universe—is ever separate from the Ideal. He distinguishes the public man of action from the private man of art, placing them in separate worlds that interface, but never intermingle.

"(T)he imitator knows nothing worth mentioning about what he imitates, but his imitation is a kind of play,"[6] says Socrates about the artist. And then in an apostrophe to Homer, he challenges that epic poet to claim otherwise:

> My dear Homer, if you are not really at a distance three removes from truth in the matter of virtue, just the manufacturer of images whom we defined as an imitator, but if you are even at the second, and were able to know what pursuits make men better or worse in public and private life, tell us this: What city was ever governed better because of you . . . ?[7]

Socrates then passes his verdict on the great epic poet:

> He did nothing in public matters, then; what of private life? Is Homer reported to have been himself a leader of education for any, while he lived? . . . [I]f Homer really could educate men and make them better, if he had been able to understand and not simply to imitate, do you suppose he would not have gathered a band of disciples who would have honored and loved him? . . . Then, if Homer had been able to bless men with virtue, would the men of his time have let him or Hesiod travel about reciting poetry? Would they not rather have clutched them closer than gold, and compelled them to reside with them in their homes? . . . We may take it then, that all the poetic company from Homer onwards are imitators of images of virtue and whatever they put in their poems, but do not lay

hold of truth. Indeed, as we said just now, the painter will fashion an apparent cobbler, although he knows nothing of cobbling himself, nor do his viewers who judge from the colors and shapes. . . . Just so, I think, we shall say that the poetic workman dabs on certain colors by using the words and phrases of the various arts, but all he knows himself is how to imitate; so that others are ignorant as himself, taking their view from words, think he is speaking magnificently when he talks in metre and rhythm and pitch about cobbling. . . .[8]

And then Socrates concludes:

Look here, then: The maker of the image, the imitator, as we say, knows nothing of the real thing, but only the appearance. . . . Then, in the name of heaven, just think! . . . This imitator is only concerned with the third remove from truth, isn't that so?[9]

This would be so if, like the ancient Greeks, we held a static view of the universe; with everything and every person in a fixed position. However, it was not only classical Greek philosophy that influenced Socrates' reasoning in banishing the poet/artist from Utopia. It was also the ancient Greek concept of art which influenced him.

If we read Socrates' words carefully, we will see that he equates imitation with art. As his following words about artistic creation confirm:

. . . if you just pick up a mirror and carry it about everywhere. You will then quickly make a sun . . . quickly an earth, quickly yourself . . . and everything else I mentioned.[10]

To the classical Greek mind, all art was realism. Art was mirror images. The artistic and literary styles of impressionism, allegory, absurdism, surrealism, etc. were outside the realm of possibilities to the ancient Greek poet/artist. Even their gods were depicted in the flesh and blood of realism.

Yet despite this "literal" approach to art as realism, we will never see a Greek sculpture looking anything like the modern sculptor Duane Hanson's man on the street. This is because in the classical Greek view of the universe, an ideal or unchanging substance underlay all the varied outward manifestations of creation. And this Ideal was the ultimate reality, no matter that man could not approach or attain it. The subject of art was to be this Ideal of the real. Therefore, all ancient Greek sculpture is of the idealized man. And all Greek tragic theatre deals with kingly characters. For a king, although flawed as a "real" man, was the highest degree of real man who came closest to the Ideal. A modern tragedy, such as Arthur Miller's *Death of a Salesman*, chronicling the tragic life of an average citizen, was inconceivable as subject matter for the classical Greek artist. If an ancient Greek dramatist wanted to even bother to portray the common man, he had to reserve such portrayals for comic theatre; a genre which wasn't even considered an art form to the Greeks, as Aristotle's omission of it from his analysis of art, *The Poetics*, demonstrates.

Therefore, since the universe was unchanging and static, and since all art was realism—relegated to still life images of static reality that always fell short of the Ideal (man being of the "real" or flawed world as he was), what positive purpose would be served—Socrates reasoned—what positive public role within a utopian Republic could the artist have in depicting flawed reality and ignoble passions? Better to not even permit such art to enter the utopian city's gates. As a moral philosopher, restricted by static Greek views of art and the universe, Socrates saw no other choice. Bound by the dualism of the Greek "Ideal" and "real"—which would later reappear in Christian theology as the dualism of soul and body—Socrates banished the poet from his ideal Republic except "to give poetry entry into our city as far only as hymns to the gods and encomiums of the good are concerned."[11]

Nonetheless, as an unbigoted man and as an appreciator of art, Socrates lamented the philosophic choice he had felt compelled to take. After all his labored reasoning as to why art had no place in the utopian Republic he concludes his argument by saying:

> ... let it be said plainly that if imitation and poetry made to please can give some good reason why she ought to be in a well-ordered city, we should be glad indeed to receive her back home, since we are quite conscious of her enchantment for us. Yet to betray the truth as we see it would be wrong.[12]

The Renaissance Response. The European Renaissance gave Socrates the "good reason" he was looking for.

Too much emphasis is given to classical influences regarding the circumstances contributing to the Renaissance, and not enough acknowledgement is given to Islam. Yet it was by way of Muslim society that the classics arrived in Europe. It was Arabic translations of the Greek texts that made their way to Europe, and from which the European scholars became familiar with the classical world.

At the same time, far from acknowledging Islamic artistic influences on the European Renaissance, most scholars are quick to point out the paucity of Islamic artistic contributions citing the complete absence of the theatrical arts as an example. Greek art is given most of the credit for artistic influence on the Renaissance. It is not the purpose of this paper to deal with the Islamic influences on the European Renaissance. Nonetheless, one crucial point is worth mentioning.

We have seen through Socrates' argument the limits of realism as an art form in a well-ordered utopian society. It was the Islamic world that began the extensive social experimentation that was the search for new art forms—other than realism—that would be conducive to a well-ordered utopian society. And it did so by shunning all representational art. This fallow period of artistic realism in Muslim society served the purpose of plowing under many of the weeds of realism that had been stifling artistic development.

Unlike ancient Greek philosophy Islam did not teach a static view of the human condition. On the contrary, similar to all divinely revealed religions, it taught that the essential purpose of man's life is to improve his character and perfect himself and society. It taught a dynamic concept of man. Therefore, it did not want man's spirit to become imprisoned within a picture frame, or to be constrained by the four walls of a stage. Rather than worshipping idealized icons, or personalities, or other manifestations of the material world, man was meant to turn towards the Ideal itself, to turn towards God. Therefore, art was to be a door leading towards the Source. Just as nature could wing the soul upwards (compare the palpable peace of the falling water and fragrant gardens of Islamic society with the cold conclusion of the early Church—derived from Greek dualism—that all nature is the workplace of the devil), art too was seen as a liberating instrument. Hence, the lack of linear form to Islamic architecture, and the geometric and vegetal arabesque designs with neither beginning nor end. And although Islam shunned representational art and did not ostensibly, "technique-wise" influence Renaissance art, its artistic philosophy was what opened this door on the Source and let in a breath of fresh air in Europe that blew the cobwebs from the closed mind of the Church and its dictums affecting nature and art.[13]

Rather than giving classical Greece the credit for the Renaissance, it is more telling to point out the classical Greek influences on the static, hierarchal, dualistic early Church, from whose fetters the Renaissance freed Western man.

It is well-established that early Christian theology was derivative of Greek philosophy. The concepts of the man-god and of original sin (the tragic flaw) are the most obvious examples. But more importantly, the early Church fathers, most notably St. Thomas Aquinas, depended heavily on Aristotelian logic for their world views. Unfortunately, Aristotle's logic was faulty. Nonetheless, his misguided dictum that physical bodies are naturally at rest and that motion is abnormal (a result of disturbance), and that this abnormal movement and change only applied to the attributes and never the substance of an object, not only gave philosophic legitimacy to the mistaken Greek concept of human nature's stasis, but also gave a theological rationale to the early Church's acceptance of a feudal social order and for burning Bruno and imprisoning Galileo for their suggesting the earth was in motion. Happily, the Christian humanism of the Renaissance with its "imitation of Christ" (*imitatio Christi*), or "becoming" concept of the individual, threw off the static world view of the Greek-influenced medieval Church that classified man, along with everything else in the universe, in a fixed place or state of "being."

Briefly stated, the Renaissance concept of man's "becoming" exempted him from the fixed laws of nature. All else in creation was in a "being" state. That is to say, all of creation upon coming into existence has inherent within it the necessary raw materials for the eventual perfection of its form. The seed contains all that the tree will eventually need to branch and flower and bear fruit. The egg in the nest encapsulates all that will one day have the bird on the wing and instinctively feathering its nest and feeding its young. Philosophically speaking, all of creation is in a state of "being": what it is, was, and will be is involuntarily locked on "automatic pilot" for as long as it exists. Moreover, each and every thing in creation epitomizes one attribute or quality of God. In the animal kingdom, for example, we see the lion as the epitome of courage and the donkey of patient long-suffering. In contrast to this, man stands alone out of all creation as in a state of "becoming." Made "in the image of God," he contains inherent within him all the qualities of God lying latent, waiting for him to add the element of volition to develop them. This was the "imitation of Christ" concept.

Unlike the rest of creation, man—it stated—embodies the

epitome of no single attribute of God, rather he contains the seeds for epitomizing all of them. Hence, he is in a state of "becoming" his true spiritual nature, rather than of "being" in his true state.

The Christian humanism of the Renaissance did not create or invent this concept; it resuscitated and reinterpreted it in terms of Christian life. However, what it also resuscitated and brought to remembrance to an equally significant degree was the place of art and the artist in the "becoming" process of mankind. Freeing man from the fetters of Aristotelian philosophy and early Church theology which bound him to a fixed place, Christian humanism now showed how human knowledge, added to faith, could lead man towards the Ideal. No longer was the tragic flaw, or original sin, to lock earthly man forever in an imperfect condition. He could "become" better. And most significantly, art was viewed as an important aid in inspiring man to attain such heights. Socrates had been answered. He had been given the "good reason" why art and the artist had every right to enter the Republic, the New Jerusalem. It was because art and the artist would play a vital role in establishing this Ideal City.

The Modern Dilemma. Unfortunately, however, the delicate balancing act of holding faith and science on an equal par, as early Islam and later the European Renaissance managed to do in the name of all inclusivity, has once again been upset. Once again, the equilibrium between the two scales of the human balance has been lost. One pan on the scale has been elevated to prominent position at the expense of dragging the second pan in the dust. Just as, previous to the Renaissance, religion was held up while science was downgraded, ever since the happy equilibrium of the Renaissance, enlightened Western thought has elevated science to the downfall of religion. Dualism reigns once again. Where before, society was child-like with its passivity and dependence on the will of God and other unknown forces, modern man has an adolescent sense of omnipotence due to his great new-found knowledge which is largely derived from modern science. And he has developed an adolescent-like, exaggerated pride in this knowledge which blinds him to the vastness of his ignorance as he assumes that all control of his destiny lies in his own hands. Where before man thought he was all-encompassed, now he believes he is all-encompassing. Each attitude betrays the lack of maturity necessary for mankind's adulthood or coming of age.

And so for all our advancement from the days of the man-gods of ancient Greece, and from the scientist-burning days of the Catholic Church, we still wear the tattered rags of dualism handed down to us by our two older-brother schools of thought. What was the dualism between the Greek Ideal and the real, and later between the soul and the body, is now a dualism between religion and science. We see evidences of religion without scientific rationality degenerating into fanaticism and mindless superstition, whereas we see evidence of science without ethics and faith degenerating into materialism and destruction. The most vivid contemporary example of this dualistic advocacy is the hasty lining up on either side of the creationist/evolution controversy without giving dispassionate reflection to how both theories may interface in agreement.

Nonetheless, the resurgence of fundamentalist Christianity and fundamentalist Islam notwithstanding, today's world is a secular world. So secular that our dualism is not even really between religion and science anymore. It is between the two bastard children of science. It is between capitalism and communism: the two materialistic philosophies that fail to address the affective and spiritual needs of man as they bicker over whether it is the individual or the society which must first be made comfortable. As Karl Marx would say, it's all a question of economics.

But, of course, it isn't all a question of economics. There is a grain of truth to what Marx said. However misguided or mistaken he may have been with many of his theories, one very positive innovation and contribution that he made to civilization was his economic interpretation of history. To the political, heroic, idea, war, and religious interpretations of history, Marx added the insight that economics shapes our laws, government, culture, religion, and art. This is why he railed against capitalism. For capitalism is based on competition—rather than cooperation—and emphasizes the individual and his inalienable right to make a profit.

Certainly capitalism has influenced art and religion. Consumer-oriented, disposable novels and films are the Western norm. However, Karl Marx's theory of economic determinism can be taken to the point of absurdity. And it often has been. It is not uncommon for a Soviet production of *Romeo and Juliet*, for example, to portray the star-crossed lovers as young people of the future undone by bourgeois parents. The social realism of Mainland China and of Stalin's Soviet Union, ever depicting the triumph of the worker, are well-known examples of how communist economic theories can influence art forms. What is not as obvious though is how capitalist economic theories can influence art forms. Nonetheless, the Guardian of the Bahá'í Faith, Shoghi Effendi, made oblique reference to this:

> The chief idols in the desecrated temple of mankind are none other than the triple gods of Nationalism, Racialism and Communism, at whose altars governments and peoples, whether democratic or totalitarian, at peace or at war, of the East or of the West, Christian or Islamic, are, in various forms and in different degrees, now worshipping. Their high priests are the politicians and the worldly-wise, the so-called sages of the age; their sacrifice, the flesh and blood of the slaughtered multitudes; their incantations outworn shibboleths and insidious and irreverent formulas; their incense, the smoke of anguish that ascends from the lacerated hearts of the bereaved, the maimed and the homeless.[14]

When we reflect that racialism and irrational nationalism are oftentimes an outgrowth of undue emphasis on the individual at the expense of others, and that defining oneself in terms of race or nation is often a further fall-out of the "Us" and "Them" way of looking at the world—which capitalism encourages, then it is not too free an interpretation of the above text to read it as an indictment of both communism and capitalism. And then to see that the new dualistic bind that is shackling the world is between the bases of capitalism and communism. Namely, between philosophies emphasizing the individual and philosophies emphasizing the state. The First World glorifies the individual and the Second World glorifies the state, while the Third World is bullied into jumping on the band wagon of either one or the other. God forbid we eschew dualism and champion both the individual and society!

Alas it is, then, that the world's artists have chosen sides and joined either the artistic school of individualism (civil liberty, self-discovery, personal freedom, sexual freedom, etc.) or the artistic school of political and social responsibility. On the one hand, we have American novelists writing within a minimalist framework about the angst and sexual habits of Hamlet-like, self-involved surburbanites and dissociated 7-11 sales-clerks, while Eastern European and Latin American writers sprawl awkwardly across their extended canvases of socialist and sociological art. And it often seems—to paraphrase Rudyard Kipling—that never the twain shall meet.

Nonetheless, although it is a valid point to mention economic systems as having an effect on artists and their subject matter, it would be belabored and futile to argue that capitalism alone is the reason for Western artists' subjective preoccupation. As the poet and critic W. H. Auden has pointed out, there are numerous universal factors which have combined to shrink the canvas of the modern poet/artist, regardless of whether he is of the First, Second, or Third World:[15]

1) *The loss of belief in the eternity of the physical universe.* In a world under the threat of nuclear weapons, with advanced sciences (physics, geology, biology) that depict nature

as a process in which nothing is now what it was or what it will be, in which nature itself is transformed by pollutants, chemicals, and technology (while real estate developers revamp every neighborhood), it is becoming more and more difficult for the modern artist to believe he can make an enduring object based on any model of endurance. He is more apt to abandon the eternal and the perfect as subject matter and to be content with sketches, improvisations, and slice of life portrayals.

2) *The transience and mutability of society, its values, and its enjoyments.* Before the Industrial Revolution, a person grew up where his grandparents had been born, on the same plot of land, maybe even in the very same house as they. Things changed slowly. And a person could imagine his grandchildren as people who would live the same kind of life as he did, possessing the same needs, desires, and entertainments as himself; perhaps as even eating fruit from the very same tree as he ate from. But technology has radically transformed modern man's way of life. In a mobile society with excellent mass transportation and mass communication, with urban centers of employment, families uproot and even separate at a rate literally unthinkable one hundred fifty years ago. Not only are our lives vastly different from those of our grandparents, but we cannot even imagine what life will be like twenty years from now for our own descendents. Consequently, the artist no longer has any certainty when he creates something that even the very next generation will enjoy it, or even understand it. So the artist concludes that all he can be true to are his own subjective feelings and impressions, and he paints his minimalist canvas accordingly.

3) *The disappearance of the public realm as the sphere of revelatory personal deeds.* In the preindustrial, agricultural past, man sustained himself—"earned his living"—at home, in private life, as farmer or craftsman. It was in the public realm—when he went into the city, to the market place, when he sat and sipped tea, beer, or coffee and listened to songs,

stories, or poetry, and when he serendipitously heard gossip about the goings-on of the community—that he disclosed and revealed his own private persona and personality and talents to others. However, today man earns his living away from home in a public place. It is when he returns home, in his private life, that he is free to express his personal self. Consequently, the subject matter of earlier market place art—the tragic hero, the epic hero, the romantic hero—has been replaced by the "modern hero." This is not "the Great Man," the world explorer, the conqueror, or doer of extraordinary deeds, but the man or woman in any field, from any walk of life, who, in spite of all the cumulative impersonal pressures of modern society, manages to persevere and maintain an individualized face of his or her own.

4) *Writers and other artists have lost their social status.* To quote Auden:

> Some writers, even some poets, become famous public figures, but writers as such have no social status, in the way that doctors and lawyers, whether famous or obscure, have.
>
> There are two reasons for this. Firstly, the so-called fine arts have lost the social utility they once had. Since the invention of printing and the spread of literacy, verse no longer has a utility value as a mnemonic, a device by which knowledge and culture were handed on from one generation to the next, and, since the invention of the camera, the draughtsman and painter are no longer needed to provide visual documentation; they have, consequently, become "pure" arts, that is to say, gratuitous activities. Secondly, in a society governed by the values appropriate to Labor[16] (capitalist America may well be more completely governed by these than communist Russia) the gratuitous is no longer regarded—most earlier cultures thought differently —as sacred, because, to Man the Laborer, leisure is not sacred but a respite from laboring, a time for relaxation and

the pleasures of consumption. In so far as such a society thinks about the gratuitous at all, it is suspicious of it—artists do not labor, therefore, they are probably parasitic idlers—or, at best, regards it as trivial—to write poetry or paint pictures is a harmless private hobby.

In the purely gratuitous arts, poetry, painting, music, our century has no need, I believe, to be ashamed of its achievements, and in its fabrication of purely utile and functional articles like airplanes, dams, surgical instruments, it surpasses any previous age. But whenever it attempts to combine the gratuitous with the utile, to fabricate something which shall be both functional and beautiful, it fails utterly. No previous age has created anything so hideous as the average modern automobile, lampshade or building, whether domestic or public. What could be more terrifying than a modern office building? . . .

In all societies, educational facilities are limited to those activities and habits of behavior which a particular society considers important. In a culture like that of Wales in the Middle Ages, which regarded poets as socially important, a would-be poet, like a would-be dentist in our own culture, was systematically trained and admitted to the rank of poet only after meeting high professional standards.

In our culture a would-be poet has to educate himself; he may be in a position to go to a first-class school and university, but such places can only contribute to his poetic education by accident, not by design. This has its drawbacks; a good deal of modern poetry, even some of the best, shows just that uncertainty of taste, crankiness and egoism which self-educated people so often exhibit.[17]

This then is why so many First World artists today speak with such a subjective voice. Their characteristic style is an intimate tone. It is the speech of one person addressing one person, not a large, mass audience. So while the world is wracked with fratricidal war, while children's bellies swell with starvation, political protesters are tortured in prisons, and passion crimes proliferate on the streets and in the daycare centers, the American novelist discourses on the personal frustrations of a young professional in Manhattan and the modern artist paints soup cans.

"But what is an artist to do?" protests the socially conscious Western poet/painter with vague traces of guilt in his voice. "Of course I can't help but agree that everyone should get enough to eat, that it's necessary to reduce the arms build-up, and that the drug problem has gotten very serious indeed. . . . But what do these sociological problems of the average man have to do with art, which is of the individual man? Art is concerned with individuals as they struggle alone to succeed in coping with their personal challenges and problems."

And there is something to this justification for and defense of subjective art. Especially when one regards its opposite. For it so often seems that when an artist today raises his sociological voice, he sounds phony. Tolstoy is a case in point. After the miracles that were the creation of *War and Peace* and *Anna Karenina*, Tolstoy underwent a religous conversion. In his old age, he renounced his property estates, his aristocratic title, and even his copyrights, and made an effort—a sincere effort, however unsuccessful—to escape from his privileged class and to live the simple life of a peasant. He then developed a new theory of art to complement this spiritual conversion. He decreed that great works of art—to be declared so—had to treat subject matter "important to the life of mankind."[18]

> . . . his main aim, in his later years, was to narrow the range of human consciousness. One's interests, one's point of attachment to the physical world and the day-to-day struggle, must be as few and not as many as possible. Literature must consist of parables, stripped of detail and almost independent of language.[19]

Perhaps Tolstoy was right in decreeing that "when the gratuitous and the utile are divorced from each other, there can be no art."[20] However, this doctrinaire intellection caused him to be critically dishonest. He tried to persuade his readers—and himself—that the spiritual, moral, socially conscious "utility" in a work of art was more important than "gratuity" (that is, entertainment). Consequently, he praised spiritually thematic works which aesthetically he must have despised, while at the same time he dismissed as artists both himself, as the author of *War and Peace*, and Shakespeare.[21]

George Bernard Shaw was another hostile critic of Shakespeare for similar propagandistic reasons. But his aesthetic dishonesty was the product, not of a spiritual platform, but of a political one. And thus we come to the second variety of that disease of aesthetic dishonesty which afflicts the socially conscious artist. The variety that the Mexican poet Octavio Paz says breaks out when an artist allows himself to become "a tool of politics." And that's the case with many European and Latin American writers such as Mr. Pablo Neruda and Mr. Garcia Marquez, who are instruments of political propaganda."[22] One might add the name of Bertolt Brecht to this list of well-intentioned but misguided artists, so socially concerned that they lower their aesthetic standards to allow for the proliferation of inferior propagandistic art. Artists like this at the same time condemn great art such as Shakespeare's because—as Tolstoy claimed—it "corresponded to the irreligous and immoral frame of mind of the upper classes of his time and ours."[23]

And yet were not Dante, Milton, Byron, Whitman, Goya, and even Picasso with "Guernica" politically minded in their art? What has gone wrong with socially concerned artistic work? Where did it go off track?

Perhaps socially conscious art has become too "utile." There is not enough of the gratuitous about it. And yet every human being has the basic right to enjoy himself. "*Eat ye, O people, of the good things which God hath allowed you, and deprive not yourselves from His wondrous bounties."*[24]

The peasant may play cards in the evening while the poet writes verses, but there is one political principle to which they both subscribe, namely, that among the half dozen or so things for which a man of honor should be prepared, if necessary, to die, the right to play, the right to frivolity, is not the least.[25]

Nonetheless, we cannot place all the blame on the politically and spiritually motivated artists. For while their art has become too "utile," its opposite—subjective art—has become too "gratuitous." Post-modernist writers of the West, with their cynicism and bleak view of human nature have snuffed out the humanitarian spirit that is the spark igniting, and the breath of life animating, any body of political or moral philosophy worth considering. Then, putting down their murder weapons (that is their pens), these same artists look up, regard with aplomb the lifeless corpse of current moral/political solutions, and shrug innocently, "Well, there you have it. Can you blame me?" But is this not unlike the bold-faced murderer who after killing his parents appealed to the clemency of the judge on the grounds that he was now an orphan?

Despite the Renaissance, dualism persists. Dualism between the artistic proponents of an art with a private, subjective subject matter, and those proponents of a politically and morally responsible art. Not quite as wise as King Solomon, we've cut the baby in half; and neither half by itself has been found to be sufficiently alive. On the one hand, the moral order called for by the "socially conscious" artists has degenerated into socialist propaganda or sociological case studies. While on the other hand, despite the humanism of the Renaissance, we see artists—for the most part in the First

World—portraying a mechanistic or nihilistic picture of humanity. Much of this "subjective" modern art and literature is as little disposed to the "becoming," *imitatio Christi*, concept of man as the static ancient Greek "being" view of man had been. Bereft of any vision of man as having a part in a greater scheme of things, this subjective art, not only has muted its metaphysical commentary, but has silenced its voice on social issues, retreating rather into either the psychological angst of its characters or remaining satisfied with keeping a mere record of the external motions they go through. And thus dependent on their own subjective impressions of man and reality, these artists have become like the three blind men in Sa'dí's story. As one touches the elephant's trunk, another the elephant's leg, and the other the elephant's flank, each one in turn declares the answer to be a snake, a tree, or a wall.

So, insofar as much of current art is concerned, Socrates' bold decision to ban the creative artist from the Ideal City is once again justified. For the private artist is once again failing to provide a public service.[26]

The Bahá'í Response. If Bahá'u'lláh's Revelation had brought no other revolutionary change in the ordered life of humankind—if there had been no Covenant, no progressive revelation interpretation of history, no authentic Scripture for the first time in religion—the fact that its teachings have dissolved all dualistic notions of man, nature, and reality would be miracle enough. Religion and science, man and woman, church and state, work and worship, inspiration and administration, contemplation and action—all previously perceived opposites have been joined together as complementary supporting pairs. Neither a sabbath day nor a church building have been set aside as exclusive times and places for the worship of God. The seat of adoration is the throne of the human heart,[27] and the occasion every day of our lives. It is no mere poetic image that *"the Nightingale of Paradise singeth upon the twigs of the tree of eternity.*"[28] Creation and spirit intermingle in the Bahá'í Dispensation. Consequently, we should not be surprised to learn that the dichotomy between "subjective" art and political art has been bridged by the Bahá'í Revelation. The private artist has been given the means for once again providing a public function. The challenge remains within to do so.

Such integrated art has been created in past epochs. And although such isolated examples of a dynamic, community-based, integrated art may not have had the far-reaching global effects that Bahá'í art[29] will one day have, it is worth referring to these isolated examples—not only out of a sense of justice, but out of a desire to learn from them. For all art (like all religion) is a torch race, not a furious dispute among heirs.

An American Indian rain dance, for example, might be called a religious observance, might be admired for the aesthetics of its dance movements, or might be regarded as an economic ritual—a way to ensure a good harvest. In fact, it is all three. Living in an age today of specialization—or, to speak perjoratively, "categoritis"-afflicted—we might go to Mass, or to a synagogue service, for our religious "theatre" and consider it irrelevant whether it be poorly or well sung, because what matters most is the attitude of our will towards God and our neighbor; we might go to the ballet to be entertained and enjoy ourselves, demanding only that the choreography and performance be aesthetically pleasing; or we might watch from the balcony of the Stock Exchange the theatrics on the floor below as economic matters are determined, knowing all the while that whether the computers be beautiful or ugly or whether the participants be agnostics or believers is irrelevant to the system's criteria for their success or failure. The danger threatening modern man is that instead of being a complete person at any given moment, he will be split into unrelated fragments which are continually jostling for dominance: the religious which goes to a church service, the aesthetic fragment which goes to the ballet, and the practical which earns its living. It is not only artists who are alienated and fragmented, producing nihilistic, neurotic, existentialist works. The entire modern world is fragmented; as W. H. Auden rhetorically laments:

> Yes, I can see all the works of a great civilization; but why cannot I meet any civilized persons? I only encounter specialists, artists who know nothing of science, scientists who know nothing of art, philosophers who have no interest in God, priests who are unconcerned with politics, politicians who only know other politicians.[30]

In bemoaning the categoritis that afflicts modern society, F. Buckminster Fuller supposedly snapped, "specialization is for insects." Although somewhat exaggerated (after all, if I require a coronary bypass operation, I will certainly prefer a heart specialist to a General Practitioner), his point is well taken. For if true civilization is the precarious balance between atavistic regimentation and trivial classification, we are currently suffering from an acute case of trivial order's soul-less specialization. Primitivism is unified but uniform, lacking diversity; classification is diverse (specialized) but lacking in any central unity. The ideal of civilization is the integration into a complete whole, with minimum friction, the maximum number of distinct activities.

> If a civilization be judged by this double standard, the degree of diversity attained and the degree of unity retained, then it is hardly too much to say that the Athenians of the fifth century B.C. were the most civilized people who have so far existed. The fact that nearly all the words we use to define activities and branches of knowledge, e.g. chemistry, physics, economics, politics, ethics, aesthetics, theology, tragedy, comedy, etc. are of Greek origin is proof of their powers of conscious differentiation; their literature and their history are evidence of their ability to maintain a sense of common interrelation, a sense which we have in

great measure lost as they themselves lost it in a comparatively short time.³¹

And the ancient Greeks lost this balanced interrelation because the flaw was bred in the bone. In a society which held a static worldview, the Ideal was Ideal, the real was real, and the imitated (art) was always and only the imitated. Never were the three to meet. Categoritis—to use the vernacular—was the Greek malady too. So in the end, Socrates opted for the dualistic solution:

> . . . we must give poetry entry into our city as far only as hymns to the gods and encomiums of the good are concerned.³²

Ideal and real, spiritual and practical, were viewed as ever separate and distinct. Art could not treat the world of everyday events and still be spiritual.

This was an ironic verdict handed down by Socrates when we consider that with the dramatic theater of ancient Greece "for the first and last time in history, an art, drama, became the dominant religious expression of a whole people, the dramatist the most important figure in their spiritual life."³³

But a religious exercise elevated to theater need not necessarily be a spiritual experience. We need only refer to the Catholic Mass as proof. The ritualized presentation of the martyrdom of Jesus at Calvary repeated daily without variation precludes a transcendent experience of that event. It is not living theatre. The solution is not the artistic treatment of a spiritual/political theme. The answer is the infusion of works of art with a spiritual/political consciousness and conscience which includes a belief in the nobility of man. The Bahá'í Faith offers the believing artist a pattern of living which can make him an instrument capable of sounding such sublime chords of harmony.

First of all, through a subjective belief in Bahá'u'lláh's divine station and His divinely revealed Scriptures the Bahá'í artist can hurdle over two of the biggest obstacles waylaying the modern artist. The two obstacles—as mentioned earlier—that detour the artist down a minimalist, sketchy path:

> 1) loss of belief in the eternity of the physical universe;
> 2) the transience and mutability of society, its values, and its enjoyments.

For the Bahá'í artist knows, despite any destruction and devastation that is yet to accompany the Lesser Peace, that the physical universe will endure. Also, despite the advances in technology and the benefits of a multicultural society, he knows that Bahá'í values will set the tone of the future. More quickly than any other genres of art becoming obsolete, any art with values narrower than those of the Bahá'í Dispensation will become obsolete. Consequently, the Bahá'í artist knows that if he expresses values consistent with a multicultural, spiritually based, unified world society, and his metaphors and images are drawn from nature and not from machines and other man-made things of the moment, there is a good chance that his work will have future relevance, regardless of style or genre. The comfort that comes to an artist from such an assurance cannot be overstated. In fact, this is precisely what today keeps many Bahá'í artists persevering, as their work is repeatedly rejected in the modern market place of ephemeral and consumer art standards.

Faith in the future, in himself, and in the relevance of his art, is a haven and harbor that any artist would sell his soul for. For it is debilitating doubt that causes so many of the suicides, the alcoholism, the drug dependency, and the destructive life styles that cut off so many artists' talents before they are fully realized.

And beyond receiving once again some semblance of a status in society due to Bahá'u'lláh's exaltation of the work of the artist, the Bahá'í artist occupies a unique niche today distinct from that held by other artists. The Bahá'í artist, as believer, is automatically (albeit bountifully) given access to "such power . . . as can generate, through successive ages, all the manifold arts which the hands of man can produce." Bahá'u'lláh elaborates: *"This, verily, is a certain truth. No sooner is the resplendent word [Fashioner] uttered, than its animating energies, stirring within all created things, give birth to the means and instruments whereby such arts can be produced and perfected."*[33] This is akin to the power for which Faustus sold his soul to the devil! And it is beholden to any Bahá'í artist.

On one condition.

Subjective faith must be complemented by cooperative action for faith to have relevance in this age. After recognition of the Manifestation of God, the Bahá'í must obey His every ordinance. "These twin duties are inseparable. Neither is acceptable without the other." However, obedience is not a private or a passive condition. This becomes immediately clear when we learn that *"the most meritorious of all deeds,"* one that is *"prescribed unto every one"* is *"the duty of proclaiming His Message."*[35] So by the obligatory act of teaching, the artist engages in cooperative action and raises himself up to the level of "doer." He is not the mere "imitator" Socrates thought all artists were. And since before he can teach others he is required to *"teach his own self"*[36] which implies an interaction with Scripture and the divine Revelation which is of the Godhead, the Bahá'í artist actually interfaces with the "Ideal," and justifies to Socrates his admittance into the Ideal City.

So the Bahá'í artist—as any Bahá'í—must teach the Faith, pioneer, serve in the Administration, and be "public" as a civil/social servant in obedience to Bahá'u'lláh. And since every single divine command has a spiritual significance,[37] this obedience draws man into association with the Godhead, with that Ideal which Socrates assumed the artist must ever be separate from. In fact, the public nature of faith in this age is its essence. Service to mankind is the only true expression of faith. So through his public service, the Bahá'í artist draws ever closer to the Essence/Ideal/Godhead. Thus through his first hand experience of It (however limited or proscribed) the artist frees himself from mere iconic imitation or sketchy slice of life, solely subjective, impressionistic, fragmentary art. For now the artist speaks "of," not "about." For he knows. Perhaps but through a glass darkly, but he sees. And a dim view of the divine—such as Paul's at Damascus or Dante's of Beatrice—can be enough to implant a certitude and purposefulness in an artist (and in anyone) which an imagined, deduced, intuited imitation can never give as well. For the latter is constructed upon a foundation of doubt—based as it is on the self's subjectivity.

However, surety is not enough. The fire of conviction can also fuel Auschwitz ovens and burn witches. It was conviction, not correctness, that inspired Machiavelli's *The Prince*, Marx's *Communist Manifesto*, and Hitler's *Mein Kampf*. No one can come away from Neitzsche's work unimpressed by his self-confidence and the conviction of his beliefs. But was he always correct? It was Dante's conviction that charged his *Divine Comedy* with a power and beauty that makes it one of the greatest literary works of all time, not his correctness. His metaphysics were awry, for certainly Muhammad does not belong in hell.

And so Bahá'u'lláh has given the artist some standards to which his work must measure up. Through service to mankind and obedience to these standards, the Bahá'í artist can foster the vigilance to keep his ego in check and be assured of approaching the light of conviction and not the megalomaniacal darkness of self-delusion.

Specifically, Bahá'u'lláh says that only *"such arts . . . as are conducive to the well-being and tranquillity of men have been, and will remain acceptable before God."*[38]

These few words imply a wealth of moral responsibility. It is no longer aesthetically acceptable for a stand-up comedian such as Eddie Murphy to be merely funny; not if his routine reinforces obscenity, racism, and sexual promiscuity. Mick

Jagger might be the quintessential performer. But are the aesthetics of performance enough? We cannot hold him responsible for the stabbings during the *Gimme Shelter* concert while he was singing the song "Sympathy For the Devil." Or can we? Andy Warhol might be the artist as quintessential consumer. But the artist as passive spectator is not a role without inherent evils. Some might say he watched his groupies rather than watching over them, and some died of the excesses that characterize our current society.

Duality has been debunked. Bahá'u'lláh has exploded the myth that artistic endeavor is separate and removed from moral responsibility. The day is dawning in which the makers of movies such as *Raiders of the Lost Ark* and *Emerald of the Nile* will realize that they are responsible for the racism and sexism which their films reinforce. Just as Sylvester Stallone, in knowing *Rocky IV* inspires a patriotism built more upon hate for other nations than on love for one's own, will conclude that such films are not "conducive of good results."

Happily, behind Bahá'u'lláh's specific words about art's function, there is a wealth of teachings to further guide us. He has given us extensive spiritual guidance which fleshes out His criteria for art. First and foremost Bahá'u'lláh teaches us that man is a noble being.

"Noble have I created thee . . . [39]*"*
"Noble I made thee . . . [40]*"*

Man is neither an animal that must gratify his every desire, nor a machine that needs to let off steam. The importance of this teaching—for the novelist and playwright in particular—cannot be over emphasized. For a compassion and love for all characters—such as Chekhov's—is more important than any "religious," Western-Union message. The work of many political writers who purport to love "the people" often drips with hatred for certain social classes. Just as many religious writers veil their disgust for mankind with the disguise of a love for God.[41] But hatred and disgust for mankind will not do. Recognition of the nobility of man is the touchstone for all great art. Shakespeare was of this mind, and therein lies an element of his greatness.[42] He defied religious classification, but he celebrated the nobility of man. This was what baffled the literal Christian Tolstoy who late in life clung to creed rather than to belief in God's human creation.

> The morality of Shakespeare's later tragedies is not religious in the ordinary sense, and certainly is not Christian. Only two of them, *Hamlet* and *Othello*, are supposedly occurring inside the Christian era, and even in those, apart from the antics of the ghost in *Hamlet*, there is no indication of a "next world" where everything is to be put right. All of these tragedies start out with the humanist assumption that life, although full of sorrow, is worth living, and that Man is a noble animal—a belief which Tolstoy in his old age did not share.[43]

The Bahá'í Writings continually remind the artist of man's nobility. There is no room to doubt the capabilities of the grassroots populace ("Thou hast endowed each and all with talents and faculties . . . "[44]).

> According to the words of the Old Testament, God has said, "Let us make man in Our image, after Our likeness." This indicates that man is of the image and likeness of God; that is to say, the perfections of God, the divine virtues are reflected or revealed in the human reality. Just as the light and effulgence of the sun when cast upon a polished mirror are reflected fully, gloriously, so likewise the qualities and attributes of divinity are radiated from the depths of a pure human heart. This is an evidence that man is the most noble of God's creatures. . . . [45]

The on-going, evolutionary "becoming" concept of man—as juxtaposed with the static "being" state of the rest of creation—that infused the endeavors of the Renaissance is reaffirmed by Bahá'u'lláh:

> *Whatever is in the heavens and whatever is on earth is a direct evidence of the revelation within it of the attributes and names of God, inasmuch as within every atom are enshrined the signs that bear eloquent testimony to the revelation of that Most Great Light.... To a supreme degree is this true of man, who, among all created things, hath been invested with the robe of such gifts, and hath been singled out for the glory of such distinction. For in him are potentially revealed all the attributes and names of God to a degree that no other created being hath excelled or surpassed.*[46]
>
> *Upon the inmost reality of each and every created thing He hath shed the light of one of His names, and made it a recipient of the glory of one of His attributes. Upon the reality of man, however, He hath focused the radiance of all of His names and attributes, and made it a mirror of His Own Self. Alone of all created things man hath been singled out for so great a favor, so enduring a bounty.*[47]

In the oft referred to chapter, "The Grand Inquisitor," in his masterpiece, *The Brothers Karamazov*, Dostoevsky comments on that cleric that, "He does not believe in God. Therefore he cannot believe in man." There is a world of meaning in that remark. For it clarifies the modern problem. The artistic problem is not so much that some artists do not believe in God. It is that they do not believe in man.

Taking at random a few of the authors who are "believers" in the nobility of man—such as Dickens, Chekhov, Shakespeare—we immediately notice the astounding vitality of their created characters and the vibrant power, energy, and enthusiasm of their writing styles. Then if we look at the work of the doubters, the hesitaters, the existentialists (some of whose talent is unquestionable and whose craftsmanship is masterly) such as Kafka, Sartre, Virginia Woolf, we come to a series of flat character creations which lack substantiality. These characters seem to fall short as creations for the same reason that their creators' styles falter. There is an uncertainty or hesitancy imbuing both.

It is a commonly encountered criticism that Charles Dickens' characters are unreflecting or "unphilosophical," and that he is really the creator of caricatures rather than of characters. However, it is the *joie de vivre*, the enthusiasm, and the conviction of his presentation of these characters that keeps him perennially popular as an author. While the "lost soul" characters of so many modern authors are as immediately forgettable as they are chronically unrecognizable as people the reader has known (which perhaps accounts for why so few of these artists' works are clutched to the breasts of succeeding generations). When a Dickens character crosses a London street, we have a distinct sense of having seen Fagan or Uriah Heep in the flesh (even if we don't see what's on their minds). Whereas when Virginia Woolf's Mrs. Dalloway is, say, doing her shopping, for all our awareness of what is on her mind (through the technique of stream of consciousness writing), she leaves us uninvolved and indifferent. She leaves our minds as easily as she herself leaves Harrods.

The Bahá'í teachings concerning the nobility of man are but one example of how the artist may interact with the divine through an association with such divine wisdom, and subsequently demonstrate the good effect of such an association upon his art work. We see then that far from being oppressive or repressive, association with the divine Revelation of religion is liberating. This was why Socrates believed it was so important for the artist to have some relation to the divine Ideal. However, his static view of the universe precluded the artist from ever having such a relationship. But through Bahá'u'lláh's teachings, we now see that active public service to the Cause is not mere "busy work" that will bring about the realization of the New World Order, but that it is the stuff for facilitating personal spiritual growth, which in turn the artist can translate into art of a greater scope.[48]

The impact then of the Bahá'í Faith on the Bahá'í artist is that, far from merely giving him a "cause" to proselytize (all propaganda failing as art anyway), it gives the Bahá'í artist a sense of purpose and a realization of man's nobility. The former validates the artist's subjective experience while the latter spiritualizes his social philosophy. Consequently, since a Bahá'í's subjective values have a universal correlation and his broad social solutions are founded on individual transformation, the man-made barrier between "subjective" and "political" art is obliterated. A Bahá'í author's five hundred-page novel about the personal sacrifices and trials of one character can conceivably effect change in society. Just as the transformation of one Bahá'í's character is part of the transformation of society in general. Artistic dualism has been undone by Bahá'u'lláh.

In addition, the sense of purpose and the realization of man's nobility beholden to the Bahá'í artist in turn ennobles his own self. For his belief in his fellow man's (and in his own!) potential, not only infuses his art with hope, but encourages him as an individual to "go public" and actively serve mankind's best interests with instruments other than his pen or paint brush. This obedience to Bahá'u'lláh—complementing one's subjective faith with cooperative action—keeps him in association with the divine which then guides him, and in so doing, justifies the ways of the artist to Socrates.

And thus it is then that the artist as romantic loner (*"He that secludeth himself in his house is indeed as one dead"*[49]), or as pamphleteering propagandist (*"The wise are they that speak not unless they obtain a hearing"*[50]), has given way to the Bahá'í artist as citizen. He who, while privately creating a synthesis of subjective/political art, will publicly proclaim the Faith, teach it, serve its institutions. For ultimately, the only profession and pursuit common to all of us is that of being a citizen and a philosopher—to exercise our social responsibilities and our minds with the play of ideas. To be a doctor, writer, or car mechanic is not an inalienable responsibility. To be a citizen and a philosopher is, however. These two professions are another way of describing the public and private nature of the artist—or of anyone.

The integrity of our private art is dependent on ideas (craftsmanship goes without saying), and the integrity of our public persona is dependent on being a good citizen—which has nothing to do with how often we are interviewed or on how many talk shows we appear, and everything to do with typing minutes, taking time for others, and travel teaching. And although at times—perhaps oftentimes—these activities might appear mundane and even unimportant, yet we are told that the future of the planet depends upon these details of working, and learning to work together lovingly.[51] And so the Bahá'í artist then, in both his work and his example, must be an active, Bahá'í citizen. The side effect of such devotion and consecration could be an artistic flowering such as *The Divine Comedy* of Dante or the Islamic architecture of the Golden Age of Islam. But the main result will be a catalyzed coming into being of the Most Great Peace and a fully realized personal life of godly service.

Notes

1. "*The essence and the fundamentals of philosophy have emanated from the Prophets.*" Bahá'u'lláh, *Tablets of Bahá'u'lláh*, p. 145.
2. Ibid. pp. 52 and 26.
3. *Tablets of Bahá'u'lláh*, p. 52.
4. Ibid., p. 146.
5. Ibid., p. 147.
6. *Great Dialogues of Plato*, "The Republic," Book X, p. 402.
7. Ibid., p. 399.
8. Ibid., pp. 399, 400.
9. Ibid., pp. 401, 402.

10. Ibid., p. 395.
11. Ibid., p. 407.
12. Ibid., p. 408.
13. Perspective, the painting technique for representing three-dimensional objects on a flat plane by receding parallel lines, which was developed during the Renaissance, far from being a mere technical innovation, is an indicator of this "openness" of Renaissance thinking. And in sculpture, for all the ostensible classical Greek influence on Michelangelo's work, there is a distinctly non-linear, non-temporal aspect to the psychic energy which endues his figures and which seems to strain for release. "The Rebellious Slave" seems to be struggling to break out of the bonds of the very block of marble itself.
14. Shoghi Effendi, *The Promised Day is Come*, pp. 117–18.
15. W. H. Auden, *The Dyer's Hand*, p. 78–80.
16. Labor's consumer values ("What the mass media offer is not popular art, but entertainment which is intended to be consumed like food, forgotten, and replaced by a new dish." Ibid. p. 83)
17. W. H. Auden, *The Dyer's Hand*, pp. 74–75, 76.
18. George Orwell, *The Portable Orwell*, "Lear, Tolstoy, and the Fool," pp. 302.
19. Ibid., p. 307.
20. W. H. Auden, *The Dyer's Hand*, p. 75.
21. For this reason we cannot be sure if Isabeela Arkadevna Grinevskaya's dramatic poem *The Báb*, which was performed in St. Petersburg, was aesthetically and technically pleasing to Tolstoy or satisfying for simply being consistent with his own moral philosophy. ("Very happy that V. V. Stasov has conveyed to you the fine impression your book made on me. . . . I sympathize with all my heart with Babism, insofar as it preached brotherhood and equality between all men, and the sacrifice of material life in the service of God." Count Leo Tolstoy, quoted in *Leo Tolstoy and the Bahá'í Faith*, pp. 32–33.)
22. Octavio Paz, as quoted in the *Miami Herald*, Sunday, January 25, 1987.
23. Tolstoy, as quoted by George Orwell, *The Portable Orwell*, p. 303.
24. Bahá'u'lláh, *Gleanings from the Writings of Bahá'u'lláh*, p. 276.

25. W. H. Auden, *The Dyer's Hand*, pp. 88–89.

26. The majority of "artists" providing a public service forfeit their title of "artist" by becoming tools of politics. They create propaganda, not art.

27. *"Thy heart is My home..."* Bahá'u'lláh, *Hidden Words*, Arabic #59.

"The temple of being is My throne..." Ibid., #58.

28. Bahá'u'lláh, as quoted in *Bahá'í Prayers*, p. 209.

29. To label any Bahá'í artistic expression at this early stage in history as "Bahá'í music," "Bahá'í theater," "Bahá'í architecture," etc., would be inaccurate and incorrect. Bahá'í art will be the flowering expression of a Bahá'í World Order that is still well in the future.

30. W. H. Auden, Introduction to *The Portable Greek Reader*, p. 7.

31. Ibid., pp. 8, 9.

32. *Great Dialogues of Plato*; "The Republic," Book X, p. 407.

33. W. H. Auden, Introduction to *The Portable Greek Reader*, p. 12.

34. Bahá'u'lláh, *Gleanings*, pp. 141–42.

35. Ibid., p. 331 and 278.

36. Bahá'u'lláh, *Gleanings*, p. 277.

37. "Know thou that in every word and movement of the obligatory prayer there are allusions, mysteries, and a wisdom that man is unable to comprehend, and letters and scrolls cannot contain." 'Abdu'l-Bahá, *Malaysian Prayers*, p. 19. . . . Muhammad's injunction to Muslims to pray five times each day at specific times facing a specific direction resulted in the founding of the science of astronomy, which had Muslim astronomers calculating accurately the circumference of the earth five hundred years before the likes of Columbus went sailing, unsure if the world was round.

38. Bahá'u'lláh, *Epistle to the Son of the Wolf*, p. 17.

39. Bahá'u'lláh, *Hidden Words*, Arabic #22.

40. Ibid., Arabic #13.

41. "Jesus Christ is the Lord of Compassion, and these men call themselves by His Name! Jesus is ashamed of them!" 'Abdu'l-Bahá, as quoted in *'Abdu'l-Bahá*, by H. M. Balyuzi, p. 152.

42. "What a piece of work is a man! how noble in reason! how

infinite in faculties! in form and moving how express and admirable! in action how like an angel! in apprehension how like a god! the beauty of the world, the paragon of animals!" *Hamlet* II, ii, 319–323.

43. George Orwell, "Lear, Tolstoy, and the Fool," from *The Orwell Reader*, p. 311.
44. 'Abdu'l-Bahá, *Bahá'í Prayers*, p. 103.
45. 'Abdu'l-Bahá, *The Divine Art of Living*, p. 24.
46. Bahá'u'lláh, *Gleanings*, p. 177.
47. Ibid., p. 65.
48. This art of a greater scope does not yet exist. Therefore, examples of it cannot be cited. Experiments in this evolving art do exist. But a discussion of these is beyond the scope of this paper. Two points, however, made by the Guardian of the Bahá'í Faith, Shoghi Effendi Rabbani, are worth noting. First, not all artistic experimentation is ground-breaking for the future; much of it only mirrors the breakdown of present society. Second, such art of a greater scope will be a fruit of the World Order of Bahá'u'lláh.
49. Bahá'u'lláh, in *Tablet to Napoleon III*.
50. Bahá'u'lláh, *Hidden Words*, Persian #36.
51. "God loveth those who are working in His path in groups." 'Abdu'l-Bahá, *Bahá'í World Faith*, p. 401.

CONFLICT OF THE SATANIC AND CELESTIAL EGOS
by Mark Tobey, 1918.

Restating the Idealist Theory of Art

by Geoffrey Nash

I DO NOT INTEND in this essay to offer a Bahá'í theory of art. I have already discussed elsewhere the proposition that great art is the product of advanced stages of civilization, and that now is not the time for profound works of art inspired by Bahá'í beliefs to appear.[1] Increasingly, I feel that the essential ingredients of significant art in any age do not vary, even though the media may be multifarious. Nor do I believe that any direct influence of religion upon art is necessary before work of value can be produced. In fact, it seems to be that this influence is more subtle and elusive than I had earlier thought, for the reason that art—like religion—is an eternal faculty of human nature which has its own laws and which, while it can be greatly enhanced by any inspiration of a religious nature, must remain autonomous and free if it is to be true to its mission.

Indeed, it may be doubted if there could ever be a specifically "Bahá'í" theory of art, anymore than there exists or has ever existed a specifically Buddhist, Muslim, or Christian one. If Bahá'u'lláh's Faith is, according to His claim, *"the changeless Faith of God, eternal in the past and eternal in the future,"* then the art that it will eventually inspire must also inevitably draw from those ancient wellsprings that art has always drawn upon. Truth is always one and the same, albeit the forms in which it incarnates itself are various and many.

That the Prophet of God does not appear in the world to articulate, among other things, the principles of a new artistic theory is supported by this statement by Mírzá Abú'l-Faḍl, the noted Bahá'í scholar:

> It is clear that the prophets and Manifestations of the Cause of God were sent to guide the nations, to improve their characters, and to bring the people nearer to their Source and ultimate Goal. *They were not sent as historians, astronomers, philosophers, or natural scientists.* Their position in the world of creation is like that of the heart in the body: it has a universal position *with a general effect.*[2]

What is said for the various disciplines mentioned must also apply to art. However, since the Bahá'í Faith is in its essence a restatement of the eternal truths of religion, I feel that it must stand in relation to art in a place similar to where religion has stood in the past.

The greatest art appears in ages of affirmation and belief; epochs of doubt and anxiety give rise to contrary perceptions of the meaning and role of art such as we see today. Though man is a being perennially subject to the laws of change, there is that within him which pursues the eternal and the changeless. Often, there appears to be a direct link between great art and religious inspiration. Nor is it an accident that religion employs a similar language to that used by art: the language of symbol, image, and metaphor. Indeed, it might be argued that both are preoccupied with the same reality—Ideal, Spirit, Essence—which in this world cannot be apprehended except by reference to the sensate. States of being and of feeling must be spoken of in sensuous terms. The divine world is figured in the natural world: "Natural and supernatural with the self-same ring are wed."[3] Earthly love mirrors the divine love. Paradise (in Islam) is the sustained sexual union of men and women in gardens of delight.

Both poet and Prophet are purveyors of the nonmaterial. Both celebrate what Yeats called the "wasteful virtues," meaning those human attributes which cannot be calculated and weighed according to a scale of material advantage. It is the poet who signs into being such ideal values as bravery, beauty, love, wonder for nature, and so on; just as the Prophet articulates what the materialist philosophers and doctors of science can never speak to: the deeper longings of man's inner self. In so doing, he adopts the language of the poet, even as he soars into realms unexplored by the latter.

Precisely to what extent the inspired Word moves us because it is beautiful, and to what extent it moves us because it is true, is a profound question. But it need not detain us there, for we have already accepted that the power and range of the Prophet is of another order to that of the artist. And yet as far as the souls of men are concerned, poet and Prophet are engaged in a common enterprise. This is evidenced by the fact that both are banished from the feast served up by the savants and apologists of the contemporary world, who in turn determine what degree of scepticism the masses should imbibe. A materialist age can see in them naught else but the delusions of a childish, "unscientific" epoch. Poetry and religion are thus the stuff of "ruder ages" and cannot be sustained under the cold dissection of rationality.

Even poets themselves have been unable to withstand this century of sociology, planned warfare, and bankrupt traditions. The poets of the interwar years affected a tone that utterly disparaged the idealistic, heroic categories of prewar verse. The new tone "was ironic, could be bitter or angry, and could hate and condemn, but it avoided the upper register of emotions, the range of nobility and splendor and high tragedy. . . . The new rhetoric was the language that Owen had commended, stripped of the high-flown abstractions that had faded on the recruiting posters, reduced to the plainness of fact."[4]

The atomization of human faculties experienced in modern times was addressed by Friedrich Schiller nearly two hundred years ago. Against the materialist view of man, which reduces him to the mere creature of his immediate circumstances, we find in Schiller an understanding of man as a being created to be in harmony with his surroundings—but subject to the fragmentary organization of society in the modern world. The development from the integrated communal life of ancient Greece to the divided life of industrialized Europe was, however, a necessary experience in man's evolution, part of a dialectical process whereby human society could progress to a more advanced and integrated whole. But in the meantime, humanity becomes alienated from its former wholeness, and loses all sense of harmony:

> Eternally chained to only one single little fragment of the whole, Man himself grew to be only a fragment; with the monotonous noise of the wheel he drives everlastingly in his ears, he never develops the harmony of his being, and instead of imprinting humanity upon his nature he becomes merely the imprint of his occupation, of his science.[5]

Materialist philosophy rejects the transcendental dimension of man's being; an idealist theory of art is based on transcendentalism, and is therefore unacceptable to the materialist. But materialism, which is the result of an acceptance of only a part of man, is itself the reflection of the fragmentary state of society mentioned by Schiller. The integrated and harmonious is the norm; the bifurcated and fragmented is an expression of limitation.

The goal of all true art is transcendence. Art, through its realization of man's spiritual faculty in the realm of the material, appeals to us through the senses while at the same time it aims to transcend them. It shows us that the beautiful and the moral are attributes of the same transcendent reality. Such is the classic idealist axiom of art that goes back to the Greeks. Art is seen as the highest human activity, in as much as it records the imprint of man's eternal mind on the ever-changing forms of matter. Detached from the constantly mutating world of matter, the individual mind or soul would have no arena in which to realize itself. In the following passage, from Schiller's letters *On the Aesthetic Education of Man*, read for "personality," "mind" or "soul":

> [Man's] personality, regarded in itself alone and independently of all sense material, is merely the potentiality of a possible infinite expression; and so long as he neither contemplates nor feels he is still nothing but form and empty capacity.[6]

On the other hand, mere sensual man is indistinguishable from the world in which he is placed; he must use the faculty of mind in order to give individuation to his acts:

> So long as he only perceives, only desires and acts from mere appetite, he is still nothing but *world*, if we understand by this term simply the formless content of time. It is indeed his sense faculty alone which turns his capacity into operative power; but it is only his personality [i.e., mind] which makes his operation really his own. Thus in order not to be merely world, he must lend form to his material; in order not to be merely form, he must make actual the potentiality which he bears within himself.[7]

For Schiller, whose concern is with both man as moral being and man as artist, reason or the ideal has to struggle with the anarchic and capricious instincts within man. "Every individual man, it may be said, carries in disposition and determination a pure ideal man within himself, with whose unalterable unity it is the great task of his existence, through all his vicissitudes to harmonize."[8] While in social terms, the pure, rational part of man can find its representation in the state, the individual will nevertheless still retain his freedom and idiosyncrasy. What Schiller suggests, is that even were the philosopher's dream of the ideal state to actually be achieved, there would still remain the quirkiness and imbalance of the individual. Moreover, the demands of the state, even though they conform with the principle of reason, cannot be imposed too forcefully on the idiosyncratic individual without contravening the principle of freedom.

It is here that Schiller proposes an aesthetic education whereby what is individual in men and what is rational, what is moral and what is artistic, is dissolved in the concept of Beauty. Beauty, Schiller's *summum bonum*[9] accomplishes the relaxation of the disparities and tensions within the human personality. The solvent of an aesthetic education is to harmonize man both with himself and with his environment. It is within the artistic process that man endeavors to utilize and express both of his natures. This implies a disciplining of both the mind and of the senses. It is achieved by giving form to the material, by imprinting mind upon matter.

This activity is not limited to art alone, however. It is repeated again and again in the act of living. Man conquers and orders his material environment by allowing his spiritual faculties to have reign in the world of the senses. While the mind is the potter, matter is the potter's clay. Man is the artist who through the instrumentality of soul, mind, and sensation creates the world in which he lives. Were he to balance these three instruments he could create a perfect world, or a world susceptible to the manifestation of endless perfections. Schiller: "Beyond question Man carries the potentiality for divinity within himself; the path to divinity, if we may call a path what never reaches its goal, is open to him in his *senses*."[10]

All men are artists and creative beings, if they only knew it. To say so is not, I think, to stretch Schiller's aesthetic ideas beyond their proper realm. All are waiting to fulfill their ideal potential in the world of being. In the life of every human should exist the opportunity to achieve moments of joy during which creativity seems to realize its aim, beauty is made tangible, and the innate human powers seem to be harmonized. The role of art is to make this possibility real in its presentation of an image of the harmonization of human powers, and so act as an inspiration and stimulation for men to achieve this harmony in their lives. In its highest form, the rendition of the beautiful, Schiller affords to art the power to cancel antimonies and enter into the realm of the infinite.

We have taken Schiller's letters *On the Aesthetic Education of Man* as our text because the work well expresses the fundamental tenets of the idealist credo on art. Of course, there are many other aspects and variations within the general principles that we do not have the space to consider now. One example is Schiller's own dramatic theory of tragedy; another is the Romantic idea of the poet as seer, "whose eye," according to Carlyle, writing under the influence of Goethe, "has been gifted to discern the godlike Mystery of God's Universe, and decipher some new lines of its celestial writing . . . for he *sees* into the greatest of secrets, "the open secret."[11] Certainly, for the German Idealists among whom Goethe was the greatest artist, art was spiritual nourishment, almost a religion. Goethe would have us worship at the shrine of art everyday by looking at one fine picture or reading a line of poetry. *Wilhelm Meister* educates the reader in aesthetics, but also leads him back to participation in life.

But, are moral ideas and aesthetic culture the same thing? Even if we accept that Beauty and Truth are one and same reality, as idealist philosophy maintains, the fusion of moral and artistic values in a common aesthetic theory would be quite another matter. Schiller's attempt to do so is too ambiguous and unclear to achieve this. Yet we do feel that Schiller has come close to articulating an important association between truth and man's moral character, on the one hand, and sensibility and motive force on the other. In some way, we are all aware that Beauty has the power to ennoble man, while cold reason and moral exhortation are slow to move him. When his sensibilities are engaged, he is able to do much. And, as the word implies, sensibility has to do with the senses.

Yet where the senses are concerned, there is always the fear that man will be led toward indulgence and forsake his higher impulses. Plato "with the pursuit of Beauty and the Good as his primary concern, . . . is notoriously suspicious of art, fearing, and not without cause, its power to incite the passions: nevertheless, a great artist himself, he is clearly fascinated by Homer and the poets, he allows into his Republic art that conduces to stillness . . . and in texts like the *Ion* concedes that art can be the result of divine inspiration."[12] The notion that art is a powerful instrument indeed which can easily seduce humans and lead them into the paths of unrighteousness is one reason why the pious fear it. But the high claims that artists like Blake and Shelley make for art might appear almost equally unorthodox. Blake's exaltation of the creative Imagination, which he associates with the Logos or Christ, could be taken as blasphemous; while Shelley's claim that poets are "the unacknowledged legislators of mankind" flies in the face of a more mundane understanding of order and government.

Is the sort of art we have been talking about so far—the art which harmonizes and lifts to the encounter of Beauty—necessarily a sanitized art, which only engages the senses where they are least vulnerable to "lower impulses?" And if this is so, if art is concerned mainly with the good and, by implication, only the kind of subject matter and ideas that lend themselves to moral upliftment, how can there be room for the interdependence of light and darkness? Yeats would have it that the true artist attains to a "Vision of Evil" wherein he beholds the dark forces of the world working for ultimate good. Where the pious believer, in obedience to religious command, fears the magnetic pull of evil, the great artist marvels at the part played by evil within the order of things, acknowledging the creative power of God the Artist. As Rumi wrote:

> To make that evil
> Denotes in Him perfection . . .
> Could He not evil make, He would lack skill[13]

Darkness has its role within the scheme of things, though it be but the absence of light. And if every atom in existence has been ordained for man's training, then all experience, whatever its darkness, must hold within it something of value. It is invariably the artist who has the innate sensitivity to experience, directly or vicariously, the multifarious nuances of human existence and to express them. So it becomes important that, whatever else it does or does not do, art must remain faithful to human experience. Moral ideals and the pursuit of the beautiful are perhaps the essential terms of reference for the greatest art; but these cannot be portrayed and apprehended save in relation to the ugly and the evil.

Yet art must never give us a more apparent or more easily perceived representation of these qualities than is present in life itself. Take the case of Balzac: feared and reproved by Victorian moral sensibility, he remains one of literature's greatest moralists, even though he articulated many of the darkest feelings of the human soul. A great part of the truth of art resides in its faithfulness to human experience, to the actual human states, from despondency to exultation, eroticism to transfiguration. The universal artist, Shakespeare being the obvious example, has command over the greatest range of human experience. A telling criticism of so much that is written or produced in modern times is that only a distorted, truncated representation of human experience and human potential is offered.

Yet it would be equally limited to exclude all that is unpleasant or ugly, in the cause of "spiritual upliftment." Art recognizes the truth in Blake's dictum: "without contraries is no progression." If the aim of religion is the detachment of men from their self-centered, appetitive natures by contrasting the material with the spiritual, the goal of art is very similar. But where the one makes the point by reference to dualities, the other softens these dualities—on the one hand in pursuit of verisimilitude, and on the other in order to achieve the harmonization of mind and sensation discussed above. Didacticism of any hue is a great enemy to the artistic conception behind a work. Art cannot be made to fit the axioms of a particular political or religious movement without fundamental damage being done to the final execution.

The value of the idealist theory of art is that it proffers an ultimately transcendental explanation of the artistic process which need not exclude the regard for verisimilitude that we have just argued for. Artistic models might be representational or abstract, so long as they derive from the only referent mankind can know: the example of the natural world, which is the manifestation of the ideas or attributes of Divinity in the domain of the senses. Cut off from this referent, man so easily becomes a meglomaniac who negates his own essence and thus turns out inhuman. And so we return to the central concept of mind, the eternal organizing principle, acting upon matter in the fundamental endeavor to realize its full potential.

Dealing as it does with form and material, art is a joining of theory and practice and is therefore the most salutary kind of praxis. This praxis must eventuate in actual products, the *works* of art themselves, which are their own testimony. Aesthetic training and a climate in which great art can be produced lends to man the impulse to rise to even greater things. Art teaches not through its message—for it has no message as such—but through its awakening of sensibility and awareness. The Greek Parthenon, Gothic Chartres, Ummayad Alhambra—each speaks a universal language that transcends the preciousness of moral homilies and religious systems precisely as it lifts us through our senses and delivers our spirits to the heavens.

But this is not to say that art is aloof from the central ordering power of Divine Revelation. 'Abdu'l-Bahá explains:

Although to acquire the sciences and arts is the greatest glory of mankind, this is so only on condition that man's river flow into the mighty Sea, and draw from God's ancient source His inspiration.[14]

For W. B. Yeats, the great artist attains to "Unity of Being"—the awareness that when all contrary states, paradoxes, and cycles of development, growth and decay have been taken into account, the ordering principle behind all things is one. For idealist philosophy this fits the recognition that behind all appearances is a Supreme Reality that is both ineffable and unknowable—the Ultimate Good.

We have seen how idealist philosophy can provide the artist with a transcendental term of reference. In its broad outline this is totally acceptable to the Bahá'í. This should hardly be strange, given the fact that both Bahá'u'lláh and 'Abdu'l-Bahá use ideas and metaphors common to the transcendentalist tradition which came to Islamic culture by way of the classical authors. In essence, it might be considered applicable to the thought of all the higher religions.[15] For the Bahá'í artist of the future, as for the great artists of the past, the world will continue to be the manifestation of the qualities of a Higher Reality, and he himself possessed of a spirit-mind that can reflect the attributes of divinity within the realm of the senses.

The moral and the beautiful cannot fail to be apparent to this Bahá'í artist given the loftiness and splendor of the Bahá'í holy writings. What perhaps needs to be emphasized from the issues raised in this essay is that art is concerned with the real as much as with the ideal. The application of moral theories is better left to religious tracts. For the present, as a reviewer in the British *Bahá'í Journal* (May 1986) put it: "Novels written about the Faith by Bahá'ís have seldom been satisfactory. The desire to teach, to give lectures on the history of the Faith often leads characters into dissertations on Bahá'í subjects out of keeping with their role and situation." Notions about what exactly the term "prostitution of art" means sometimes lead to preciousness among both the Bahá'í public and would-be Bahá'í artists. The following observations on the art critic John Ruskin might provide a salutory contrast to this way of thinking:

> For a period at least, he revolted against his early evangelicalism and expressed an embarrassed and puzzled admiration for the robust and sensual in art. Homer, Shakespeare, Tintoretto, Titian, Michelangelo were boldly animal, while St. Francis and Fra Angelico were poor weak creatures. "I don't understand it," Ruskin confesses in an 1858 note after hearing a dreary nonconformist sermon in Turin. "One would have thought that purity gave strength, but it doesn't. A good, stout, self-commanding, magnificent animality is the make for poets and artists." Later, however, he returned to his earlier view and found that "Religion," in Giotto, "instead of weakening, had solemnized and developed every faculty of his heart and hand." But the basic theory remains the same.[16]

Because he is a composite being, man belongs to two worlds at the same time: the ideal and the material. Both must receive their due. For the Bahá'í artist, inspired as he is with a vision of the perfect, the danger lies in detaching himself from the real world. Indeed, it might be argued that this bifurcation between the ideal truth of the Bahá'í Revelation and the actuality of the material world is an established, probably inevitable fact in present-day Bahá'í communities. If there is one major theme that presents itself to the would-be Bahá'í artist in the foreseeable future, it must be the tension set up by the potential held out to mankind by Bahá'u'lláh, contrasted with the preponderantly negative forces present in the world around him. The tension between the ideal and the real has always existed, but for the Bahá'í artist it will appear all the more stark. At times he will find it unbalancing and bewildering; at other times it will be a source of inspiration and awe. His system of ideal values will sustain his artistic vision, but he will need to face the reality of the world in which he is working.

It is the job of the artist to express opposites, irreconcilables, growth, and pain. Pious verse, paeans of joy, and cypress trees can cloy when the larder is empty. Truth to life is the foundation of art. To deny the real, to censor the harrowing or the ugly, would render the efforts of the artist vain. By facing the antimonies, the positives and negatives that constitute the whole, he may achieve a real victory; he may succeed in reconciling truth and reality, beauty and ugliness, hope and despair. But in doing it he will have to face all that is. And he will need, as well as an original talent, courage and strength to sustain him in this awesome vision.

Notes

1. See "Can there be a Bahá'í Poetry?" introductory essay in *Response to the Revelation: Poetry by Bahá'ís*, Bahá'í Studies Series (Ottowa: Association for Bahá'í Studies).

2. *Miracles and Metaphors* (Los Angeles: Kalimát Press, 1981) p. 9. Emphasis added.

3. W. B. Yeats, "Supernatural Songs," *Collected Poems of W. B. Yeats* (London: Macmillan, 1961) p. 64.

4. Samuel Hynes, *The Auden Generation: Literature and Politics in England in the 1930s* (London: The Bodley Head, 1976) pp. 23–24.

5. Friedrich Schiller, *On the Aesthetic Education of Man* (London: Routledge and Kegan Paul, 1954) p. 40.

6. Schiller, *Aesthetic Education*, p. 63.

7. Ibid. A parallel line of argument outlining the development of human powers in terms of an association between body and spirit is advanced by 'Abdu'l-Bahá:

The wisdom of the appearance of the spirit in the body is this: the human spirit is a Divine Trust, and it must traverse all conditions, for its passage and movement through the conditions of existence will be the means of its acquiring perfections. So when a man travels and passes through different regions and numerous countries with system and method, it is certainly a means of his acquiring perfection, for he will see places, scenes and countries, from which he will discover the conditions and states of other nations. He will thus become acquainted with the geography of countries and their wonders and arts; he will familiarize himself with the habits, customs and usages of peoples; he will see the civilization and progress of the epoch. . . . It is the same when the human spirit passes through the conditions of existence: it will become the possessor of each degree and station. Even in the condition of the body it will surely acquire perfections. (*Some Answered Questions* [Wilmette, Ill.: Bahá'í Publishing Trust, 1981] p. 200)

8. Schiller, *Aesthetic Education*, p. 31.
9. That is, his highest value.
10. Schiller, *Aesthetic Education*, p. 63.
11. Thomas Carlyle, *Critical and Miscellaneous Essays* (London: Chapman and Hall, 1896–1899) vol. 2, p. 377.
12. Peter Malekin, "Art and the Liberation of Mind," *Temenos* no. 5 (London: Element Books, 1984) p. 139.
    'Abdu'l-Bahá also distinguishes between the form of music which is a "ladder to the soul" and that which promotes lustful feelings.
13. *Rumi, Poet and Mystic*, trans. and ed. by R. A. Nicholson (London: George Allen and Unwin, 1950) p. 150.
14. Compilation on *Bahá'í Education* (Oakham: Bahá'í Publishing Trust, 1976) p. 12.
15. Cf: ". . . the human spirit, whose mysterious nature inclines it towards transcendence, a reaching towards an invisible realm, towards the ultimate reality, that unknowable essence of essences called God." The Universal House of Justice, *The Promise of World Peace* (Wilmette, Ill.: Bahá'í Publishing Trust, 1986).
16. Rene Wellek, *A History of Modern Criticism 1750–1950* (Cambridge University Press, 1983) p. 139.

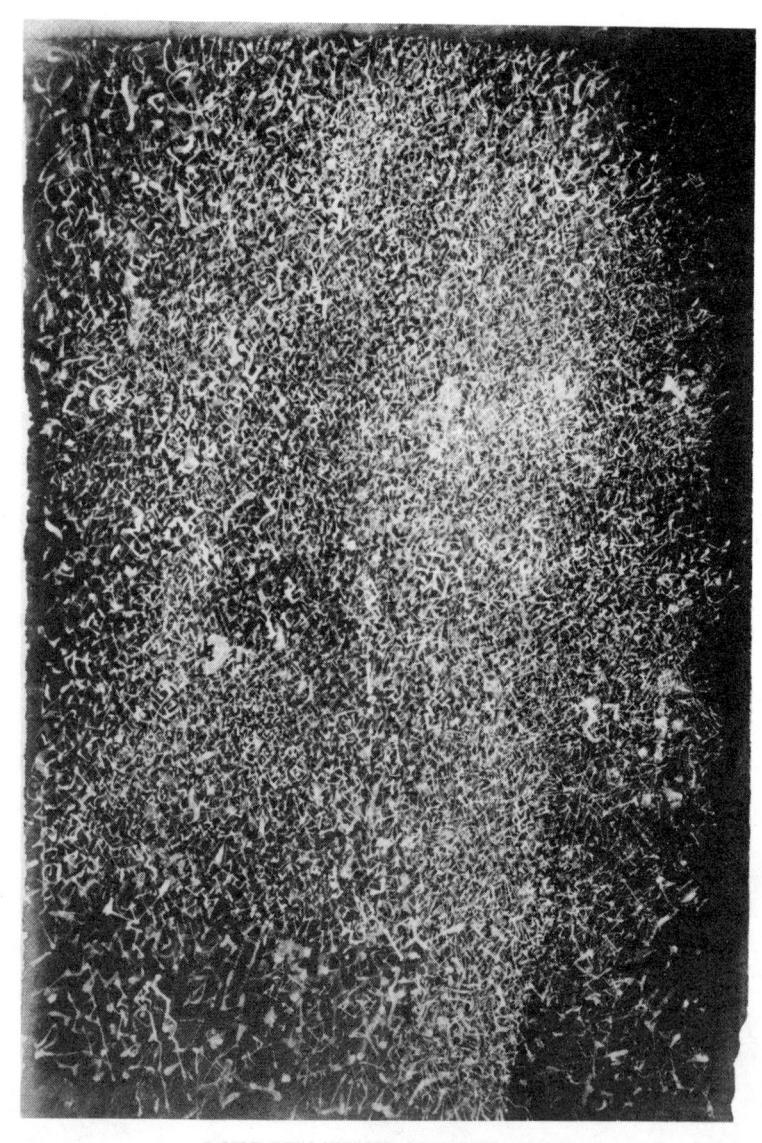

MEDITATIVE SERIES VIII
by Mark Tobey, 1954.

Poetry and the Arts in Rebuilding Society

by Duane L. Herrmann

THE AMERICAN BAHÁ'Í Community has been wrestling with the question of poetry and the other arts for a great many years. The problem is that poetry is not generally seen as part of religion in America. And worse, poetry is seldom considered as an active or "real" part of modern society. Yet the Bahá'í community faces the statement written of behalf of the Guardian in 1932: "Shoghi Effendi wishes . . . to encourage those who are talented to give expression to the wonderful spirit that animates them. We need more poets and writers for the Cause . . . "[1] More specifically: "In Persia, the Cause gave birth to many poets of national standing. Let us hope that the west will follow suit and produce similar results."[2]

The status of poetry is exalted in the Bahá'í Revelation. Even before the ministry of Bahá'u'lláh, the Báb remarked to a companion as they passed a fellow traveler reciting some lines from Hafez, one of Persia's greatest poets: "It is the immediate influence of the Holy Spirit that causes words such as these to stream from the tongue of poets, the significance of which they themselves are oftentimes unable to apprehend."[3] He also reaffirmed a well-known tradition of Islam:

"Treasures lie hidden beneath the throne of God; the key to those treasures is the tongue of poets."[4] Poetry has definitely been considered, since the very beginning of the Bahá'í Era, a spiritual enterprise.

Where does that place poets in the second century of Bahá'í history? Nearly fifty years ago, single voices in the American Bahá'í Community were trying to explain the naturalness of poetry to their fellow believers. Mark Tobey, internationally acclaimed for his paintings, but as yet unknown for his poetry, explained: "The potentialities of art appreciation and creation are present in some degree in almost every child, and when the right approach is made to liberate the adult . . . we still find that element alive."[5] It was obvious to him that the capacity for creativity is inherent in one's humanity.

Even earlier, in 1935, Henry P. Eames wrote: "In my study and research of sources of art-impulses, aims and manifestations, I have found . . . the emotional depths they sound and the elemental problems and purposes they present are universal, common to the life of humanity."[6] Worldwide, human beings are a creative species. No matter where on the planet we are born and live, or under what conditions, we are in some way creative. Creativity is a basic component of our human nature, fundamental to our essence.

Yet, where are the poets and other creative artists in the Bahá'í community? Most Bahá'ís cannot name any Bahá'í poets. Roger White and Robert Hayden, perhaps. How many know that Hand of the Cause of God Adelbert Mühlschlegel wrote poetry? Regretfully, it remains in German, untranslated. Who remembers that his fellow Hand, George Townshend, also wrote poetry (as well as prayers, essays, and books)? Who else is there in the Bahá'í community with similar unknown treasures?

There exists a heritage of poetry in the American Bahá'í community, but it is hard to find. Regretfully, the same can be said of our contemporary poetry. To find it one must search long and hard. Very few titles are currently carried by the Distribution Service; a few more are available elsewhere. One can't help feeling: there must be more.

Some poetry is scattered in the *Bahá'í World* volumes, issues of *World Order*, and the publications of the Association for Bahá'í Studies. But individual poems are hard to locate, and it is impossible to find specific poems by topic or author. Even less accessible is the poetry of *Star of the West* and the early *World Order* (1935–1949). We have a corpus of poetry in the Bahá'í community, but it is uncollected and largely unusable. How can current poets know where they are going if they do not know where they have been? No one can safely travel any road in isolation.

If poets hold the key to the "treasures beneath the throne of God," why are they not a visible part of the life of the Bahá'í community? Why are poets not a regular and expected part of the programs of conventions, conferences and other gatherings? Poetry can even be appropriate at Feasts and Holy Days. A letter on behalf of the Guardian specifically stated: "With regard to your question concerning the use of music in the Nineteen Day Feasts, he wishes you to assure all the friends that not only he approves of such a practice, but thinks it even advisable that the believers should make use, in their meetings, of hymns composed by Bahá'ís themselves, and also of such hymns, poems and chants as are based on the Holy Words."[7]

It is *advisable* to use *hymns, poems and chants* that are composed by Bahá'ís themselves. In every community the Bahá'ís can, and should, use in their programs the work they create themselves. And if such works have not yet been created, it is not too late to begin.

The Guardian appears to have defined a new and specific genre of poetry: that which is "based on the Holy Words." In time, undoubtedly, this will grow into a sizable body of devotional literature. This distinction should separate "regular" (secular?) Bahá'í poetry from the devotional kind. But even such a distinction should not hinder any creative efforts; rather, knowledge that there will be a specific body of devotional *hymns, poems, and chants* should spur us on to begin to develop such a literature.

In the Lawḥ-i Maqṣúd, Bahá'u'lláh comments favorably on some poetry written by Maqṣúd which He was pleased to have read. Could these comments of the Blessed Beauty not set a standard for poetry of any kind written by Bahá'ís? Bahá'u'lláh wrote: *"Every word of thy poetry is indeed like unto a mirror in which the evidences of the devotion and love thou cherishest for God and His chosen ones are reflected."* He concluded by noting that poetry reflects the human relationship with God: *"Its perusal hath truly proved highly impressive, for it was indicative of both the light of reunion and the fire of separation."*[8] Might not this be a goal for which all poets and other artists strive?

But where is the poetry now? At some larger community events we have begun to witness a growing presence of some of the arts: exhibits of paintings, a dramatic musical or two, even ballet, and (sometimes) singing. But where is the poetry? And where is the sculpture, the weaving, and the other original expressions of our human creativity within the Bahá'í community?

Even in the outline of the major goals of the Six Year Plan, the Universal House of Justice, under the goal "Carrying the Message of Bahá'u'lláh to the generality of mankind," has stated that one of the devices whose use is to be encouraged in the teaching and deepening work and in Bahá'í meetings is "drama and singing."[9] "And poetry . . . " I continue the thought, but in some ways that would be redundant. For what are songs but poetry set to music? And what is drama but poetry acted out? In each case the House of Justice is encouraging, almost insisting, that the entire Bahá'í world community utilize the regenerative power of poetry in our efforts to revitalize humanity.

Later in the outline, under the goal "Greater involvement

of the Faith in the life of human society," we find the statement: "Encourage Bahá'í youth to move towards the front ranks of those professions, trades, arts and crafts necessary to human progress."[10] It is our lives, our professions, our daily actions which will bring about the transformation of this planet.

Our active involvement in the arts and other occupations is essential, not only to the development of this world, but to our own progress in the next. 'Abdu'l-Bahá very clearly stated this in Paris in 1911: "Our actions will help in the world, will spread civilization, will help the progress of science, and cause arts to develop." "Without action," He continued, "nothing in the material world can be accomplished, neither can words unaided advance a man in the spiritual kingdom. It is not through lip service only that the elect of God have attained to holiness, but by patient lives of active service they have brought light into the world."[11]

The connection between physical action and spiritual development is clear. A quarter of a century after the Master's ststement in Paris, and American Bahá'í author examined contemporary society in this light. Bertha Hyde Kirkpatrick explained the correlation: "This field (art) is perhaps the most sensitive index we have of the life of the spirit in a community or nation. It quickly responds to new spiritual energies by giving new creations. In its every phase it is closely connected with the life of a people."[12] Art is the barometer of the spiritual condition of a society. Each society, conversely, supports the arts that most clearly reflect or sustain its spiritual condition. And yet the creativity of the artist infuses new elements into the society. This infusion of creativity perpetuates the further development of the whole. For this reason the involvement of Bahá'ís in the arts is crucial to the rebuilding and rebirth of human society all over the planet.

Perhaps, we need a common definition of poetry and poets. Many otherwise reasonable people (even some Bahá'ís) are frightened by their image of "The Poet" and their idea of poetry as inapplicable to daily life. But wait! Bahá'u'lláh was a poet. "He is the archetypal Poet."[13] His Writings are poetry of the most lofty kind. Mark Tobey described it thus:

> What expansion! What rivers of inspiration pour from the greatness of Bahá'u'lláh's Being as He attempts to acquaint us with this vision of Oneness, this sublimity of the One Great Power!
>
> It is, as though from every leaf and doorway, from every cloud and flower, from the mystery of sun and shadow, rain and heat—multiple mystic voices poured into His Heart the Glories of God. It is as though His eye beheld and knew the mystery hidden by the ardor of Its own manifestation!
>
> How He laments! How the sacred pen weeps that our capacity is not able to receive more! What a grief must be His, as He feels all things turned back upon himself as though the confines of His very being would break when there is no ear to hearken, no heart to receive these poems of the spirit![14]

Likewise, God is a Poet: the True Original Poet/Creator of Beauty and of The Word. "Art is the projection of the divine will into our human world," wrote H. Rozenhofer in 1937. "A manifestation of divine happenings, the creator being the very first artist who formed through the medium of 'logos,' his master-piece, the world."[15]

Doris McKay earlier explained, "To clothe with the familiar the new-old Truth the prophets took symbols. They too spelled a word—they called it the Word of God. So we may say that the prophets were the first symbolic poets. . . . " She commented further on the use of symbols, "through the language of the symbol the prophets and poets of all ages have sought to make Truth articulate. . . . "[16]

Robert Hayden (in an interview video taped at the House

of Worship) concurred saying, "Poetry is very close to religion." And he added: "I might say tangentially, that when we speak of the Prophet, and Bahá'u'lláh in particular, as being a poet, in a sense this is very true, because the Prophet uses symbols, speaks in parables, uses metaphors, and all the devices we associate with poetry."[17]

And so it would not be out of place to entertain the idea of the Word of God as poetry; and conversely that poetry can be like the Word of God, since "The speech of poets and prophets is a continuous flash of metaphor, often self-explanatory."[18] This was recently affirmed by Geoffrey Nash in his essay, "Can there be a Bahá'í Poetry?":

> By keeping poetry alive he (the poet) bears witness to the divine impulse within and may enrich society by increasing other men's perceptions. For he knows poetry is akin to the revealed Word itself (albeit of infinitely lower rank); that the poet also in his limited way testifies that in the beginning was the Word; that man's speech is also a mark of his divine descent, and poetry the utterance of his deepest nature.[19]

Although that which a human may compose can never rank with the Scripture revealed by a Messenger of God, human poetry nevertheless can be uplifting and inspiring. This understanding could have been incorporated into the life of the Bahá'í community years ago. Over half a century ago the Guardian asserted to Mark Tobey while on pilgrimage, "Art must inspire. Personal satisfaction [of the artist] is not enough."[20] This was echoed in "The Divine Origin of the Arts," written less than ten years later: "How manifold is the meaning of creative art. Its ultimate end is to lead to the Lord and to serve Him."[21] The creative impulse has a purpose and should be used for that purpose. To deny that purpose is to deny the gifts of God.

Commenting on the current disintegration of our society, the House of Justice has stated: "Even music, art and literature, which are to represent and inspire the noblest sentiments and highest aspirations and should be a source of comfort and tranquillity for troubled souls, have strayed from the straight path and are now the mirrors of the soiled hearts of this confused, unprincipled, and disordered age."[22] The arts can be perverted, like anything else at our disposal, and we have to guard against that in our efforts. We have been created for glory, not humiliation: *"Noble I made thee, wherewith dost thou abase thyself?"*[23]

Music, art and literature are "to represent and inspire the noblest sentiments and highest aspirations." How much more clearly can we state the role of the arts in a divinely guided society? Our creative expressions will be a cause for the healing of humanity when the arts are eventually used as "a source of comfort and tranquillity for troubled souls." If the Bahá'í community is to help heal mankind, we must begin to encourage expression of the talent latent within every individual Bahá'í and make it a part of our community life. And this, in turn, will teach society.

With this in mind it is logical to consider that the poetic response is one sign—perhaps, because of its relationship with the Word of God, the highest—of our likeness with our Creator. 'Abdu'l-Bahá Himself said,

> Ye must therefore put forth a mighty effort, striving by night and day and resting not for a moment, to acquire an abundant share of all sciences and arts, that Divine Image, which shineth out from the Sun of Truth may illuminate the mirror of the hearts of men.[24]

We are able to create because God first created, and our creations are likewise, a sign of our likeness to God: "... *I created thee, have engraved upon thee Mine image.* . . . "[25] That image gives us our humanity. This link, our creativity (that element of divinity within us) is one of the distinguishing characteristics of humanity. No other creatures can similarly create. The arts are the essence of our humanness expressed in physical forms. Without art we would not be human—that is to say, spiritual—beings. Our ability to create is the greatest indication of our essentially spiritual nature.

Creativity springs from the human being irrepressibly and unbidden. We must be taught other behaviors, attitudes, and virtues: kindness, love, selflessness, prayer, respect, fear, hatred, etc. These must be taught or brought from the potential to the actual, but creativity is like breathing: we just do it. The results may not always be appreciated. Parents, no matter how hard they try, cannot prevent their babies from trying to alter their environment, to create a new arrangement of their given surroundings. It is as inherent as the need to explore, which we share with animals. Only severe restrictions limit the expression of our creativity—as extreme physical handicap or profound mental oppression or abuse. Even then, the limits sometimes have been overcome.

To create is to allow the divine impulses to flow through our being. The Master explained this in a letter to George Townshend, "These heavenly susceptibilities of thine form a magnet which attracts the confirmations of the Kingdom of God; and so the doors of realities and meanings will be open unto thee. . . . "[26] To deny this is to deny our true selves, that channel to our Creator. In essence, it is to deny God. Any society which denies the human capacity for creativity is gravely ill. This link with the creative power and the uplifting nature of the arts can serve as an indicator of the role poetry can play in the rebuilding of society.

Robert Bly, one of America's better-known contemporary poets, emphatically asserts, "My feeling is that poetry is also a healing process, and that when a person tries to write poetry with depth or beauty, he will find himself guided along paths which will heal him, and this is more important, actually, than any of the poetry he writes."[27] For this reason alone, poetry writing should be part of our school curriculum.

This healing process applies not only to individuals, as Henry Eames pointed out to the Bahá'í community decades ago. "The perception and realization of beauty in space or beauty in time are not monopolized by any one people or period," he observed in an article in *World Order* magazine. "Nor are the forms and content of the arts—material or immaterial—the exclusive possession of any race or nation. The message of beauty is the message of truth, and as such is for the healing of nations as well as individuals."[28] Too few of us have paid attention.

This healing is necessary within the Bahá'í community as well as outside it. In fact, we need it *first* in order to offer a healthy and spiritual alternative to the world. Now that we have emerged from the protective cloak of obscurity, we need healing and spiritual renewal in our communities more than ever.

Poets are in a unique position to participate in the rebuilding of society, not only as creators of poetry, but as visionaries for society. A scholar of poetry outside the Bahá'í community. M. L. Rosenthal, voiced a statement similar to 'Abdu'l-Bahá's about the faculty of human receptivity when he wrote: "Poets are the verbal antennae of a people. The awareness they distill and convert into the dynamics of language is somehow present in the populace at large." He concluded with the warning: "We neglect it at our peril."[29]

The role of poetry can be stated in even more timely fashion as we begin to move into the realm of social and economic development. "The poet will lead mankind into the future," Glyn Eyford declared a number of years ago, "by giving expression to hopes and visions that are often poorly articulated and little understood by most men. Poets serve as interpreters and prophets by giving definite shape to feelings, to thoughts only dimly perceived by others."[30]

This was also Bahíyyih Nakhjavání's conclusion in her paper "Artist, Seeker and Seer." She offers that the poet's "aim should be to speak with the tongue that whispers in the bones and arteries of his audience, in such a way that the isolated and speechless elements in the community find their voices in his harmony."[31] In both cases their affirmation of the role of poets was clear: "They provide the images by which man moves into the future.[32]

In this position, of articulating the dreams of humanity, the poet has a moral role or responsibility. Geoffrey Nash explained it this way: "The poet is individual and subjective, but he is mankind's conscience. Mystically initiated to the divine order of things, he registers man's departure from his nobler nature and his higher ideals."[33] Of course, not every poet fulfills this ideal to the greatest degree possible, but those whose work has endured certainly have been in touch with the spiritual balance necessary for the promotion of the race.

This could be one reason why poets have been so overwhelmingly shut out from the life of the current mass culture, a situation that reflects the sickness of the age. "Society as a whole has shut the door to the artist and creative person," reflected Mark Tobey. "Because they [people in general] have shut the door to their own feelings."[34] This is true even in the Bahá'í community. After all, we have emerged from, yet we still live in and work in, that larger society. How could we have known differently? But now, as rebuilders of society, we have the responsibility to open that door, unite the inner and outer hearts of humanity, and heal the nations.

We have a long way to go. "In practically every aspect of society," wrote Dennis Schimeld a few years past, as he addressed the Bahá'í community, "one sees the arts being ignored or misused. Individuals and institutions of society pay little attention to the perceptions expressed by the artist. Perhaps even the Bahá'ís themselves, struggling to organize a way of life in numerous small groups throughout the world, are still but dimly aware of the significance of the arts and their use in the education and awakening of society."[35]

Why else would Robert Hayden have been so ignored by the Bahá'í community in general. Why else would he have had to endure such thoughtless comments as "[I] used to write poetry [too] but gave it up to do 'Bahá'í work.' "[36]

Surely it is Bahá'ís, though, who can most directly express the orientation necessary for arriving at a peaceful society. We are the only ones who have accepted the guidance of Bahá'u'lláh's Revelation, whose goal is a harmonious world where all persons can develop their full potential as spiritual beings in a physical realm.

"Poetry appeals to the spiritual nature of man," wrote Glyn Eyford. It "goes to the very roots of his being, and therefore, can exert a profound effect upon his perception of reality. It results in nothing less than the moral improvement of the race."[37] And it is this moral improvement of the human race, as well as its development in all other aspects, that we are trying to stimulate, assist, and accomplish.

The Bahá'í community is beginning to awaken to the need for a fuller expression of the arts in its community life. We have begun to explore ways in which we can assist in the rebuilding of society. We have been told, in the Sacred Texts, the changes that must come about for all humanity to realize their spiritual potential. In 1972, the question was raised: "Is it not possible, then, that the arts can serve at this time a twofold purpose: to help bring about a change in mankind and to help tell mankind that a change is happening?"[38]

Not that art is to be perverted into propaganda. But art, in its highest form, will call humanity to God. As Robert Hayden himself stated, "Poetry, all art, it seems to me is ultimately religious. . . . It grows out of, reflects, illuminates our inmost selves."[39] And so it should, for the arts proceed from God.

Bahá'u'lláh unequivocally exclaimed:

> *Every word that proceedeth out of the mouth of God is endowed with such potency as can instill new life into every human frame, if ye be of them that comprehend this truth. All the wondrous works ye behold in this world have been manifested through the operation of His supreme and most exalted Will. His wondrous and inflexible Purpose. Through the mere revelation of the word "Fashioner," issuing forth from His lips and proclaiming His attributes to mankind, such power is released as can generate, through successive ages, all the manifold arts which the hands of man can produce.*[40]

This power flows through God's intermediaries to receptive human souls. "*The light which these souls* [the Prophets and Messengers of God] *radiate is responsible for the progress of the world and the advancement of its peoples.*" The Blessed Beauty continued, "*They are like unto leaven which leaveneth the world of being, and constitute the animating force through which all the arts and wonders of the world are made manifest.*"[41] These exalted souls are the channels of God's grace to humanity.

But to receive these creative impulses one must be receptive to their influence. Our minds cannot be passive and expect wondrous results. "*The source of crafts, sciences and arts is the power of reflection,*" asserted Bahá'u'lláh. "*Make ye every effort that out of this ideal mine there may gleam forth such pearls of wisdom and utterance as will promote the well-being and harmony of all the kindreds of the earth.*"[42]

Here we find the role of the poet, writer, and speaker linked directly by the Manifestation of God for this age to the rebuilding of human society: ". . . *such pearls of wisdom and utterance as will promote the well-being and harmony of all the kindreds of the earth.*" How much more clearly can we be told? Is there any room for doubt or question, that those who create with words will be in the forefront of the efforts to turn humanity towards our Creator?

How is it that artists, and writers in particular, can accomplish this when, possibly, engineers and technicians cannot? The artist is most clearly a channel for the spirit. He brings concepts and ideals into focus from the unseen realm through the power of reflection. He deals with emotions and their expressions, the essentially spiritual nature of humanity. He can transmit the lofty ideals in various ways into a variety of physical representations which can, in turn, affect the ideals, emotions, and expressions of the one receiving, viewing, or partaking of the art. "The artist," Dennis Schimeld commented, "affect[s] changes in the consciousness of society."[43] These expressions of creativity change the way people perceive their world. And thus progress results.

The artist probes into the human spirit, and emotions, with the divine spark. When the human condition is not in tune, the experience can be painful, but conducive to healing. The artist highlights the discrepancies between our behavior and our morals. "Hence the artist, like the surgeon at times, probes deeply and cleansingly into the disease," Schimeld continued, "attempting to 'tone up' the mind of man so he will be capable of the insight necessary to effect changes of attitude in society." The question remains: "But is the artist heeded?"[44]

It is the change of perception that the artist can best facilitate. "By its very nature, art, Mr. Hayden taught, is revolutionary, because it seeks to change the consciousness, perceptions, and very beings of those who open themselves to it," remembered Julius Lister.[45]

Anaïs Nin, one of the more perceptive observers of our society, reached to the heart of the transforming role of the poet when she wrote in her diary in 1955: "a poet transfigures all he touches and he discards the appearance to penetrate beyond, to the essence."[46] It is the poet who sees past what appears to be, to what is, and beyond that, to what is possible. The poet is the seer for human society. We need Bahá'ís who are poets.

Poetry and the other arts are much more subjective areas than other disciplines. The poet and other creators have to be in tune with the Spirit, otherwise there is no creation. "The best of poets have always dealt with intangibles, with spiritual values," agreed Geoffrey Nash. "The modern age is grossly materialistic and utilitarian, and above all atheistic; poets, if the evidence of the last century's poetry is to be trusted, cannot do without God."[48] It is the poets link with our Creator which makes all the difference.

So we have a channel in the arts, and poetry in particular, for the healing and rebuilding of society. For the poets and other artists to be effective and productive, they need to know their importance, but the rest of the community needs to know it more so. There needs to be a recognized, permanent and honored place in our community life for our poets and other artists. Why not let the walls of our Bahá'í Center double as art galleries? (Bare walls are ugly anyway.) Let us have classes in our schools where *everyone* is encouraged to exercise creativity, and thereby appreciate what true humanness is. And give time on our programs to poets, dramatists and others. They need our patronage and encouragement. Above all, why not support those who are actively trying to create by providing space (in time and responsibilities) to do so. The healing of the planet is at stake. We will all benefit.

The purpose of the Revelation of Bahá'u'lláh is to change the life of mankind from what it was to what it can be. This change is the purpose of our lives as well. We are to bring humanity back into an awareness of its relationship to its Creator. Bahá'u'lláh taught that our true human nature and purpose are so noble and exalted that every effort should be made to strive to attain our fullest potential. Poets can create this awareness among humanity more directly and effectively than any other people. But we must allow them and encourage them to do so. Are we up to the challenge?

POETS CRY

All the Poets cry aloud;
    the earth is in its weeping.
Among the silent, deaf and dumb,
    the Poet/Singer knows
The earth in its travail
    begetting a new vision.
Mankind groans in silence,
    as hearts die, one on one.
Traditions creak and crumble,
    their age cannot sustain . . .
Now the Scattering Angels
    work their mercy-vengeance.
Can order come from chaos?
    And all the poets cry aloud.

Notes

1. Shoghi Effendi, *Unfolding Destiny* (London: Bahá'í Publishing Trust, 1981) p. 429 (letter on behalf of the Guardian to an individual dated 2 January 1932).
2. Ibid., p. 429 (letter to an individual, dated 10 January 1932).
3. Shoghi Effendi, trans., *The Dawn-Breakers* (Wilmette, Ill.: Bahá'í Publishing Trust, 1974) p. 258.
4. Ibid., p. 258-59.
5. Mark Tobey, "Art and Community," *World Order* (April 1939) p. 34.
6. Henry Purmort Eames, "The International Aspect of the Arts," *World Order* (July 1935) p. 127.
7. Universal House of Justice, comp., *Bahá'í Meetings/The Nineteen Day Feast* (Wilmette, Ill.: Bahá'í Publishing Trust, 1976) p. 25 (letter on behalf of the Guardian to an individual, dated 7 April 1935).
8. Bahá'u'lláh, *Tablets of Bahá'u'lláh revealed after the Kitáb-i-Aqdas* (Haifa, Bahá'í World Center, 1978) pp. 175-76.

9. Universal House of Justice, "Outline Summary of the Six Year Plan's Major Objectives," (study Sheets) np, nd.
10. Ibid.
11. 'Abdu'l-Bahá, *Paris Talks* (London: Bahá'í Publishing Trust, 1971) pp. 80–81.
12. Bertha Hyde Kirkpatrick, "Social Trends in American Life: Part 8: Art," *World Order* (December 1935) p. 355.
13. Bahíyyih Nakhjavání, "Artist, Seeker and Seer," *Bahá'í Studies*, 10 (Ottawa: Association for Bahá'í Studies, 1982) p. 4.
14. Mark Tobey, "The One Spirit," *World Order* (August 1935) p. 175.
15. H. Rozenhofer, "The Divine Origin of Creative Art," *World Order* (June 1937) p. 114.
16. Doris McKay, "Through the Invisible," *World Order* (September 1935) pp. 207–208.
17. John Hatcher, *From the Aural Darkness* (Oxford: George Ronald, 1984) p. 69.
18. Doris McKay, "Invisible," p. 209.
19. Geoffrey Nash, "Can There be a Bahá'í Poetry?" *Bahá'í Studies 7: Response to the Revelation* (Ottawa: Canadian Association for Studies on the Bahá'í Faith, 1980) p. 4.
20. Marzieh Gail, "The Days With Mark Tobey," *World Order* (Spring 1977) p. 13.
21. H. Rosenhofer, "Creative Art," p. 115.
22. *Bahá'í National Review*, no. 117 (January 1982) p. 1 (letter from the Universal House of Justice to the Iranian Bahá'ís living in other countries around the world).
23. Bahá'u'lláh, *The Hidden Words of Bahá'u'lláh*, Shoghi Effendi, trans. (Wilmette, Ill.: Bahá'í Publishing Trust, 1985) pp. 6–7.
24. 'Abdu'l-Bahá, *Selections from the Writings of 'Abdu'l-Bahá* (Haifa: Bahá'í World Center, 1978) p. 140.
25. Bahá'u'lláh, *Hidden Words*, p. 4.
26. George Townsend, *'Abdu'l-Bahá: The Master* (Oxford: George Ronald, 1987) p. 12.
27. Joe David Bellamy, ed. *American Poetry Observed* (Champaign: University of Illinois Press, 1984) pp. 66–67.
28. Henry Eames, "Arts," pp. 126–27.
29. Macha Louis Rosenthal, *Poetry and the Common Life* (New York: Oxford University Press, 1974) p. xviii.

30. Glen A. Eyford, "Aesthetics and Spiritual Education," *World Order* (Fall 1979) p. 39.
31. Bahíyyih Nakhjavání, "Seer," p. 14.
32. Glen Eyford, "Education," p. 39.
33. Geoffrey Nash, "Bahá'í Poetry," p. 2.
34. Mark Tobey, "Art," p. 34.
35. Dennis Schimeld, "The Presence of the Arts," *World Order* (Spring 1972) p. 19.
36. John Hatcher, "Darkness," p. 72.
37. Glen Eyford, "Education," p. 39.
38. Dennis Schmield, "Arts," p. 18.
39. John Hatcher, "Darkness," p. 74.
40. Bahá'u'lláh, *Gleanings from the Writings of Bahá'u'lláh*, Shoghi Effendi, trans., (Wilmette, Ill.: Bahá'í Publishing Trust, 1976) pp. 141–42.
41. Bahá'u'lláh, *Gleanings*, p. 157.
42. Bahá'u'lláh, *Tablets*, p. 72.
43. Dennis Schimeld, "Arts," p. 9.
44. Ibid., p. 17.
45. Julius Lister, "In Memorium: In Gratitude for Robert Hayden," *World Order* (Fall 1981) p. 53.
46. Anaïs Nin, *The Diary of Anaïs Nin, volume six, 1955–1966* (New York: Harcourt Brace Jovanovich Publishers, 1976) p. 26.
47. Geoffrey Nash, "Bahá'í Poetry," p. 2.

Ladder of the Soul

an interview with Lasse Thoresen

Lasse Thoresen (b. 1949) is one of Europe's outstanding young composers. He has had works commissioned by all the major Norwegian Philharmonic Orchestras and the French National Radio, among others. His compositions incorporate different modern mediums and several have been recorded and published. Mr. Thoresen has also developed his own musical theory and method of analysis that focus on the aural perception of musical order. His method has drawn international interest, and Mr. Thoresen has lectured and given seminars on it in several European countries. Mr. Thoresen has served on the National Spiritual Assembly of Norway for twelve years.

In the following article, Mr. Thoresen is interviewed by Trym Bergsmo, a professional photographer. The article has been edited by Margaret Warden Maytan, a teacher of piano and music history.

TB: Inspiration is a central aspect of any artist's way of expressing himself. What do you think the nature of artistic inspiration is, in the light of the Bahá'í Writings?

LT: I think that musical or artistic inspiration is basically the same kind of inspiration that people who are not musicians or artists can get when they pray or meditate on a certain subject or problem. All of us feel inspired when we get ideas we have never conceived of before, but it is evident that a creative artist especially must cultivate this ability to receive new ideas. He must learn to open himself to thoughts, visions, and ideas and must cultivate an ability to formulate these in an artistic medium. But neither the artist nor the non-artist can ever fully know the nature of the inspiration he receives: he may feel or think that a certain idea is divinely inspired, but later he may realize that the idea was entirely his own imagination.

As a Bahá'í and an artist, my ideal is of course to convey some spiritual insight through my music, hopefully without my own ego too much in the way. To purify the mental sources of inspiration, to open the right channels, so to speak, one has to submit oneself to some spiritual discipline, and the Bahá'í Faith has offered me many means and opportunities to do that. It still does—this process never ends. I choose to listen to my inner voice, knowing full well that it is not always reliable or divine, because at the same time I am practicing spiritual disciplines to purify myself as a channel. I accept the imperfections in my inspiration and in my composition because I accept my own humanity and the dynamic evolution of spiritual qualities.

There is another way to relate to one's inner source of inspiration, which I have not chosen for myself. This way is to construct some general ideas about what spiritual music should be like and then censor one's inspiration when it seems to deviate from that idea. However, there is no doctrine about the character of spiritual music in the Bahá'í Faith. There is no tradition in this field yet, and there is no reason to assume that one's intellectual construct is superior to one's intuition in assessing spiritual music. My music is at times more a confession, a diary of my own life, than the presentation of an ideal. My music pictures a spiritual struggle, rather than a state of spiritual perfection.

TB: Do you think that developing the intuition and improving the ability to become a pure channel for inspiration will replace much of the technical training that the musician goes through today?

LT: No, I definitely don't think so. Both types of training are necessary. I think Johannes Brahms explained this very well when he stated in an interview that, although musical ideas came to him after prayer and meditation, their realization depended completely on his technical ability, his discipline, and his mastery of the musical material. In expressing an idea, divinely inspired or not, he could not go beyond what he himself had mastered as far as the techniques of composition are concerned.[1]

TB: Bahá'u'lláh says: *"We have made music a ladder by which souls may ascend to the realm on high."*[2] How does music fulfill this function?

LT: Music does this in many ways, and it is hard to answer the question briefly. Let me demonstrate one way. To attain mastery in music, let us say in order to play an instrument well, you have to discipline your senses and your physical ability. This discipline can make you feel as though you are always limiting yourself. For example, you have to train yourself to play scales, to play chords, to read music. Many people experience this type of discipline as a sort of dark tunnel—when they get into it they become afraid. They feel uninspired, "unspiritual," unable to express their own emotions freely. They see no light at the other end of the tunnel. So they often escape by returning the way they entered.

However, if you have the courage to pass through that tunnel of discipline, then you will find that you are attaining a mastery which actually means freedom.

You regain the spontaneity that seemed to be lost in the middle of the tunnel. Of course, you can choose not to master anything and be very spontaneous. But most often, in that case, you will not be able to find the right technical channels for what you wish to express. To put it differently, before you are trained, you are confined to expressing only very elementary, often crude meanings. Training and discipline give you the capacity to say more refined, more elevated, more human things.

For us who are Bahá'ís, or indeed for anyone, the criterion of true spiritual nobility is the ability to act according to ethical principles. These principles, or divine laws, must be trained and become part of our new nature, so that when we act spontaneously, we also act ethically. This ethical training process is exactly parallel to what I have already described in music.

I contend that it is easier to learn symbolic behavior as a prelude to learning it in real life. This, I think, is what Bahá'u'lláh is suggesting when He says concerning the Fast: "*With it Thou didst adorn the preamble of the Book of Thy Laws.*"[3] The Fast is basically symbolic—through it, we learn detachment from desires and obedience to spiritual laws. We practice these virtues symbolically by abstaining from food and drink. The Fast itself is not the goal.

Similarly, passing through musical training in the way I have explained need not be a goal in itself. Rather, it can be a symbolic learning process by which one can attain freedom through discipline and through the internalization and mastery of laws.

TB: So this is one way in which music is a ladder for the soul's ascension. But isn't there a simpler way? For example, through the listener's immediate appreciation of a piece of music?

LT: Yes, I would say that most classical or "Serious" music is a language—a nonverbal language—in which profound meanings can be found. I would say that in the music of the great European masters—Josquin, Monteverdi, Bach, Haydn, Beethoven, Schubert, Bruckner, Brahms, Messiaen, to mention some of my favorites—one can really find mysteries embodied in metaphors of structured sound. These composers communicate through a language that requires that the listener be willing to exert himself. The language has to be learned; the more or less concealed meanings have to be found and interpreted. It is like the Bahá'í Writings: they are not something you understand without making an effort and diving into them. Music—like the Writings—rewards your efforts by revealing meaning after meaning, delight after delight, though not until you have given it devoted attention for some time. When people feel they understand a piece of music—particularly one without a text, for example a symphony or a sonata, they have proven themselves capable of understanding a nonverbal message.

Music can thus be a means for developing an individual's capability for understanding nonverbal messages. This capability is essential for any religious individual, since the Holy Writings tend to express their meanings through symbols and metaphors,[4] images rather than abstract concepts. Bahá'u'lláh uses a very poetic language by which He evokes wonderful images and inner vistas. In order to understand these images and draw on the spiritual power they can release, we must first of all call forth these images from our imagination—using our inner senses rather than the outward ones. Thus, when Bahá'u'lláh speaks of *"the rustling of the Divine Lote-Tree and the murmur of the breezes of thine utterance in the Kingdom of Thy Names,"*[5] He suggests auditive impressions that we can imagine internally.

In order to evoke the spiritual potential of these images, in this case sound images, we have to dive into them mentally, listen to them, penetrate them, ultimately dissolve them in the clarity of understanding. We have to find out, though not necessarily explain intellectually, why exactly these sound impressions, these images, were chosen as metaphors by Bahá'u'lláh. Of course, to divine the meaning of these images ultimately becomes a very subjective and personal thing. Yet, the process of finding these personal meanings should be cultivated, as it stimulates the spiritual development of the individual. Art can play a vital role in this development, since the arts work with nonverbal symbols and images within the subjective, personal sphere.

By the way, it is interesting to note that the entire earthly experience can be viewed as a metaphor from the Bahá'í point of view.[6] Learning to find the meaning of metaphorical expressions in art or in the Writings, then, becomes a way to learn symbolically the process of passing from physical reality to metaphysical reality.

TB: Could there be other reasons why art and religion communicate so often through nonverbal images rather than well-defined, precise statements?

LT: Fundamentally, when we conceive of ourselves, we have an image of how we relate to other human beings, how we relate to objects around us, what the world is like. These images govern our behavior. Some of these images may be conscious, others may be hidden deep in our souls. To develop ourselves spiritually, we have to change ourselves; and to change ourselves means changing our images—both the conscious ones and the unconscious ones. I suppose there are two basic strategies for changing mental images: one, to make our unconscious images conscious; and two, to make our conscious images unconscious.

Psychoanalysis is an example of the first strategy. The individual in psychotherapy will become aware of previously unconscious images that have controlled his behavior. This awareness gives him the freedom to then change that behavior. For example, a person may discover in therapy that he has an image of his father as an infallible dictator. As soon as he becomes aware of the image, he can then better control and understand his own behavior as a father.

The second strategy, making conscious images unconscious, means taking an intellectually understood spiritual principle and internalizing it so that its practice becomes automatic. For example, the image of humanity as a flower garden whose beauty is found in the diversity of the flowers and colors can become so much part of our unconscious that we are no longer aware of it, yet we cherish peoples of other races. When meditating, when reading the Writings, when studying them, we are actually internalizing certain images. The internalized images often represent alternative ways of relating to other human beings, ways that are not necessarily biologically natural, but ways that are ethically and humanly more valuable. In a very few words, for example, Christ, by asking us to turn the other cheek, has suggested a completely new ethic that departs from centuries of biologically conditioned responses to aggression. Thus religion enables us to conceive of ourselves in new relationships to the world and to our fellow human beings—relationships that may be more fruitful and more benign.

Art also has this ability to induce a certain ideal in people, but of course whether that ideal is ethically and spiritually valuable depends on the intention of the artist, as well as that of the listeners. Art can have two opposing functions: it can reveal an unconscious potential—positive or negative, and it can present an ideal—

positive or negative, and contribute to its being absorbed in the minds of people. Unfortunately, these opposite functions are often confused and can appear unreconcilable. One can trace this conflict back to Aristotle and Plato. Aristotle tanded to emphasize the cathartic effect of art, that is, its capability to evoke negative emotions from people in symbolic, thus harmless ways. In this way, it releases tensions and increases their happiness. Plato, on the other hand, insisted that art should set up an ideal, and he went so far as to recommend that certain musical modes should be forbidden because of their detrimental effect on the character of the youth.[7]

TB: But isn't it in many ways a disadvantage that nonverbal languages—the use of images and symbols—never allow the formulation of a precise and unambiguous message?

LT: This is a disadvantage in, for example, administrative matters, or in questions of essential doctrine. In dealing with these questions, one should use precisely defined words and concepts, not poetic images. This is of course done in the Bahá'í Writings, as well as by the present administrative institutions of the Bahá'í Faith.

But for the spiritual development of individuals, I think ambiguity plays an important part. All understanding of nonverbal poetic images—for which no precise code of interpretation or authoritative tradition of interpretation exist—must necessarily be based on very personal interpretations. These interpretations are most often projections of thoughts and ideas that the individual already has or has conceived of subconsciously. So his understanding will suffer from the limitations of his own mental and spiritual faculties. The symbolic image that this individual feels he relates to and understands thus becomes a catalyst for his own understanding to become more explicit, more conscious. As his understanding becomes more conscious, he can then better apply that understanding to daily life and the pace of his spiritual growth will quicken.

As he continues to grow, however, his understanding will change, and so probably will the meaning he finds in the same symbolic images. Actually, the same symbol may change its meaning several times during a lifetime, thus time and again serving as a catalyst for new insight. In this way spiritual growth is stimulated. Without the ambiguity, a symbol could not contain several strata of meaning. A good work of art is one that suggests a maximum of concentric meanings by employing a minimum of words, notes, etc.

TB: But for many people music is more than a personal experience. Music has a social function, bringing people together, creating unity.

LT: The most striking example I have ever heard of this function is a recording of Pygmy music I came across.[8] It records a ceremony performed when the hunters return to the tribe with game. In this incredible music, you can hear virtually every class of that society participating. You have the children, the old men, the hunters, the women, and so on, each with their characteristic motives. They all join in an overall pattern that unifies them. It is to me a completely heavenly vision of ideal community living. These people make their social order audible through music. Their music is not anything they can examine and discuss as a separate object or entity. The music transcends completely the individual point of view, as it is a manifestation of a social reality or order that includes and encompasses the individual. There is no audience for this music, only participants who, through the music, make themselves feel as one with a greater social organism. That is a beautiful experience and one that has much to do with what we Bahá'ís call unity. It allows individual expressions of differences, yet shows that the interplay of these differences form a totality displaying qualities not to be found in any of its constituent parts.

TB: It seems that the music of these poeple is a tool for recognizing spiritual values in life.

LT: It definitely is. And I think this is true of a lot of other music, including our European classical tradition. This music often expresses different attitudes and emotions, such as drama, anger, serenity, etc., all of which correspond to behavior patterns and attitudes in human beings.

But more than that, we can look at many of these different expressions as somehow reflecting attributes of God. There is an enormous spectrum of God's attributes—for example, justice, wrath, beauty—whose expression we can also find reflected in the human temperament. And then of course also in music. True music teaches us some of the alchemy of God's names. It shows us how certain of God's attributes can be visualized, be made audible and tangible. What is a merciful gesture? What is a wrathful gesture? What is justice, beauty, and so on? All of these can be made visible for us in a music that at the same time induces this gesture in us and makes us experience that gesture physically or mentally. This helps us to identify ourselves with and to adopt these qualities.

TB: One wonders why the Manifestations of God did not themselves compose music, or become great artists, instead of using words to illustrate the qualities of God.

LT: Well, in actual fact, I would say that Bahá'u'lláh is very much an artist. The music in His use of words is fabulous. I even believe that God, in selecting the languages of revelation, considers the sounds of those languages.⁹ There are words in our Western languages we describe as onomatopoetic. These are words whose sounds imitate a certain phenomenon we know around us, such as *sizzling* or *rustling*, words that are sound images of other sounds. And I personally think that many of the words that describe God's attributes in the Persian and Arabic languages are onomatopoetic for the spiritual realities that constitute the meaning of the words. The sound and rhythm of these words suggest to the inner ear and eye of man certain archetypal forms related to God's attributes.

The use of mantras in Eastern religions, such as Hinduism and Buddhism, corroborates this view. In Muslim tradition, we also find a similar usage of sound. The reason the Qur'an was not translated until very recently was that the sounds of the Book were considered to be the sounds that the Prophet Muhammad heard from the angel Gabriel. Implicit here is the fact that the Muslim traditions actually value the *sound*, the *music* of the Revelation, just as they value the conceptual and verbal aspect of the Revelation.¹⁰

Sometimes I have wondered if there is a set of sound symbols used for conveying spiritual meaning that is more universal than the actual spoken language it appears in. For example, consider that in the Christian tradition one uses the word *amen*. This is a word that is essentially meaningless; it does not denote a certain concept, but it is often used for endings. Thus, *amen* is a "sound" more than an ordinary word. If we turn to Buddhist and Hindu traditions we find a word which is often used in closing formulas and which has a very similar sound: *aom* or *om*. Looking into the Bahá'í Writings, we find that Bahá'u'lláh often closes paragraphs or prayers (such as the short obligatory prayer) with the word *qayyum*, meaning "Self-Subsisting." Again, here is a similar use of similar sounds. Both *aom* and *qayyum* have been used in meditation, in the Far East as mantras, and in the Middle East in the *Dhikr* of the Muslim Sufi tradition.[11]

I think these observations can be valid for many other words. There is perhaps a universal language of sounds of which the Revealers of the religions avail themselves. We know also, that some words from the Bahá'í Revelation are not translated, such as the Greatest Name, and that these mostly are words used for meditation or contemplation.

TB: You are suggesting that the Revelation has an aural dimension incorporated into the revealed word itself. But this aural dimension is lost when the text is translated to other languages.

LT: Bahá'u'lláh asks us to recite, or intone, His words,[12] thus indicating perhaps that He considered the aural aspect of His words to be important. Of course, the aural aspect is not essential, otherwise the Bahá'í Writings would not have been translated at all. When we listen to the believers from the Middle East chanting their prayers, we are all enraptured by the beauty of sound and rhythm. We know that the first believers became completely ecstatic when reading prayers and Writings. That was, of course, partially because of the mere magic of the sound. They were spellbound by these fabulous utterances that were themselves so rhythmical, so beautiful, so suggestive.

But languages are different, and I don't think that all languages have these evocative, onomatopoetic words describing metaphysical realities. For example, I find that the Norwegian language lacks these sound symbols. Norwegian has a fabulous repertoire of words that describe natural phenomena, but not metaphysical ones. In this case, I think that the role of music might even be to compensate for the lack of music in the language, by adding to the revealed Word the dimension that is lost in translation. This compensation is perhaps among the major contributions that future art can make in enriching the Revelation of Bahá'u'lláh by adapting that Revelation to different people and local mentalities around the world.

TB: What position do you feel music and art will have in a future Bahá'í society?

LT: Today, music in the Faith has its most important function in proclamation activities. In order to satisfy and to attract people to the Faith, the music has to appeal to current styles and popular tastes. But music can also be an important means for deepening the believers in the profound, spiritual aspects of the Faith. This is of relatively little importance now, but in the future it will become of immense importance. When the society functions according to Bahá'í principles and the focus is on the spiritualization of the masses of people, individually as well as collectively, music and the arts in general will play a prominent part. During this state of development Bahá'í art is going to emerge.

There will probably never be a fixed liturgy for the services in our Temples. A liturgy implies the authorization of one set of artistic symbols. While the Bahá'í Faith accepts that spiritual realities can be made visible in symbolic and artistic forms, it seeks to avoid the authorizing of one type of artistic expression. I believe there will be a lot of flexibility and possibilities for different approaches in the services. Accordingly, a plurality and multiplicity of artistic expressions based on individual as well as cultural or national differences may develop. This differentiation will occur as different native national cultures find adequate interfaces between their own temperaments and the universal spirit of the Faith.

TB: Then art of the future will play a much broader role in

achieving a more total understanding of existence. However, as a Bahá'í artist living today and composing music for a world in which materialism is a predominant force, what do you think an artist of today actually can achieve?

LT: I think that a spiritual artist has potentially much to contribute in our current situation, as he represents a few feathers on the wing of religion that 'Abdu'l-Bahá says has to be developed in order to balance the wing of science. Scientific discovery has become predominant in shaping the way we in Western civilization perceive the world. Often our world, therefore, is lost in numbers and calculations, and we forget to regard it in a spiritual and symbolic way. The Báb, Bahá'u'lláh, and 'Abdu'l-Bahá often use images and symbols taken from nature. As far as I can see, they were concerned with nature in a way that is more phenomenologic than scientific. They turned simple perceptions into metaphors for spiritual reality. They did not concern themsleves with the scientific explanations of these perceptions.

For example, the Báb and Bahá'u'lláh often talk about the rising sun, and this image is a very central and archetypal one in our Faith. From the scientific point of view, we know that the sun does not rise. It is our planet that spins, so that the sun becomes visible. However, the perceptual illusion that the sun rises is enough for the Manifestation to be able to use it as a metaphor and a symbol for spiritual reality. The Báb goes so far as to affirm that this *symbolic* reality is the sun's essential reality. He says: "Verily, the sun is but a token from My presence so that the true believers among My servants may discern in its rising the dawning of every Dispensation."[13]

The artist today can play a vital function in making the phenomena we experience around us appear to be the wonders that they really are and in helping us unravel their symbolic and spiritual potential. In doing so, he (or she) strengthens a spiritual perception of the world, and counteracts a tendency reinforced by contemporary science to regard the world exclusively as material.

TB: But certainly it is legitimate to regard the same object both as an object of scientific research and as a symbol or metaphor for spiritual reality. This dual perspective can be applied to music as well.

LT: That is true. 'Abdu'l-Bahá Himself makes that distinction when saying: "Musical melodies are a certain something which prove to be accidental upon etheric vibrations, for voice is nothing but the expression of vibrations, which, reaching the tympanum, affect the nerves of hearing. Musical melodies are, therefore, those peculiar effects produced by, or from, vibration. However, they have the keenest effect upon the spirit. In truth, although music is a material affair, yet its tremendous effect is spiritual, and its greatest attachment is to the realm of the spirit."[14]

There is a dichotomy between physical and spiritual reality, and in this dichotomy lies the great spiritual challenge, brought about by the development of science and technology, both for the arts and society in general. There are dangers as well as potentialities. Music composed in strictly scientific ways may sound awful. The sensitivity to what the music expresses symbolically is blunted by an obsession with technical procedures. This music epitomizes the kind of hell a society ordered in purely scientific and materialistic terms could become. Despite its internal logic and order, the result is chaos.

However, it is possible to extract sound materials from the contemporary scene and use them for spiritual purposes. Technically, there are lots of things to learn from contemporary music and music technology. And as an artist and Bahá'í, one can use all this to express some aspects of the spirit of the new age. But this is a difficult task, because there is no tradition of Bahá'í music, no Bahá'í culture. All this will come into being in the future. Now we simply have to start working with what past and present culture can offer, and make the best out of it by applying Bahá'í principles as we work.

I have considered that, since the Bahá'í Faith views the world as being governed by divine laws, music must somehow also be governed by laws, laws that should be audible to the listener. Contemporary music that sounds chaotic and ugly is often very highly structured. The problem is that it is not possible to hear the underlying structure, and therefore such pieces are perceptually chaotic. So I have made a thorough theoretical study of how sound can be organized so as to seem ordered and governed by laws. This isn't enough to solve all the problems facing serious contemporary music, but I believe it is a step in the right direction.

TB: Technological research has affected serious music profoundly, even more perhaps than pop, rock, and jazz music. Would you say, then, that materialism has had a lesser influence on the music of the popular scene?

LT: No, absolutely not. But whereas in serious music the challenge may be an excess of intellectualism, in modern popular music it is an excess of sensuality. Of course, all art appeals to the senses, the question is whether such an appeal is the means, or an end in itself. It seems to be an end in itself in some rock music, where the sheer volume of the sound forces itself on the listener with enormous physical power, forcing a reaction in a stimulus-response pattern. This is a pattern in which the possibility to choose one's reactions, i.e. to exercise one's free will, plays little part. And when one reduces the range of one's free will, one becomes more animal-like, less like a spiritual, fully developed human being. This is, of course, hardly an ideal situation from the spiritual point of view.

But we have to admit that people are different and that they like different kinds of music. I know there are many people who find classical music too intellectual. I myself see in this music a perfect balance between emotional involvement on the one hand, and distance—providing space for reflection—on the other. However, I can also see that in the pop and rock music styles there may be potential that can be utilized for spiritual ends. I think that the essential difference here is ultimately in the intention with which the music is produced, more than in different styles and ways to express these intentions.

It is evident that all art appeals to the senses and communicates through the senses. Art, however, is a means not only of refining the senses but of transcending them. By transcending them, I mean that one goes from one's external senses—that is, from listening with the physical ear, seeing with the eye, etc.—to one's internal senses, that is listening and seeing with the mind and soul, and with our imagination. Our external senses are the tools of the soul for developing an inner vision and an inner audition. In this way, experiencing an artistic discipline and working on our external senses, can lead in the end to a transcendence of the external senses and a development of the faculties of the soul, particularly the faculty of inner vision.[15] This is one of the most exciting and important aspects of how music and art in general can help us spiritualize ourselves.

Music is nonverbal, symbolic language that allows us to understand spiritual dimensions that go beyond words. The understanding of music helps us in our understanding of God's Revelation, because the revealed word also contains non-verbal dimensions of expression. Music is of vital importance in mankind's spiritualization, as it may aid us to transcend our physical senses and to develop the faculties of the soul.

Notes

1. Cf. Arthur M. Abell, *Talks with Great Composers* (New York: Philosophical Library, 19--).
2. The whole quotation reads: "We have permitted you to listen to music and singing. Beware lest such listening cause you to transgress the bounds of decency and dignity. Rejoice in the joy of My Most Great Name through which the hearts are enchanted and the minds of the well-favored are attracted.

We have made music a ladder by which souls may ascend to the realm on high. Change it not into wings for self and passion. I seek refuge in God that you be not of the ignorant." Bahá'u'lláh, from the *Kitàb-i Aqdas*, cited in a compilation of extracts, *Bahá'í Writings on Music*, p. 1.

3. See *Prayers and Meditations of Bahá'u'lláh* Wilmette, Ill.: (Bahá'í Publishing Trust, 1938).
4. A metaphor is a "term or phrase applied to something to which it is not literally applicable, in order to suggest a resemblance." (*The American College Dictionary*).

A metaphor is different from a mere comparison: a sentence such as "Achilles fought as a lion in the battle" is a comparision; whereas "Achilles was a lion in the battle" is a metaphor.

5. *Prayers and Meditations*, p. 291.
6. John S. Hatcher, "The Metaphorical Nature of Physical Reality," *World Order* (Summer 1977) pp. 31–56.
7. Aristotle's ideas about music are, for example, found in "Politica," Book VIII. Plato presents his viewpoints in "The State," Book IV.
8. Song of rejoicing after returning from a hunt. UNESCO collection: *An Anthology of African Music*.
9. See Shoghi Effendi's characterization of Bahá'u'lláh's Revelation: "Such testimonies bearing on this theme are impregnated

with such power and reveal such beauty as only those who are versed in the languages in which they were originally revealed can claim to have sufficiently appreciated." (*The World Order of Bahá'u'lláh* by Shoghi Effendi [Wilmette, Ill. Bahá'í Publishing Trust, 1955] p. 103).

10. See Jean During, "Revelation and Spiritual Audition in Islam," *World of Music*, ed. by Schott Mainz (Berlin: UNESCO, 1982–83).

11. See Laleh Bakhtiar, "Sufi Expressions of the Mystic Quest," p. 38—Thames and Hudson (1976).

12. See, for example, *Bahá'í Prayers* (Wilmette, Ill. Bahá'í Pub Trust, 1982).

13. *Selections from the Writings of the Báb* (Haifa Bahá'í World Centre, 1976) p. 159.

14. Table Talk by 'Abdu'l-Bahá, cited in compilation of extracts, *Bahá'í Writings on Music*, pp. 3–4.

15. "Know that the power and the comprehension of the human spirit are of two kinds: that is to say, they perceive and act in two different modes. One way is through instruments and organs; thus with this eye it sees, with this ear it hears, with this tongue it talks. Such is the action of the spirit, and the perception of the reality of man, by means of organs. . . .

The other manifestation of the powers and actions of the spirit is without instruments and organs. For example, in the state of sleep without eyes it sees, without an ear it hears, without a tongue it speaks, without feet it runs. Briefly, these actions are beyond the means of instruments and organs." 'Abdu'l-Bahá quoted in *Bahá'í World Faith*, p. 50.

"Therefore we must thank God that He has created for us both material blessings and spiritual bestowals. He has given us material gifts and spiritual graces, outer sight to view the lights of the sun and inner vision by which we may perceive the glory of God. He has designed the outer ear to enjoy the melodies of sound and the inner hearing wherewith we may hear the voice of our creator. We must strive with energies of heart, soul and mind to develop and manifest the perfections and virtues latent within the realities of the phenomenal world . . . " 'Abdu'l-Bahá quoted in *Bahá'í World Faith*, p. 267).

FRITZ A. MANN
Bahá'í artist.

Photo by Walt Martin

Looking Forward in the Visual Arts

by Fritz A. Mann

AS FAR BACK AS I can remember I have always aspired to be an artist. The inner discoveries I have realized, through what the creative drive produces, have confirmed this identity. The obsession with visual art has been there all my life because art is both the vehicle and the avenue by which I best express my greatest feelings in ways others can appreciate.

My artwork reveals that my main interest is in people. As a Bahá'í, I feel compelled to uplift and dignify humanity in my work, reflecting aspects of man's nobler and gentler nature in order to inspire hope and a sense of the mysterious in my viewing audience.

Because creativity is often a highly subjective experience, my thoughts are never without humbling suspicions of self-delusion as I pursue my chosen tasks. My inner voice tells me I have a talent that I should put to good use whenever worthwhile opportunities present themselves. Perhaps I am only hearing the prompting echos of the encouraging words I heard years ago from my artistic mother and the school teachers of my youth who recognized my potential.

It would be a mistake for an artist like myself to pay undue attention to society's general indifference. On the other hand, it would make me shudder to think that the road I have embarked upon since childhood leads to a dead end, that my cause had been lost before its worth had been realized. I believe it is too late now to turn back, and I must continue facing the risk of delusion while listening to that voice within. I don't know any other instinctively true roads to follow.

I depend on my artistic talent as if it were a very close and special friend. It is always near, loyal, entertaining, and full of surprises. Like I suppose the soul is, talent can be a very quiet presence that makes itself felt through you before finding some tangible expression of its own in a work of art.

Though I am driven to create, I am my own harshest critic. Sometimes I am so particular about the quality of my work that I am the first one to depreciate it. By the time I hear a second critical opinion, it begins to sound rather comical. Most people are never as critical about my work as I am. Initially, I try to create art to please my tastes, and then afterwards I consider its relevant public value before I decide to publish or exhibit it. One can spend years on a piece that turns out bland, or one can knock out a piece in a week that looks grand. The time spent can be of little consequence.

As a painter I often work in the isolation of my studio, focusing as much on the abstracted world within me as on the observable one outside. Trance-like in deep concentration, much of my brain shifts into neutral, as my mind drifts along a stream of creative exploration. I am alone in my work, but never lonely: cut off from the rest of the world and working for hours on end, frequently experiencing an elevated sense of completeness with my being and all thoughts invading my consciousness. At such times, I am in touch with the song of my soul, that driving animator called creative inspiration. Beyond this, I am just another seeker knocking on the doors of his imagination. Naturally, this kind of work suits me, but I make no pretense that it is superior to any other kinds of work people do in a spirit of conscientious servitude. When we are describing the creative nature of the beast, artists are very introspective creatures.

As a religious person, I am susceptible to making occasional requests of the disembodied spirits of Bahá'u'lláh and 'Abdu'l-Bahá (both true Artists in the Creative Word)—or Leonardo da Vinci and Vincent Van Gogh—prayerfully beseeching them to inspire my soul with that certain twist of vision that dispels mental blindness. In spite of this wish, I am never certain whether the inspiration thus received arrived via the hidden world or merely from the well-read but static pages of my studies. Because art was my first religion, so to speak, I can be as deeply moved by a Van Gogh painting as I am by a passage from Bahá'u'lláh's Writings. Similarly, I find it difficult to distinguish between the poetic majesty of Van Gogh's paint brush and the magnificence of Bahá'u'lláh's reed pen.

During the 1880s, while Bahá'u'lláh was living at Bahjí, in Palestine, His Dutch contemporary, Vincent Van Gogh, was struggling to make a life for himself as an artist in Belgium and France. Not too remotely, both of these men, a Persian Messiah and a humble artist, shared lives of bitter hardship as social outcasts because of the ideals they believed in.

The genius and tragedy of Van Gogh emerged most prominently when he came deeply in touch with his innermost feelings while losing grasp of his emotional stability. Manias tormented him to the point of disrupting his painting. In the end, at the age of 37, Vincent killed his pain with a pistol: a victim of suicide.

In the course of his brief art career, Vincent expressed his feelings brilliantly through his dazzling artwork and an outpouring of a thousand letters he wrote to his dear brother Theo, who supported and encouraged him from afar. In sharp contrast to the philosophically deep intellect that he manifested in his writings, Vincent's utility of the spoken word usually betrayed his impetuosity and bluntness. Well-read and initially quite religious, he still lacked an adequate ability to communicate socially. (After many frustrated efforts, he gave up trying.) He suffered from being misunderstood in his time and among his peers. "There may be a great fire in our soul," he wrote, "yet no-one ever comes to warm himself at it, and the passers-by see only a wisp of smoke coming through the chimney, and go along their way."[1]

He had good reason to grow cynical in the face of society's rejection. His religious convictions, once an energizing force in his life, eventually took a subordinate role to his art because of the hypocrisy he saw in the church leaders and their stand against him. Throughout these ordeals, however, his love for humanity, particularly the humble and poor, remained.

Vincent eagerly sought spiritual salvation in his discovery of the transcendent power visible in the beauty and order of nature—an approach to the mysterious which he substituted for the traditional God. This was all that remained from his earlier beliefs as a Christian missionary. Within a few years, even this philosophy failed to satisfy him. One of the underlying causes of his suicide was his loss of faith in God. He even began to envy those who had this faith, because he knew it gave them the vitality of spirit that he now longed for in vain.

Despite artistic obscurity during his lifetime, Vincent Van Gogh's art continued to touch people's hearts and minds in everwidening circles following his death. Within a century his work would become celebrated the world over. In 1985, his "Landscape With Rising Sun" was purchased for $9.9 million. In the spring of 1987, his "Sunflowers" sold for a record $39.9 million. Later that same year, his painting of a garden of blue irises, painted in 1889, stunned the art world when it sold for $53.9 million. Van Gogh had received less than a hundred dollars in his lifetime for anything he was able to create as an artist. (He sold only one painting and a few drawings.) Destitution and stinging rejection were his only rewards. His life made the unrewarded genius proverbial. Today his work is internationally recognized for having had a profound influence on twentieth-century artists and has become almost priceless. Perhaps there is a strange justice in this turn of events, an artistic pariah becomes a cultural icon with the passing of a few generations. Some revolutionary minds are not received in a day but in a century. A few years before his death, while corresponding, Vincent wrote prophetically: "These eyes have discovered a new vision of the world; now we see it with those eyes."[2]

No one can escape this life without some kind of hardship and suffering, but this fact does not cease our fascination with how certain patterns of tragedy lead to greatness. Old questions still haunt us. Why does society continually treat so many of its creative minds in this way? Why are the prophets of humanity, great and humble, being spurned in their own time and by their own people in perpetuity? Obviously, because they advocate various degrees of change in the perception and behavior of others.

Most visionaries, whether they be creative artists, seers, philosophers, or obstinate idealists, suffer the same fate. They have a flair or genius that is continually being upstaged by their more obvious deficient traits and their message, perhaps unfairly, loses its credibility after having been perfunctorily branded as dull, hypocritical, or deceptive.

Western civilization has been historically biased in favor of thinking in the linear, analytic, left-cerebral hemisphere of the brain. But within the last fifty years new research has emerged to suggest that we have been hemispherically imbalanced as a result. Human intelligence is being redefined by discoveries about the imagistic and intuitive powers of the right hemisphere of the brain, the hemisphere responsible for man's creative and spiritual capabilities.

In her popular book, *Drawing on the Right Side of the Brain*, artist and author Dr. Betty Edwards illustrates how everyone can unleash their hidden creative potential. By following her instructive drawing exercises, based on specific methods of observation, special functions within the right hemisphere of the brain are utilized, producing remarkable results for the learner.[3]

THE WILLING PRISONER
by Fritz A. Mann. A depiction of the Báb's arrest on the road to Shiraz done as an illustration for the Bahá'í children's magazine *Brilliant Star*.

Our genetic inheritance places limitations on our capacity for doing certain things, however. Ongoing studies of identical twins who have been reared apart for many years without contact, reveal similar patterns in their lives. Personalities, beliefs, and career choices are often the same. This would suggest to the rest of us just how much we are programed by our genes in spite of all the variables of education and environment.[4] According to 'Abdu'l-Bahá: "... all mankind possess intelligence and capacities, but the intelligence, the capacity, and the worthiness of men differ." He also attributed these variations to "inherited qualities,"[5] from the parents to their offspring, genetically.

Signs of artistic endowment may appear in early childhood or remain dormant until adulthood. A creative learning environment that offers incentives and the rewards of encouragement will do the most to bring these qualities out. The process is a continuous one. Just as the Bahá'í community would not hesitate to nurture each and every child in its charge in the knowledge that every individual is unique before God, Bahá'ís should not cease this encouragement once these children become adults. 'Abdu'l-Bahá said that the heart of each person has the potential to "become even as a mirror disclosing the secrets of the universe, penetrating the innermost reality of all things."[6] We must reach the point where we can praise the child in each adult without distinction, without fearing the myth that this will foster a distorted ego in the recipient. At best, it will lead toward strengthening the community by instilling in each individual feelings of greater self-worth and confidence. Members of the community will learn to take more pride in their association with each other, lessening the chances for the kind of distrust that evolves out of jealous relationships.

Though creative talent is genetically innate, appreciation for the arts is not. It is learned. Hence, the Bahá'í Writings emphatically encourage everyone to study the arts sometime in the course of their education. The arts have everything to do with our feelings as human beings—feelings that might range from the universal to the distinctly individual. They solicit emotional and intellectual responses with the possible benefit of nourishing our souls, bringing peace, happiness, enlightenment, and stability to our lives. The arts may even challenge us with controversy, which is sometimes necessary for progressive social change.

Without cultivating our feelings as we grow older, we risk distancing ourselves emotionally from the rest of humanity, and frozen feelings are just as tragic and crippling as frozen limbs. Because art appreciation is really the art of feeling, being in touch with one's innermost feelings becomes a requisite to the study of art. Bahá'u'lláh has described this pursuit and its vocation as "identical with the worship of God."[7]

Our experience of the arts depends primarily upon what we have stored in our memory at any given moment. A visual work of art stimulates countless neural connections in the brain of the viewer that are associated with some of his deepest emotions and may well comprise his collective experience. Nothing actually "happens" on the surface of a painting. Everything that could possibly happen occurs in the brain, mind, and soul of the observer. And there are as many different reactions to a piece of art as there are people. Without this interaction between the spectator and a piece of art, the art itself means nothing. However we attempt to define it, art can only be given life and meaning in the responsive mind insofar as art remains a primary outlet for human communication. Great art is just a different way of seeing reality and its quality is more easily demonstrated than defined. If a picture is worth a thousand words, it may also need a thousand words to explain it.

Since the middle of the last century, legions of art critics have emerged to assume a prominent and sometimes dubious function in the world of art. Often convinced that criticism is an art in its own right, art critics attempt what few others are willing to risk saying publicly by judging the worth or taste of an artist's creative output. Their verdict in the name of constructive criticism often stirs up certain resentment, producing love-hate relationships with the artists they write about. Any resentment artists feel toward their critics might stem from the fact that liking or disliking a creative work doesn't necessarily mean it is or isn't art. "A creator needs only one enthusiast to justify him,"[8] said Surrealist Man Ray.

On the other hand, art criticism can be a vital feature of the art world, offering well-intended and honest assessments of the direction and change brought about by the latest artistic styles, trends, and movements. Artists can choose to ignore them at their own expense or translate the rhetoric into something useful. Art critic for *The Denver Post*, Irene M. K. Rawlings, summed up the problem this way:

> Ideally, criticism should not be written to influence opinions but to stimulate others to have opinions. I have the same dialogue with a work of art publicly that everyone should have with it privately. In the end, it matters less whether I am right or wrong than that I have stimulated discussion. But the art critic who doesn't understand that he is being used in some way as a threshing machine to separate the best from the worst is being naive . . . life needs two forces to sustain it, although they are in total conflict. One is the need for the old, the continuing, the familiar, the dependable. The other is the need for the new, the unknown, and different. And while newness itself isn't always a virtue, openness to it is. It carries over into other areas. It gives me a tolerance and capacity to enjoy the new and strange in life outside art.[9]

Today we must chart the future course of mainstream art with universal guidelines based on society's growing global awareness. Visual art has of late been too often characterized by triteness, being locked into a norm of repetitive themes

PERSECUTION IN THE SABZIH-MAYDAN
by Fritz A. Mann. Conflict between Muslims and Bábís in a nineteenth-century market place.

© 1975 by Fritz A. Mann

and mundane sentimentalities. The very popular artist can sometimes influence or change public taste, but the majority of artists can only suggest imaginative possibilities to the public, which itself decides on the direction of change. A society that yearns for cowboy-and Indian paintings will get them in droves; if the public's fancy is still lifes, flying ducks, or weeping clowns, there will be a bandwagon of artists ready to supply the demand *ad nauseam*. If people want famous art, at affordable prices, counterfeit art dealers will supply and exploit this craving as well. As one Colorado newspaper art critic told me in 1986: "People aren't interested in new ideas or messages, they want something neutral that will be aesthetically appealing to all." But once art becomes devoted to placating conservative opinion it has lost one of its most vital functions. In order for their vision to become society's vision, artists need to develop responsible leadership roles without being cowed by the dictates of a capricious market.

Currently, there are many more millions of people upon the earth than ever before who, each in his or her own unique way, are interacting with a flow of information. There are also more artists of every kind than there ever were who are now in the process of creative search. It cannot be too long before something explosive and wonderful happens, vindicating the highest dreams and aspirations of our time.

The knowledge explosion that began in 1844, with the revolutionary telegraph system, has ushered mankind into an information age without precedent. The real difficulty for artists is not so much the perplexity that comes with confronting new technical mediums, it is dealing with the vast array of information that so quickly transforms everyone's notions of the world around us. But few experts would disagree that this new Information Age has brought with it another springtime for the arts. According to the futurist, Melvin L. Prueitt: "When the Renaissance dawned in Europe several centuries ago, there was no trumpeter to herald the beginning of the new age. There was no radio to spread the word and no television to show the brilliant new works of art. Most people were unaware that society was undergoing lasting change. The news spread slowly. Perhaps it has taken the intervening centuries for us to fully assess the impact of the Renaissance upon the human race. Today another revolution is breaking upon the art world, and it may be as profound in the long run as the Renaissance. It is happening so fast that, in spite of globe-encircling communication networks, many people (even some in the art profession) are unaware of it."[10]

In nineteenth-century Europe, under the revolutionary forces of socialism and nationalism, the political promptings of the artist broadened and subject matter diversified. Patronage of the arts passed from royalty and the church, to the general public. Art periodicals, galleries, guilds, salons, and museums became established. As art was created for public taste instead of for the pleasure of the powerful and wealthy, the direction of the arts changed. Before long a series of renegade, heroic, and radical artists began cropping up—Pissarro, Monet, Manet, Cezanne, Degas, Renoir, Gauguin, Van Gogh, Seurat, Lautrec, and others, each distinctly different in style and yet impressionistic in technique. Artists all rejected in their own time, celebrated in ours.

In more than a few ways, the visual arts have been suffering an identity crisis. Contemporary fine artists are wondering what they can do or say that will justify their art—and at what risks. In the last century, Bahá'u'lláh had advised future generations to become fully conscious of their times and conscientiously responsive to social needs born from change. He said: *"Be anxiously concerned with the needs of the age ye live in, and center your deliberations on its exigencies and requirements."*[11] When the artist has to wonder what his function in society is, he may have lost sight of the real challenges and opportunities open to him in the contemporary world. The challenge may be intimidating to some, but the Bahá'í

Looking Forward in the Visual Arts 225

Writings offer the artist much insight into the problems afflicting our age by describing their root causes, as well as the eventual outcome.

The door for creative expression for the Bahá'í has been left wide open when one considers—in contrast to how much has been written about music for instance—how little the Bahá'í Writings mention the visual arts specifically. Without a wealth of scriptural guidance in this area, general policies will be implemented by the Bahá'í Administration at developing stages to safeguard against undignified extremes and obvious misrepresentation of basic Bahá'í values. Ad-hoc Bahá'í reviewing committees, devised at this stage of the Faith's growth to serve as checkpoints on the individual distribution of Bahá'í art, must also bear in mind the relative value of their judgments. Whether receiving or giving counsel in this regard, Bahá'ís are all students in the same school, learning the fine balance between impulse and restraint. Both artists and reviewers must share the responsibility in weighting the respective consequences of their creative and restrictive actions in order that growth and harmony will result.

The real danger comes when any of us, while acting in a given capacity, become convinced of the divine authority of our own opinions, allowing little room for sensitivity or concession. An attitude of trust should prevail, otherwise the intended purpose of screening creative works may put an end to them altogether, to the defeat of everyone. These committees should also be comprised to some extent of qualified artists (with skill and experience) to be better equipped to judge art material. Shoghi Effendi, the late Guardian of the Bahá'í Faith, said: "There is no official Bahá'í Art, as this is not a new religion but religion renewed."[12] Thus, art for the Bahá'í has been freed from the official sanctions often imposed by government and religious institutions. For an open society, art must remain free from dogmatic restrictions if it is to thrive and broaden the outlook of its people.

Generally, though, the Writings do counsel the artist to study the arts and sciences of his day and to project into his work those spiritual values that might revitalize his viewing audience. The Bahá'í Writings do offer a good deal of encouragement, inspiration and purpose to the artist as suggested in the following statements:

> . . . *the arts which the ablest hands have produced . . . are but manifestations of the quickening power released by His transcendent, His all-pervasive and resplendent Spirit.*

> You must go on with your art and improve in it; and through this very Cause you will be able to make great progress in your art, for you will be helped from above . . .

> That day will the Cause spread like wildfire when its Spirit and teachings are presented on the stage or in art and literature as a whole. Art can better awaken such noble sentiments than cold rationalizing, especially among the mass of the people. We have to wait only a few years to see how the spirit breathed by Bahá'u'lláh will find expression in the work of artists.

> . . . as the Cause grows and talented persons come under its banner, they will begin to produce in art the divine spirit that animates their soul. Every religion has brought with it some form of art.

The Bahá'í writings offer every artist a light by which to find his own way.

While the whole world is undergoing incredibly rapid social change, the traditional role of the fine artist has become even more unstable than before. Commenting upon this state of flux, the American painter, Mark Tobey, said: "At a time when experimentation expresses itself in all forms of life, search becomes the only valid expression of the spirit. I am accused often of too much experimentation, but what else

THE MARTYRDOM OF THE BÁB
by Fritz A. Mann. Pen and acrylic, in color.

© 1981 by Fritz A. Mann

should I do when all other factors of man are in the same conditions?"[17] With the emergence of photography, motion pictures, and television in the past hundred and fifty years, and the new computer graphics and special-effects studios within the last decade, time-honored art forms like painting and sculpture have lost much of the social impact they once had in previous periods of history. Now, with the advent of electronic sound recordings in this century, music has surpassed all other art mediums in its effect on the global population.

'Abdu'l-Bahá had referred to the twentieth-century in these words: "Sciences and arts are being molded anew. All conditions and requisites of the past unfitted and inadequate for the present time, are undergoing radical reform."[18] In an age of universal reformation, artists have to be involved in making changes at some point. Some artists are very creative risk-takers. But many others look for the norm, avoiding the unknown. Art must deal with both the world as it is and as it should be. Mark Tobey defined an artist as "one who portrays the spirit of man in whatever condition that spirit may be. He is one who has ever to have his antennae set toward something unknown—unknown because the 'time period' on the particular decade is unknown until it has passed."[19]

Universal standards already apply to the visual arts that are purely scientific, as in the artist's application of color, optics, perspective, anatomy, and chemistry. The degree of one's knowledge of these basic elements may well determine the outcome of one's work.

Some artists have even established their own guidelines by which they distinguish art from non-art. American painter, Audrey Flack: "Creative expression is not art, it is creative expression. Self-expression is not art, it is self-expression. Rule-breaking is not art, it is rule-breaking. A new idea does not necessarily mean it is great art; it is just a new idea. For a work to become art, it must do more than vent its spleen. Artists have two responsibilities. The first is to express themselves. The second is to communicate. If artists don't communicate, they have either been unsuccessful in their attempt, or they are being self-indulgent by not trying, unless one of those rare moments occurs when a magical poetic statement happens for oneself alone."[20]

Because the visual arts have evolved through the centuries from accumulated experience and knowledge, any work of art stands to be governed in some measure by basic rules and principles. Artists have always assumed the right to bend and even redefine the rules of art from time to time to suit their own purposes, largely because their pragmatic and intuitive instincts have governed their actions more readily than the conventional standards of procedure. Some principles about art never change, simply because many of our intrinsic qualities as human beings never change. But for the most part, the arts change along with social values. However much art may enrich society, it also reflects society's strengths and weaknesses. Like a barometer, the arts clearly reflect the intellectual, spiritual, and aesthetic conditions of the community and culture from which they emerge.

Science is producing the technology that is now leading art into a future beyond our fondest fantasies: "Computors, tied to sophisticated graphics equipment, are the bright new tools of the artists, providing expanded capabilities for the creation of new art forms that would be difficult or impossible to produce by other means. Home computers are opening exciting possibilities to millions of people for the creation of colorful art."[21]

The first computers, introduced more than forty years ago did little more than assess mundane human activities. Today's machines have evolved with the supersophisticated computer memory and speed necessary for the enhanced blending abilities of both fantasy and reality into singular images for realistic animation. Computer video-art, along with picture-perfect high resolution screens, have indeed emerged to open up a whole new field, expanding artistic frontiers with a broad range of revolutionary visual images, including 3–D.

There still remains some controversy about computer art, however, based on the fear that such technical mediums dehumanize art into impersonal gadgetry. "I think the whole field is in its infancy," said Colorado video artist, Michael Esch, while exhibiting his video-graphics at the UCCS Gallery of Contemporary Art in 1985, "but it's like photography when it first came out—it was looked at mechanistically rather than artistically. It will just take time." Esch added that the computer was "merely a tool as is a brush or palette knife for painting."[22]

Further comment came from assistant professor, Marc Berger, of UCCS's computer science department: "In order to create a beautiful picture on the computer, you have to be an artist. It's not true the computer is doing all the work. There is a lot of creativity, work, and technique involved. It's just another medium. I think more and more people are willing to accept it as art now."[23] In addition to art training, computer art students must master computer language to achieve the best results.

Artists have always worked with the advanced tools of their time. After its practical development and release to the European public in the mid-nineteenth century, photography would evolve to become the dominant tool for many artists in the creation of their work and then serve as an indispensable method for documenting and publishing that same work when it was completed. Equally important, photography produced new avenues of financial income for artists with the publication and mass distribution of their work in the printed media and motion pictures. Though it is well known that photography has had a profound influence on the artist, it isn't common knowledge that the practical application of photography was first developed and presented to the world by artists. Today the creative and technical skills of a professional artist and photographer are typically found in the same individual. Distinctions between these two pursuits often blur as contemporary artists become equally proficient photographers, with each skill feeding the development of the other. The challenge for today's artists is to use the new technological, communicative and visual mediums to capture the imagination of the human race while promoting Bahá'u'lláh's imperative for world unity and peace. Products already capturing people's attention these days are the new wave of electronic audio-visual services and products: cable television, VCRs, and computer video games. Consequently, we have become a jaded "television-society" just as much as we have become a sophisticated "information-society." Bahá'u'lláh cautions us about the unwholesome extremes that are currently seen and routinely promoted with the everincreasing varieties of entertainment: *"Whatsoever passeth beyond the limits of moderation will cease to exert a beneficial influence . . . they will, if carried to excess, exercise a pernicious influence upon men."*[24]

The artist's unfortunate predicament in all this may not seem so surprising when one considers how directly connected all art is to the age from which it emerges. Ideally, it should be at this time of global confusion that society could confidently look toward its art communities for ideas, as much as it does to its politicians, to the business sector, and to religious leaders. In many cases, this doesn't happen simply because art groups can barely keep afloat because of the meager public recognition and funding they receive. Without the credible credentials of public recognition and the influence that comes with wealth, most self-proclaimed artists are lumped together with Sunday painters and hobbyists and quickly forgotten. This situation is counterproductive when we consider just how much the arts have acted as a civilizing force within society all along. When a society and its institutions generously support and encourage the arts, this in itself is a sign of vital cultural progress and optimism.

The late John Lennon—famous musician, songwriter, author, feminist, philosophic one-worlder, and visual artist—

was a keenly pragmatic, yet conscientiously theistic man who never hesitated to defend the artist's role in society. He said: "... is under the delusion that art is something you have extra, like *crème de menthe* or something. But societies don't exist with no artist. Art is a functional part of society: if you don't have artists you don't have society. We're not some kind of decadent strip show that appears on the side. We're as important as prime ministers of policemen."[25]

Bahá'u'lláh dignifies the station of the artist in a statement supporting this view. He wrote: "*The possessors of sciences and arts have a great right among the people of the world.*"[26] In another Tablet, He writes that the believers "*must not refuse to discharge the due reward of anyone, and must respect possessors of talent. One must speak with justice and recognize the worth of benefits.*"[27]

'Abdu'l-Bahá said that through God's grace, within the various branches of knowledge including art, it was His wish that each believer "may earn worldwide fame."[28] And how could an artist influence social change directly without it? Again, in most cases, it is society that determines the fame of its artists, as a result of the power they recognize in an artist's art.

That frustration on the part of the artist still exists rather widely can be attested to in the words of the internationally recognized photorealist painter, Audrey Flack: "Why have we not been able to produce a Michelangelo, a Leonardo, a Tintoretto? Is it the way artists have been treated recently? We have become unnecessary appendages, expendable. After years of such treatment, perhaps abilities vanish, just as a limb that gets no use gradually atrophies and withers. This is an age of technology. David painted the coronation of Napoleon. Today we have video equipment to record such events."[29] It is evident that we're all constantly surrounded by the visual arts in one form or another. We have unwittingly allowed ourselves to become engulfed in manmade visual pollution, from traffic signs to the containers we buy

'ABDU'L-BAHÁ LEAVING AMERICA
by Fritz A. Mann.

our foods in. Ironically, we are more easily awed by the obscene beauty of a burning building or a nuclear explosion. For this reason, most art suffers from having little or no purpose, as it is taken for granted. We see them so much, the beautiful, the mundane, the ugly, the offensive—all at the same time—that we often become blind to the innumerable images that crowd into our daily existence. We certainly don't enjoy hearing all our favorite music at the same time—it would defeat the purpose—so why should it be any different with the enjoyment and appreciation of visual art?

Besides the routine social, political, and economic obstacles that artists must face if they intend to pursue their calling—the ultimate challenge is in finding useful interpretations of life that can sustain the artist intellectually and spiritually. Not far off is the twenty-first century, which may well be the first century to celebrate universal peace and the unity of humanity. Artists may become the visionary architects and orchestrators of tomorrow's global renaissance, if they stop supporting today's dominant culture and begin including within the scheme of their work the world-minded ideals so necessary for peace, stability, and healing. All artists have a stake in promoting world peace. When any country becomes involved in war, priceless art treasures are among the casualties. When important art is destroyed another light for civilization is snuffed out.

Art's greatest value has been social, particularly when it becomes instrumental in promoting cultural understanding and the moral purposes of civilization. A sense of affinity and oneness with peoples around the globe has been more amicably communicated through the arts than by any other medium.

The traditional motivator of creative, altruistic expression has been religion. However much the Bahá'í Era has manifested itself in the events of our times, the greatest artistic demonstrations and achievements of the Bahá'í religion and civilization have yet to be seen. History has shown that

Looking Forward in the Visual Arts 235

with every new religion comes a new spirit for the arts. According to Bahá'u'lláh, the arts have served as a primary channel by which pure and impartial souls in the other world can project their influence into this world: *"The Light which these souls radiate is responsible for the progress of the world and the advancement of its people. They . . . constitute the animating force through which the arts and wonders of the world are made manifest."*[30] Because the arts can do so much to inspire humanity toward unity and peace, they are as important as unity and peace. They go hand in hand.

Art as propaganda, however, has served a full spectrum of ideologies. Revolutionary movements, whether passive or militant, have typically employed the use of visual imagery in the form of posters, murals, and films to spread their strategy or philosophy. Unfortunately, art has been used to advocate war more often than it has been used to plead for peace. In the collective unconscious of pre-Hitler Germany, there was an unparalleled fascination with death and destruction. The arts of Germany during the 1920s and 1930s clearly reflect the fact that dark and evil forces were at work, like symptoms revealing a malignant spiritual disease. Evidently, these forces stemmed from Germany's ingrained anti-Semitism, economic despair, xenophobia, and the brutal experiences of the First World War.

The Second World War was the first conflict in history to be widely depicted by visual artists, and the country outproducing all others in this way was Nazi Germany. Hitler, who had once made trying attempts at becoming an artist, personally supervised and commissioned a program employing Germany's finest artists to create almost ten-thousand works of art to promote the militaristic spirit of the Third Reich. After most of this collection was confiscated by U.S. Forces at the end of the war, it was put in storage or on display at various U.S. military and government installations around the country, including the Pueblo Army Depot in Colorado.

Ironically, this huge body of war art outlived the ugly sham of the Third Reich. Each German artist, as it turned out, had maintained his own individual artistic standards in the work he did, in spite of Hitler's own personal dictum on art for the perpetuation of the German war machine. Each artist put his best talents to the job. Beautiful works of art were created that could stand on their own artistic merits. And many of them actually told the truth about the war—the despair and boredom that afflicted the military ranks and the devastation to cities on all fronts. It seems quite apparent now that many of Hitler's artists had mixed emotions as they went about their creative task of recording part of the demise of an old world civilization. The German war art collection is currently in the process of being reclaimed by West Germany because the value of this artistic excellence transcends the evils of war.*

A vindication of artistic idealism over war is perhaps best exemplified in Picasso's monumental painting titled "Guernica," after that Spanish town that was bombed by the Germans in 1937. The bombing destroyed most of Guernica and killed several hundred people out of a population of four thousand. It became the most internationally famous atrocity of the Spanish Civil War because of the attention Picasso's painting gave it. Hitler employed an army of eight hundred artists to promote a spirit of war, while it took only one radical Spanish artist to successfully challenge and defy the Spanish Fascists and the whole German Army. Referring to anti-war art like "Guernica," Steven Heller, co-author of the book *Art Against War*, conceded that "war is an all-too-often recurring theme in art, and that, moreover, if there is another world war—there will be no art."[31]

Art museums in some parts of the United States have low

---

*In 1976, the author personally visited the storage area at the Pueblo Army Depot in Colorado and studied the paintings and sculpture.

attendance, and government subsidies for the arts are currently in check. For most high schools in the nation, art is not a requirement for graduation. In the teaching field, subjects like English, math, foreign language, and history are given priority over art. Art teacher training programs at the college and university level, once classified as Art Education, are no longer a viable option for students entering the teaching field. University art department programs regularly get phased out because the money to support them just isn't there. Schools with their own valuable art collections cannot always maintain them due to tight budgets. Art Curator, Jean Weiffenbach, of Colorado University's Art Gallery in Boulder was interviewed in 1985 about the low priority for preserving their school's three thousand piece collection of historical artifacts. Some pieces—which are in the process of rotting—included works by such art luminaries as Picasso, Rembrandt, Matisse, and Rodin. Weiffenbach's comment was: "Art does not seem to fire people's minds around here. . . . You need art for your soul as much as you need exercise for your body. . . . We have all this art but no money to be responsible for it."[32]

Fine art galleries attract a minority of Americans and most of them are in the higher income brackets. Judging from the figures, the amount of support artists can count on from the general public at any time will depend largely on the degree of education and personal income received by each citizen. Studies show that society's wealthiest and best educated people are much more likely to support the arts than the poor and less educated.[33]

Since most artists create their work with an audience in mind, artistic expression in a work of art remains nonsocial only as long as it is isolated from a viewing audience. Picasso had a message to give which required public attention to fulfill its purpose. It mattered little whether his message was absurd or profound. Without the public's appreciation for his art, there would not have been the historical Picasso nor the cultural revolution that followed in his artistic wake. For every artist who becomes celebrated during or after his time, society should also celebrate its own expanding vision for embracing the works of such visionaries. Their vision becomes our vision. This is the integral aspect of the union between the artist and society.

Visual art is a quiet way of speaking; it is the artist speaking to the viewer without friction in between. It is a silent quickener! Mankind cannot have a Golden Age without a Golden Age of the Arts because art and society proceed simultaneously. Looking forward, we have much to see in the great promises of the arts.

Notes

1. Pierre Cabanne *Van Gogh: The Man and His Work* (translated from French by Mary I. Martin) (New Jersey: Prentice-Hall, 1963) p. 11.
2. Marc Edo Tralbaut, *Vincent Van Gogh* (Chartwell Books, 1969) p. 10.
3. Betty Edwards, *Drawing on the Right Side of the Brain* (Los Angeles: J. P. Tarcher, 1979).
4. "All About Twins," *Newsweek* (November 23, 1987) pp. 58–69.
5. *Bahá'í Education: A Compilation*, comp. by the Research Department of The Universal House of Justice Wilmette, Ill., Bahá'í Publishing Trust, 1977) p. 19.
6. *Bahá'í Education: A Compilation*, pp. 27–8.
7. *Bahá'í World Faith* (Wilmette, Ill. Bahá'í Publishing Trust, 1956) p. 195.
8. Trewin Copplestone, *Modern Art* (1985) p. 12.
9. "An art critic's year of living dangerously," by Irene M. K. Rawlings, *The Denver Post* (August 21, 1988).
10. *Art and the Computer*, from preface by Melvin L. Prueitt, 1984.

11. *Gleanings from the Writings of Bahá'u'lláh* (Wilmette, Ill.: Bahá'í Publishing Trust, 1939) p. 213.
12. *Mark Tobey: Paintings from the collection of Joyce and Arthur Dahl* (Palo Alto: Stanford University, 1967) p. 15.
13. *Gleanings*, pp. 85–6.
14. *Star of the West*, Vol. 5, No. 10 (April 9, 1917) p. 149.
15. Shoghi Effendi, quoted in *Bahá'í News*, No. 73 (May 1933).
16. In a letter written on behalf of the Guardian to Mrs. Nina Matthison, November 12, 1931, quoted in *The American Bahá'í* (July 1982) p. 3.
17. Arthur L. Dahl, *Mark Tobey: Art and Belief* (Oxford: George Ronald, 1984) p. 16.
18. *Bahá'í World Faith*, pp. 228–9.
19. *Mark Tobey: Paintings from the collection of Joyce and Arthur Dahl*, p. 15.
20. Audrey Flack, *Art and Soul: Notes on Creating* (New York: E. P. Dutton, 1986) p. 39.
21. *Art and the Computer*, preface.
22. "Bytes the Key to Creativity for High-Technology Artists," *Colorado Springs Sun*, by Judy L. Stewart (October 4, 1985) p. 3–C.
23. Ibid.
24. *Gleanings*, p. 216.
25. Ray Coleman, *Lennon* (New York: McGraw-Hill, 1985) p. 436.
26. *Bahá'í World Faith*, p. 189.
27. *Bahá'í World Faith*, p. 177.
28. *Bahá'í Education: A Compilation*, p. 28.
29. *Art and Soul: Notes on Creating*, p. 39.
30. *Gleanings*, p. 157.
31. Steven Heller, D.J.R. Brukner, Seymour Chevast, *Art Against War* (New York: Abbeville Press, 1984) p. 7.
32. *Gazette Telegraph*, Colorado Springs, CO (September 4, 1985) p. B–5.
33. *Gazette Telegraph*, by Maureen Klmmell (June 22, 1985) p. F–3.

Biographical Notes

ANNE GORDON ATKINSON, dedicated to dance, lives in Wilmette, Illinois.

MAYA KAATHRYN BOHNHOFF and her husband perform as the rock group SYNTAX. They live in California.

MICHAEL FITZGERALD teaches at Shenandoah College in Virginia and is the author of two books of poetry, *A Tree Like This* and *Living the Boundaries*. He has studied at the Iowa Writers Workshop and is a member of the Academy of American Poets.

DUANE L. HERRMANN is a writer and poet living in Kansas. He has been a Bahá'í since 1969.

THOMAS LYSAGHT, born in Brooklyn, is a writer of plays and fiction; he teaches in a private school in Florida. While living in Peru from 1983 to 1986, he organized a traveling youth theater group and served as administrator of Radio Bahá'í near Lake Titicaca.

FRITZ A. MANN, now a professional painter, was born to a military family in Anchorage, Alaska, and traveled the world as a child. He has settled in Colorado.

GEOFFREY NASH, author of several books and articles on the Bahá'í Faith, lives in Kent, England.

LASSE THORESEN is Professor of Musical Composition at the Norwegian State Academy of Music. He lives in Oslo.

LUDWIG TUMAN graduated from Harvard University and received his M.A. in music from San Francisco State University. He has taught at the Chicago Conservatory College. He is now a composer and pianist living in Venezuela.

ROGER WHITE, born in Toronto, has lived in Haifa, Israel, since 1971, and serves as an editor at the Bahá'í World Center. Author of three collections of poetry and a novel, he is also associate editor of Israel's first English-language poetry journal, *Voices Israel*.

BONNIE WILDER holds a doctorate in Education and has recently retired as an art educator. She is an active painter and writer, and divides her time each year between Texas and New Mexico. She also manages BBC publications, a Bahá'í publishing company.

CHARLES WOLCOTT, former Musical Director of Walt Disney Studios, served as a member of the Bahá'í Universal House of Justice from its inception in 1963 until his death in 1988.